Chicken Soup for the Soul.

The
Miracle
of Love

Chicken Soup for the Soul: The Miracle of Love
101 Stories about Hope, Soul Mates and New Beginnings
Amy Newmark

Published by Chicken Soup for the Soul, LLC www.chickensoup.com
Copyright ©2018 by Chicken Soup for the Soul, LLC. All Rights Reserved.

The publisher gratefully acknowledges the many publishers and individuals who
granted Chicken Soup for the Soul permission to reprint the cited material.

Front cover photo courtesy of iStockphoto.com/martinedoucet (©martinedoucet)
Back cover and Interior photo of penguins courtesy of iStockphoto.com/jtstewartphoto
(©jtstewartphoto)
Photo of Amy Newmark courtesy of Susan Morrow at SwickPix

Cover and Interior by Daniel Zaccari

Distributed to the booktrade by Simon & Schuster. SAN: 200-2442

Publisher's Cataloging-In-Publication Data
(Prepared by The Donohue Group, Inc.)

Names: Newmark, Amy, compiler.
Title: Chicken soup for the soul : the miracle of love : 101 stories about
      hope, soul mates and new beginnings / [compiled by] Amy Newmark.
Other Titles: Miracle of love : 101 stories about hope, soul mates and new
      beginnings
Description: [Cos Cob, Connecticut] : Chicken Soup for the Soul, LLC,
      [2018]
Identifiers: ISBN 9781611599800 (print) | ISBN 9781611592801 (ebook)
Subjects: LCSH: Love--Literary collections. | Love--Anecdotes. | Soul
      mates--Literary collections. | Soul mates--Anecdotes. | Dating (Social
      customs)--Literary collections. | Dating (Social customs)--Anecdotes. |
      Couples--Literary collections. | Couples--Anecdotes. | LCGFT:
      Anecdotes.
Classification: LCC BF575.L8 C452 2018 (print) | LCC BF575.L8 (ebook) |
      DDC 152.41--dc23

Library of Congress Control Number: 2018938957

PRINTED IN THE UNITED STATES OF AMERICA
on acid∞free paper

25 24 23 22 21 20 19 18   01 02 03 04 05 06 07 08 09 10 11

The
Miracle
of Love

101 Stories about Hope, Soul Mates and New Beginnings

Amy Newmark

Chicken Soup for the Soul, LLC

Changing lives one story at a time®
www.chickensoup.com

Table of Contents

❶

~Friends First~

❷

~Worth the Wait~

❸

~Love at First Sight~

❹

~How We Met~

❺

~Divine Intervention~

6

~Happily Ever Laughter~

7

~In Sickness and In Happiness~

8

~Meant to Be~

❾

~When I Knew~

❿

~When I Least Expected It~

⓫

~The Second Time Around~

⑫

~Keeping the Love Alive~

Chapter 1

The Miracle of Love

Friends First

Like That

*There is a reason why BF stands for best friend and
boyfriend, as they should be one and the same.*
~Author Unknown

The first time Adam asked me out I explained I didn't like him "like that." Even worse, I asked him if we could just be friends. Every other guy who I'd told "let's just be friends" had promptly disappeared from my life. So, you can imagine my shock when Adam took me at my word.

Adam was a tall guy with hair bleached blond by the sun. He had a goofy smile. He liked books, rugby and juggling. He was clever at making puns and graceful when he moved, whether he was walking, running, or climbing a tree. We'd known each other for a while, and I knew it had taken a lot of guts for him to tell me he liked me. I respected that courage. I've never thought guys have it easy when it comes to romance — I knew I'd hate to be the one who had to ask.

But my respect only grew when he took me seriously: He actually stuck around. He became my friend.

We hung out together in groups, and that was fine. We went to a movie together, and I made my little brother sit between us so Adam wouldn't get the wrong idea. We were both guests at the same wedding. I looked at him with his suit coat off and his sleeves rolled up, and I felt wistful that there wasn't going to be any dancing. *I would've liked to dance with Adam,* I thought.

I should have known.

Once, we found ourselves on the same retreat for a university club we both belonged to. At the end of the retreat, everyone in the group helped clean out the cabin, and Adam and I volunteered to clean out a particularly filthy fridge in a small room off the kitchen. I mean, there was dark, sticky stuff clinging to the bottom shelf that had been there long enough that it might have qualified as a new life form.

It was smelly. It was gross… and it was surprisingly fun.

I was beginning to notice that everything I did with Adam was surprisingly fun — even stuff that really shouldn't have been. Like cleaning out disgustingly dirty fridges.

It wasn't what we were doing that I enjoyed so much. It was that I was doing it with Adam. *He's such a good friend!* I thought.

I was so clueless that I started dating someone else. And even then, Adam kept being my friend.

We still hung out in the same group. We still saw each other at church and at the university, concerts and rugby games. He kept on being my friend.

I broke up with the guy I was dating that spring.

Summer came around, and one day, between work shifts, I found myself at home, complaining to my sister about boys. "There aren't any!" I moaned. "Why are there no good guys around?"

My sister just looked at me.

Then she glared at me.

And then she yelled at me. "JESSICA! What are you talking about? There's ADAM."

"Adam?"

"Yes, ADAM. He is absolutely everything you've ever said you wanted," and she named all of the requirements she'd heard me talk about again and again. "He is everything you've ever said you wanted. And he's just standing there. BEING YOUR FRIEND."

Now, I wasn't going to take this sitting down. I opened my mouth wide, ready to argue with her (What are sisters for except to argue with?) and… nothing.

Nothing came out of my mouth. Why? Because I couldn't think of a single thing to say to her.

She was right. She was completely right, and I hadn't seen it.

I swallowed hard. Now that I saw it, what was I going to do?

In the end, what made it simple was the friendship itself. I would have felt like a jerk if I treated him with anything less than honesty.

But, oh my goodness, that was harder than it sounded.

I had no idea if he still liked me… like that. It had been almost a year since he'd said anything romantic to me, and I knew people's feelings changed. After all, mine had.

But he was my friend, and I wasn't going to lie to him. I wasn't going to hide this from him.

So I asked him if we could have lunch together. I went to that lunch, and I couldn't eat a thing. My stomach was in knots. What would he say when I told him? What even were the right words to use?

The truth. This was my friend. I could tell him the truth. I knew he would tell me the truth.

Even if the truth was that he no longer liked me… like that.

"Adam," I said, "I've realized recently that, well…" I took a breath. He was looking at me so seriously. "Adam," I said, "I've realized that every time I see you… I'm really, really glad to see you."

I winced. That was the best I could do? Seriously? Was it enough? Did he understand what I was saying?

Slowly, he began to smile.

And then his smile got so big that it was hard to see anything else but the smile on his face and the way his eyes suddenly lit up like he was a kid on Christmas morning.

"Well," he said. "Well. I'm… very glad to hear that."

That turned out to be an understatement.

One marriage, four kids, and many years later, we're still friends. And we're still happy to see each other whenever we see each other.

And we still like each other… like that.

~Jessica Snell

Surprise

When two people are meant to be together,
they will be together. It's fate.
~Sara Gruen, Water for Elephants

I didn't tell my sisters that I was dating—until I told them I was getting married. You see, my husband-to-be had been a monk. I had met him when I showed up for work at the church where he volunteered.

I didn't see Scott for a few months after we met, because I was working off site at the church's summer camp. When I returned to the office at the end of the summer, life proceeded predictably. We each kept busy with our duties. In the morning, Scott usually worked in the office. No matter who came in the door—a homeless person looking for work or money, a parishioner on an errand, a visitor wanting a tour of our historic building, or the secretary and me—he showed compassion, caring, and interest in our lives.

Scott was easy to talk to and had a great sense of humor, as did the secretary, so there was a lot of laughter in the office. When he wasn't working in the office, he did anything that was needed—as long as the "order" came from one boss, our priest. Since the priest was easygoing and our church was small, Scott assisted parishioners with computer issues, tended the garden borders around the church, polished the brass candlesticks, and helped at worship. Eventually, I even requested some of his time for setting up activities for the children's programs.

One day, I told Scott I needed a dance partner for some lessons.

Suddenly, there was serious silence. Scott got a deer-in-the-headlights look and said, "I'll have to get back to you on that." He disappeared to his cell above the church offices.

I looked at the secretary and shrugged. "Stupid question, but the answer is obviously no. What's the problem?" She shrugged, too, and we both turned to our work.

Soon, I had my own deer-in-the-headlights moment. A day later, Scott told me, "I had to figure out why I couldn't answer your question right away. I didn't sleep all night. I realized I've fallen in love with you. If I put my arms around you to dance, I wouldn't be a monk anymore."

He assured me there were no strings attached, but I didn't know what to do with his revelation. Scott was a monk, and I was living like a monk myself after a rough ending to a long marriage. We were just friends. At least that was what I had convinced myself. Mostly, I avoided thinking about it. But I couldn't avoid him — we worked and worshiped together. He didn't make me uncomfortable; true to his word, he didn't mention it again.

But he did invite me to see where he called home. I thought that would settle things — I grew up in the suburbs, and he loved ranch life. I'm a tree hugger, and he loved the wide-open plains. Yet I found beauty in the place he loved. I invited him on a picnic. He took care of my dog. I wrote him poems. He wrote me poems. We started taking walks together, and then shared dinners at my home. After more conversation and time together, I realized that I had also fallen in love. Before much longer, we were engaged.

Our first "real" date was the night he asked me to marry him, so I hadn't even mentioned him to my family. We chose our wedding date about halfway between the weddings of two of my sons. Since one had occurred in August and the other was scheduled for May, we didn't expect many members of my family to attend a third wedding, especially on such short notice. But first, I needed to let them know about Scott.

I'd told my parents that I had a special friend, so their surprise when I asked them to our wedding lasted only a moment. "Yes, we'll be there!" Now to tell my siblings, who didn't know about Scott. I decided to send an e-mail because I usually express myself better in writing. Maybe not this time, though.

One of my sisters read the e-mail at work and screamed, "What?" Her friends came running to the teachers' lounge. She explained, "My sister just sent this e-mail:

> *Hi, I've been so busy that I haven't had time to tell you that I've started dating. He's a great guy, loves me and my dog, treats me wonderfully, and we're getting married in a month and a half.*

After her friends stopped gasping and laughing, they left, and she called to hear more of our story.

Another sister called to ask, "What's the closest airport to you?" When I told her I didn't expect her to use precious vacation days, especially on such short notice, she said, "Holly, we haven't heard you this happy in a long time. Of course, we're coming to celebrate with you!"

And, God bless them, celebrate we did. They came early, before the blizzard that socked in our area. They stayed to share a New Year's meal with us. And when the blizzard left, so did they. Some of our guests remember that weekend as the one when "we came for your wedding and got snowed in," but not my family. They remember hanging out with their sister again, gaining a new friend in my husband, and sharing in the beginning of our happily ever after.

~Holly L. Moseley

Thor at the Door

Also love can always find a way. It was impossible
that these two whose hearts were on fire
should be kept apart.
~Edith Hamilton, Mythology: Timeless Tales of
Gods and Heroes

The judge banged his gavel, and I followed my lawyer out of the courtroom, past my now ex-husband. My steps echoed down the polished marble corridor. Each footfall took me further from the pain of betrayal, infidelity, and alcohol abuse. I almost danced with elation. The attorney eyed me strangely. "Most people are distraught when they get divorced."

Distraught? I felt like I'd escaped from a horrible prison. Caring for my fifteen-month-old daughter Patty was my top priority. Now she wouldn't have to grow up in a dysfunctional, abusive home. We'd been set free.

A few weeks after the divorce, my best friend Debbi asked, "When will you start dating again?"

"Never," I replied. "My new mantra is, 'Every man on the planet is a conniving sneak, existing only to wreak havoc on unsuspecting women's hearts.'"

Debbi laughed at my irrational words. "You don't mean that. Someday, you'll find true love."

Love? No, thank you. I didn't want a new relationship. I didn't even want to look at a man.

Until a Norse god walked out of my neighbor's home.

Tall. Tan. Fit. Gorgeous.

A modern-day Thor was visiting Frank, my middle-aged neighbor? I looked away from the enticing vision and repeated my "all males are evil" mantra.

A few days later, Frank stopped by while I weeded the lawn. "Hey, Jeanie, I'm letting the neighbors know my buddy is staying with me for a while. He works night shift. He's a super guy." Okay, Thor was a super guy staying with Frank. Fine. It had nothing to do with me.

The next day, I glanced out my bedroom window and spotted Thor standing next to a black pickup. He looked up and down the empty street, and then hopped into the truck bed. What was this guy up to? Thor removed his shirt and stretched out to nap in the summer sun. His muscles seemed to reflect the light. I stared open-mouthed. *Whoa,* I thought, *does this guy pose for romance book covers? Yeesh.*

I dragged my hormones away from the window and practiced my man-hating mantra. Perhaps I went a bit overboard since this guy was way out of my league anyway.

Still, there was no harm in looking. Spying on Thor's afternoon tanning sessions became a daily ritual. I'd climb onto my mattress and peer out the small rectangular transom window above my bed.

After a week, guilt forced me to stop. I established Commandment Number Eleven: Thou shalt not ogle thy neighbor's guest. A round of intense house cleaning would take my mind — and hormones — off my neighbor's virile friend. While Patty napped, I threw on a ragged sundress and pushed my hair into a messy ponytail. No sense putting in my contacts or using make-up.

An hour of scrubbing later, I grabbed the window cleaner and headed toward the bedroom. *Just to tidy up,* I told myself, *not to peek at Thor.* Sure. Even I didn't believe myself. But Thor wasn't in his usual spot. A knock on the door interrupted my spying attempt.

Thor stood at the door. Had he spotted me ogling him? Fresh sweat beaded on my upper lip. I wiped it with a sudsy glove and stammered, "Oh. Yes. Hi, um…"

When I fell silent, Thor gave me a shy, easy smile. *Wow, this guy puts toothpaste-commercial actors to shame.* "Hi, I'm Jake." He pointed over his shoulder at my neighbor's house. "I'm staying with Frank."

"Uh, that's nice." Inwardly, I cringed at my inane response.

"Frank talks about what a nice lady you are."

"Um... thanks," I said.

He looked down for a moment, lifted his head, and blurted, "Would you maybe go out with me sometime?"

I stared into his electric blue eyes. It felt like I'd touched a high-voltage line. I glanced at his wide shoulders. Too tempting. I lowered my eyes. Bad move. His shorts revealed his long, muscular legs. I blinked hard and admitted, "Look, I just ended a bad marriage. I'm not interested in dating."

Thor—Jake—blew out a relieved sigh. "Same here. My girlfriend and I broke up last month. I'm not ready for a relationship. I hoped we could go to the movies or something. Just friends."

"I'll go out with you if my babysitter is available. But remember, just friendship. Nothing more."

Jake lit up like the Christmas tree in Rockefeller Center. "Great! Here's my number. Call whenever it's convenient for you." He waved goodbye. I closed the door and wondered why such an attractive man would invite me out. A glance in the mirror revealed me in all my bedraggled glory, complete with rubber gloves. Yep, his line about "just friends" made sense.

That weekend, Jake treated me to a movie and dinner, even though it wasn't a date. "Hey, I appreciate you going out with me. I'm glad to pay," he said.

Despite his handsome appearance, Jake was endearingly humble. We talked non-stop. During dinner, Jake said, "You've only eaten a few bites. Is the food okay?"

"It's great. I'll take it home in a doggy bag." Paying the sitter would bite into my limited budget. My leftovers would provide three delectable meals for Patty. Since I wasn't eating much, Jake politely stopped eating, too.

He drove me home, and I invited him in. "Patty's been asleep for an hour," the sitter said. She grabbed her pay and left. Patty awoke just as Jake and I sat down on the couch. I went to get her and when I brought her in I warned Jake. "Don't be offended. Patty shies away from men."

Patty pulled her tiny hand from mine and toddled straight to Jake. He patted the sofa and asked, "Want to sit with us?" She held up her arms. I froze, shocked.

Jake scooped up Patty and sat her on the couch. She snuggled against him. Jake grinned at me and patted the cushion again. "Are you joining us?"

We spent the evening chatting and laughing. When Patty grew sleepy, I tucked her in bed and returned to Jake. "I had a great time tonight."

"Me, too," he said.

I scooted closer. "Just to remind you, I'm not looking for a relationship."

"Me neither." He laid his arm across the back of the sofa.

I leaned toward him, "Just friends."

He brushed my cheek softly with his thumb. "Friends."

We gazed into each other's eyes. He cupped my face like precious porcelain as I lifted it toward his. Our lips met for a heartbeat of eternity.

The next day, Jake knocked at the door, his arms laden with bags. "You seemed to like the restaurant's food last night. I wondered why you didn't eat much. When you tucked in Patty, I checked your fridge." His gentle kiss eased my embarrassment over the empty refrigerator.

Jake spent the next months proving his trustworthiness. His honesty, generosity, and love silenced my man-hating mantra. When Jake proposed the following year, I don't know who was more ecstatic — me or Patty.

After thirty-three years of friendship, love and unabashed ogling, I still thank God that "Thor" came to my door.

~Jeanie Jacobson

The Project

Nobody is perfect until you fall in love with them.
~Author Unknown

When our government teacher assigned us as project partners our senior year of high school, I wanted to groan and drop my head on my desk. I was not a "group-work" kind of student, and he... well, he wasn't a "work" kind of student.

I tried to encourage him to participate — for about twenty minutes — before deciding I would be better off handling the project alone if I didn't want an F. We were assigned to design a small replica of the Pentagon, and I spent most of my weekend in the basement, designing it out of cardboard, papier-mâché, and paint.

On presentation day, all of our projects were lined up under the chalkboard. My partner, Warren, came in and shouted oh-so-covertly, "Hey, Crystal, which one's ours?" I had another head-on-the-desk moment. Then he decided to further insult me by asking if the hideous green Pentagon — which looked like a baby had upchucked spinach all over it — was ours.

We got a B. A *B*! Simply because Warren couldn't keep himself from announcing that we hadn't worked together to make it. I was furious with him.

Fast-forward five years...

My parents stopped by a Verizon store to have their phone repaired, and the manager informed them that they were hiring. My parents passed the message along, and I brought in an application. And there, sitting behind the desk, was Warren. He says that it was instant attraction for him. For me, it was instant flashback to that project.

After we began working together, we quickly became friends. We went for walks, went out for ice cream, and even played putt-putt golf. I had never dated anyone before, and at twenty-three, I had no desire to. I simply enjoyed having a guy friend to hang out with.

So when we were sitting on the couch at his house watching a movie, and he kept inhaling like he was having an asthma attack, I thought there was something wrong. I had no idea he was trying to work up the nerve to ask me out.

My first instinct was to say "no." That was my default answer for every other guy who had asked me out over the years, but I hesitated and said, "Um, sure?"

He drove me home that night, unsure whether or not he had a girlfriend. I spent the next six months trying to find a polite way to break up with him. Not because he had done anything wrong—he was amazingly sweet and thoughtful—but because being in a relationship with a man was terrifying for me. But Warren was nothing but a gentleman, which was yet another surprise for me.

After those six months passed, our relationship really began to blossom. We did goofy things like scrapbooking and pumpkin bowling (although he cheats at any kind of bowling, and I have to keep a close eye on him), and I felt a connection I had never felt before.

I couldn't tell him that I loved him. I just couldn't make my tongue say that L word, so I chose a different L word. "I *like* you… a lot."

Sometime the next year, as we were eating at Cici's pizza buffet, I realized something: I wanted to spend the rest of my life with him. I began hinting about the idea of getting engaged. Eventually, I started to get impatient and asked him what he would do if I proposed to him. He said he would say "no" because he wanted to be the one to propose.

And then came the day. He arranged everything—a trip to the zoo to see the elephants (which are amazingly beautiful creatures), feed a giraffe named Grace, and then back to my apartment. I had told him once that I wanted a fluffy, white dog. Unfortunately, my apartment didn't allow pets. Instead of a real dog, he set a white, automated one down on the patio and sent it trotting my way. Around its neck was a ring.

He told me I better not say "sure" when he asked me to marry him.

I thought about it, just for kicks, but he was so nervous that I just couldn't do it.

We got married the next October in a pumpkin-filled autumn wedding under an arbor that my father built for us. And then we climbed into a Cinderella carriage, drawn by a stunning, white horse, and were whisked away to the reception.

To this day, five years later, when people ask how we met, we look at each other and laugh before telling them the story about the papier-mâché Pentagon.

~C.C. Warrens

Not Too Big After All

More than kisses, letters mingle souls.
~John Donne, English poet

The words hung in the air. "Oh, he's big…" My wide-eyed stare captured the view of the guy from a distance — the man I came to meet.

Headphones hugged his thick neck. The young man's shoulders, biceps, and legs appeared more like tree trunks than human appendages. Everything about him, my pen pal, was body-builder big — and nothing I typically looked for in a potential husband.

Just weeks earlier, a co-worker tacked a newspaper article onto my cubicle wall. Ginny scribbled: "This could happen to you, too!" at the top. The article noted Desert Storm pen pals who had married.

At the time, I chuckled and entertained the notion briefly. After all, Tony and I were pen pals from Desert Storm, just like the couple in the article. A quick rush of reality, however, assured me my friend was crazy. Surely nothing would come of my upcoming trek to the airport. After all, my sailor and I were simply friends who met through a Dear Abby "Any Serviceperson" letter. That's all — or so I tried to tell myself.

Rewind two years earlier to a time when I sat at my college drafting table, scribbling letters to unknown military members. Several landed in the hands of sailors and airmen serving during Desert Storm. One made it to Tony's ship. His letters and mine began crisscrossing the United States and various oceans. Our friendship grew with each stamped envelope.

Those scribbled letters were our sole interaction during the first year. I tucked a picture of myself into one of those initial letters, too. Tony, however, waited for several months before offering me one in return. And so I continued writing to an unknown face.

After a year of letters and a growing ease in our relationship, Tony managed to call me. We continued our letters anyway. And then two years later, there I stood — ready to come face-to-face with my pen pal at the Atlanta airport.

That's when I saw the big guy coming toward me.

"Hi," he said.

I gulped. "Hi. Are you Tony?"

He nodded slightly.

A short, military-style haircut framed his light blue eyes nicely. He looked like the man in the sole photo I had received, but so much larger. I'd never met another man near his size.

We talked during the hour he had before his connecting flight to Charleston. Tony was quiet, and the whole situation was awkward.

For weeks, a fairy-tale daydream had flitted in my mind — a play-by-play on how our real-life, face-to-face introduction would flow. This was not it!

As Tony prepared to board his final flight, I waved goodbye. I was so disappointed. Clearly, he didn't like me.

A few days later, however, my phone rang. It was Tony. My pen pal remained interested.

Our southern cities were four hours apart. After that phone call, our cars raced back and forth with regular visits. Tony bathed me in kindness, generosity, thoughtfulness, and love. And eventually, he placed a wedding ring on my finger. That was three kids and twenty-three years ago.

~Kristi Woods

Love Restored

To be fully seen by somebody, then, and be loved
anyhow — this is a human offering
that can border on miraculous.
~Elizabeth Gilbert

R ecently, my friend and I were having lunch and discussing our families. She talked about how great her older children were doing, and my heart sank. Her children had had the best upbringing possible. They had two parents, two sets of grandparents, a lot of love and encouragement — everything that makes for well-adjusted adults.

My three children had not had the same advantages. My parents had both died before they were born, and their father's parents rarely made the effort to see them. Their father had left me for another woman. We were left with little money and had to move every two years. At one point, I was working three to four jobs to compensate for the lack of child support.

I was so busy trying to survive that I didn't have time to relax and enjoy my children. I had often felt like a failure because no matter how hard I tried, I never had enough money, energy, and patience for my children. But, somehow, we always made ends meet, and things turned out all right.

As if reading my mind, my friend stopped and said, "You are my hero, you know. I tell people about you all the time." That snapped me back to the present. *Hero? Me? Why?* She then proceeded to tell me how much of an inspiration I'd been, how she admired my courage and the way I'd raised my children. I could hardly believe my ears. Here she was, in my opinion, the epitome of an excellent mother, wife, homemaker and all I hoped to be, and she was saying how much she admired me?

Later on, as I recalled our conversation, I began to take inventory of my life. My children were now adults. My two daughters were married to wonderful spouses. They were accomplished in many ways. They were good mothers to my three beautiful grandchildren and lived in lovely homes. My son, though still finding his way in life, was a true survivor and had many skills.

My mind drifted back to when they were still young, and I was a struggling single parent, doing my best to stay afloat. With three teenagers, I was in way over my head, and I knew it. I prayed a lot and trusted that God had the stomach for all my bellyaching. I recalled one day when I was helping with an outreach event at my church. I'd been cutting up some paper for a fall carnival and made a bit of a mess on the gym floor. I asked my son to vacuum it up for me. He tossed the handle aside and said he wouldn't do it. I guess it was embarrassing for him to be vacuuming in front of his peers. A man whom I'd seen a few times at church came over and asked if he could take my son to the other side of the gym to shoot some hoops. I was relieved, as the "scene" had been quite humiliating.

The next day, we were there helping again, and the same man came up. He put his arm around my shoulder and said that he hated to vacuum when he was my son's age. His kindness caught my attention, although I didn't know if I could ever trust a man again.

The more I observed this man, though, the more I felt at ease. Every time I turned around, he was beside me. Literally! When a basement suite came up for rent behind my house, John moved in and became my neighbor. He offered to drive my son to school on his way to work, which saved me a lot of time.

For the next nine years, John and I hung out with our church friends. One day, my younger daughter noticed that I was smiling for no reason and asked if I was thinking about John. I asked her what she thought about John and me dating. She laughed and said, "You and John are in denial."

I went to my son and all I said was, "What do you think of…" He finished my sentence with, "if you and John start dating? It's about time." My elder daughter agreed.

We started officially dating in October. He decided to wait until Valentine's Day to propose. He took me to a beautiful restaurant in Vancouver. After dinner, when he got up, I assumed he was getting my coat, but instead he got down on one knee and proposed. We then went for a walk in a nearby park. It was all lit up with the words "I Love You" embedded in the gardens. After a romantic walk in the moonlight, we walked across the parking lot and looked out over the twinkling lights of the city. Suddenly, in plain view of any passerby, John took me in his arms and began to waltz me around the parking lot, singing in my ear. With the city lights in the background, and his tall frame holding me so tenderly, it felt like a scene from a Hallmark movie.

Eight months later, I had the wedding of my dreams. My son walked me down the aisle, and my two daughters were my bridesmaids. It was magical. One year later, we bought out first house. Within the past fourteen years, everything I lost has been restored. Our three grandchildren have a Papa they adore.

In retrospect, I finally saw what my friend saw. I had been through a lot of heartache and hardship, and had endured a lot of losses, but the strength she saw was my faith. I was quick to point that out to her. Without my faith, I'd have let my circumstances dictate my future. But I kept my faith, and I trusted that my story would end well.

~Carol Marks

Fast Friends

We are spontaneous when we are at our genuine best.
~Hilary Thayer Hamann

The "D word" can be almost as frightening as telling someone you have a dreaded disease. Divorce is such an ugly word. I worried that I'd be branded for life when it happened to me: a failure, someone who just couldn't get this marriage thing right. I was forty-four and made a vow to never marry again. I would be perfectly happy in my own skin and in my own little world.

Then I met Ray through a mutual friend in the glorious, cool green pines of Lake Tahoe. He was visiting my friend at the same time I chose to visit her. I'd left the dry desert of Arizona to find some solace. I had no idea that I'd find my soul mate, instead.

It started as an honest friendship, the likes of which I had never experienced before. We had so much in common. The first coincidence came when I learned he was also an Arizonan. During conversation, we realized we moved in somewhat the same circles. Both of us loved and owned horses. We were both represented by the same agency in Phoenix for radio, movie and commercial gigs. I kept my horse at the same place he frequented, and we actually had some mutual friends. Dancing was our favorite pastime, and singing was a crazy passion we both enjoyed.

For almost an entire year, we spent time with each other in friendship. I dated other guys and Ray became the one I complained to about my dates. He always gave genuine and compassionate advice. We went to movies, dinner and dances, and most of the time we went Dutch on the expenses. Ray supported me more than my girlfriends, and he listened intently. He let me cry on his shoulder in the wee hours of the morning. He never judged me.

One evening, while eating pizza, I complained about one of my dates when Ray said, "You know, don't you, that whenever you get fed up with this dating thing, I'll be waiting for you?"

I was shocked. After he went home, I pondered his words. *Really? Does Ray really have* those *kinds of feelings for me?*

Sometime later, Ray asked, "Hey, do you want to take a trip back to Tahoe to see Livia? I'm going for a few days, and if you can get off work, it might be fun. What do you say?"

We took off in his Trans Am, opened up the sky roof, and laughed and sang along with cassette tapes the entire trip. Thrilled to see us, our mutual friend constantly queried me with questions like, "Are you guys together? What's going on?"

She had no idea what Ray had asked me the day before while we were driving: "Do you want to get married?"

I had laughed. "No, not really."

"Me, neither," he said. But when we stopped in Carson City at a jewelry store, we bought his-and-hers wedding bands for less than two hundred dollars and tucked them into the glove compartment of the car.

We married in a quaint chapel in the Tahoe area with Livia and her husband as our witnesses. I can actually say I never looked back. I never questioned our quick decision to marry. Instead, I embraced having married my best friend, who became my soul mate, protector, and father of our late-in-life child. She weighed only one pound, nine ounces at birth, and it was our strong friendship that helped us through that trial.

We've been together thirty-one years and our daughter has grown into a beautiful, young woman who seems to make lots of quick decisions. We think that's just fine.

~Alice Klies

Ditto

Love recognizes no barriers. It jumps hurdles,
leaps fences, penetrates walls to arrive at its
destination full of hope.
~Maya Angelou

By my mid-forties, I had given up on love. With a long history of bad relationships, I concluded love wasn't in the cards for me. Having decided to remain single, I broke up with my latest beau, sold my apartment, bought a house in another state, and moved on.

I loved my new home and new life. After getting to know the lay of the land, I worked on getting to know my neighbors, who were friendly and welcoming. But as the first winter in my new home ended, and the trees started to show signs of life, my happiness faded. I missed my family and friends terribly.

To cheer myself up, I went to my favorite bookstore. Reading had always been my favorite hobby, and a good book would help bring me out of my doldrums. While there, I noticed a man following me. He never said a word but watched me intently as I picked up one book after the other. Hoping to prove myself wrong, I walked to the opposite side of the bookstore and waited. Moments later, he rounded the corner and stopped a few feet away, pretending to look at a book. I didn't know whether to be alarmed or flattered, so I took careful note of his appearance. He was just over six feet tall and had dark hair and blue eyes. He was dressed in jeans, a plaid shirt, and work boots. I thought, *He's ruggedly handsome and probably works outside — definitely not my type.* But I was mildly intrigued.

"Having trouble finding something good to read?" I asked him.

"No," he said. "Actually, I've been sort of following you. I want to buy a book for my daughter, but I have no idea what she likes. I thought if I followed you and saw what you picked out, I might get some ideas."

"I'm probably the wrong person to follow. I like many different subjects. What kinds of books have you seen her reading?"

"All I know is that the covers usually have some half-naked man with long hair on them, and he's holding a woman in a long, flowing dress."

Laughing, I said, "Those are romance novels." On our way over to the romance section, I introduced myself. His name was Brad. Together, we picked out several novels, and then he asked me out on a quasi-date — coffee at the café inside the bookstore.

After getting our coffee, we sat down and talked for hours. Fairly quickly, I learned Brad was a little unconventional, opinionated, and rough around the edges. But he was also down-to-earth, warm and friendly — and rather charming. I was beginning to find his earthy good looks appealing, and I was captivated by his gorgeous blue eyes. In spite of the fact that we had nothing in common, and he had no fashion sense whatsoever, I liked him. He made me laugh. So I agreed to have dinner with him the following night.

Brad was soon at my house several times a week. We took things slowly and spent a great deal of time getting to know one another. We became friends first — something I had never done in my previous relationships. It was refreshing. Brad loved to build and fix things — something we had in common. He worked in construction and had recently finished renovating his home. I had just started the renovation of my own home, but was putting off two easy projects due to some uncertainties. One of them was the paneling in my bedroom. So I asked Brad, "Do you think the paneling in the bedroom was installed directly over the studs?"

"I don't know," he said. "But there's only one way to find out." He went into the bedroom and tore down a strip of paneling — a plaster wall was behind it. So he ripped off the rest of the paneling and threw it in the corner for me to throw out. (I never could get him to take out the garbage.) When it was done being remodeled, I gazed at my beautiful new bedroom and recalled a book I once read about the five languages of love. I never did learn which of the languages was mine — all the men I dated spoke the same language. But Brad had just discovered it. And, as luck would have it, our love language was the same — acts of service. We enjoyed doing things for one another because it made the other person happy. But more important to Brad than my happiness was my safety, which included the dogs.

One of my dogs had escaped from the house and run away. For three nights, I lay awake praying she'd come home. On the fourth day, the woman who had found her saw my ad in the newspaper and called. My next date with Brad was a trip to Home Depot. He took me to the outdoor department, and together we picked out a fence that would secure the dogs in the yard. We installed it together. Afterward, we sat by the fire pit, drank a bottle of wine, and watched the dogs chase each other around the yard. It was then that I realized I had fallen in love with Brad — hook, line, and sinker. But because of all the bad relationships I had had over the years, I kept my feelings hidden from Brad for more than a year.

The stairs to the second floor of my house were steep and narrow. One cold morning, I attempted to move a table from the office upstairs to the music room downstairs. I had on my favorite fuzzy socks, and as I stepped down onto the first step, my foot slipped. While holding onto the table, I fell down the remaining thirteen steps. There were no broken bones, but I was bruised from head to toe and couldn't walk for weeks. When I was able to climb the stairs, I saw that Brad had installed a handrail, which went all the way to the top of the stairs. It was the most beautiful thing I ever saw. And like a fool, I stood there and sobbed uncontrollably. Brad came running in to see what was wrong, and with tears streaming down my face, I said, "I love you."

"Yeah, I know," he said. "Ditto." And with that, he walked away. I wanted to slug him.

That was how Brad communicated—not with a lot of words, but through acts of service and kindness. It took some getting used to, but we got along well and seldom fought. While he wasn't big on talking, he hated arguing more. In all the years we've been together, I recall having only three arguments—and they were doozies. During one, I was sure our relationship was over. He stormed out of the house, vowing never to return. But he came back hours later. I was working in my office and refused to come out. So he slid a folded piece of paper under the door and left. I opened it—in big bold letters, he had written only one word "Ditto." That's when I decided Brad was a keeper.

~L.M. Lush

The Miracle of Love

Worth the Wait

Haven't We Met Somewhere Before?

*When deep down in the core of your being you believe
that your soul mate exists, there is no limit to the ways
he or she can enter your life.*
~Arielle Ford

The first time I remember meeting him, I was dripping with sweat as I turned away yet another customer. "The freezer is broken," I said over and over to the overheated patrons who approached my snow-cone cart at Worlds of Fun, a big amusement park in northwest Missouri. The only good thing about my shift was that I made the same measly minimum wage whether I was serving overpriced flavored ice in paper cones or just standing under the cart's gigantic yellow umbrella receiving ice-cold stares.

"Why don't you just put up a 'Closed' sign and come catch some rides with us?" The boy who posed the question leaned into the cart, careful to duck so he wouldn't bump his head on the umbrella. I laughed at the thought of ditching work so I could go ride roller coasters with this good-looking guy and his goofy friends, whom I guessed to be about sixteen like me. "I promise you that we'd have 'worlds of fun,'" he added.

"Sorry, I've got to stay put. Boss's orders," I said, even though his invitation was as cute as he was, and I didn't want to say "no." Our eyes locked for a mere moment, and my heart skipped a beat.

"Have it your way," he said. "But if you're ever in Somewhere, Kansas, look me up." And then he was gone.

He really did not say "Somewhere," but for the life of me, I couldn't remember the town he said or if he'd even mentioned his name. I also couldn't forget the adorable look in his big brown eyes or the fact that it had been the closest I'd gotten to being asked on a date all summer long.

Two years later, in 1981, I was with my church youth group in Estes Park, Colorado. My friends and I tossed a Frisbee in a grassy area near where we would soon be boarding our bus. The Frisbee soared past me and into the midst of a family gathered around a picnic table.

"I guess you want this back," a brawny boy teased as he stood up while holding the Frisbee high over his head. "How about I join your game?"

The bus horn blared before I could agree. I shrugged and said, "Sorry, I've got to go." I didn't want to, though.

"That's too bad," he said, smiling as his brown eyes seemed to look right through mine. He leaned forward in a gentlemanly bow and handed me the Frisbee. Our fingertips touched, and then away I went, feeling all tingly. His eyes and smile reminded me of the boy from the amusement park. My friends teased me on the bus when I asked them if they thought he could have been the same guy. They'd already tired of hearing how I'd lost my one true chance at love at the broken-down snow-cone cart.

Thirty years passed, along with two failed marriages. I had no interest in getting involved in another relationship. I focused my energies on raising my kids in a small southern Colorado town where I'd bought a house and enjoyed my marketing job with the local hospital.

Then one day a deep voice came from the direction of my office doorway. "Can you help me with the printer?" I glanced up to see a nice-looking, middle-aged man leaning inside. He explained that he was doing some contract work for our information services department and had been set up temporarily in the office across the hallway, but he didn't have a code for the printer.

As he spoke, I couldn't help but notice his kind, brown eyes. It was January, and my office was cold, but it suddenly felt as warm and muggy as a summer day.

"Only if you have time," he said. "I didn't mean to interrupt what you're doing."

"No, it's okay, I've got time for you, I mean, to help you."

"Thanks, I really appreciate it," he said, flashing a smile that took me back to my youth.

"This may sound ridiculous, but I'm curious," I said. "Where did you live during high school?"

"Somewhere in Kansas that you've probably never heard of. A tiny town called Gridley. How about you?"

"I grew up in St. Joe, Missouri," I answered. "But I worked at Worlds of Fun over the summer, and there were always kids from Kansas there."

"You can bet I was one of them," he said.

"Did you ever happen to vacation in Estes Park?" I asked, my heart pounding.

"As a matter of fact, my first trip there was with my family right before my freshman year of college, so it must have been 1981," he said, looking quizzically at me. "Then I moved to Colorado after college. My work has me traveling all over the state, but I live in Denver now."

"I'm planning on moving to Denver soon," I said, pledging silently to myself to get my résumé together so I could begin looking for jobs in the Mile High City two hundred miles away.

"That's great," he said. "When you do, be sure to look me up."

After giving him the code to the printer, we exchanged names and phone numbers. This led to a year of long-distance dating and then to this Missouri-born girl and her boy from somewhere in Kansas finally settling down in the same Colorado home.

His memories of our possible teenage meetings have yet to meld with mine. He assures me, though, while my remembrances seem wildly crazy, he's crazy in love with me now. I feel the same way. I'm also happily thankful that even though he can't remember it, he's managed to keep his first-ever promise to me. Being together truly has been worlds of fun.

~Lisa Marlin

June 15

True love stories never have endings.
~Richard Bach

June 15, 1973: Our birthday. I was born on the East Coast. Alex was born on the West Coast.

June 15, 1986: Our thirteenth birthday. We'd met that school year, in seventh grade, in Southern California — where his family had moved when he was two and mine when I was ten. We'd become friends (with a spark, and a bit of young flirting). One day in P.E. class, standing on the blacktop numbers, I saw on his student I.D. card that his birthday was June 15. "That's my birthday!" I said. He didn't believe me, but it was true.

June 15, 1990: Our seventeenth birthday. Alex left a birthday card in my locker at our high school, and I felt my stomach flip. We hadn't talked much for a couple of years. Freshman year, our flirting had turned into hours on the phone together, then my first kiss. We dated for a few weeks. Though our feelings for each other were strong (probably too strong for our age), I hadn't been as ready for dating as he was, so I broke it off. He moved on, found a girlfriend more ready than me, and hung with the jock-surfer crowd. I hung with the theater people and didn't date seriously in high school. But our eyes often met across campus (and the spark was still there).

June 15, 1993: Our twentieth birthday. I was home from college back East. Alex was home from college in Colorado. We'd become friends again senior year, then pen pals, writing each other about college and life and dreams. I had a serious boyfriend and serious studies. Alex was enjoying the single college life. He called my house on our birthday afternoon. My mom told him I'd just found out my grandfather had died that morning, and I wasn't up for talking. It was the first time that we didn't speak on our birthday.

June 15, 1999: Our twenty-sixth birthday. I had an apartment and a full-time office job in our Southern California hometown. He had a room and seasonal jobs a couple hours up the coast (so he could take off for months-long surf trips around the globe). We'd been writing letters and talking on the phone for years, both single and dating people in our respective cities, and both harboring bigger feelings for each other that we wouldn't come out and say. We chatted on the phone on our birthday (the spark hanging in the air). When he came into town to see his dad, we'd go out to dinner, see a movie, walk on the beach, and maybe kiss goodnight. They were sort of dates, but we definitely weren't dating. Missing each other once again.

June 15, 2001: Our twenty-eighth birthday. I'd gone off to grad school in the Midwest. He was starting grad school in San Diego. He'd bought a couch, and I realized that maybe he was actually settling down. So we finally shared our long-held feelings and tried dating for real — long distance. I came to San Diego to spend my summer break with him, and it was our first birthday as a couple. We were in love, finally together after sixteen years of wondering. We toasted with champagne and carrot cake (a mutual favorite), and the future looked bright.

June 15, 2002: Our twenty-ninth birthday. It was the second time we didn't speak on our birthday, and it felt awful. We'd broken up right after that last summer. It hadn't worked for me to move into his apartment and his world, and things had crumbled between us on a disastrous trip to South America. Alex was in San Diego, I was in the Midwest, and we were both heartbroken. It hurt me too much to remain friends, so I had asked him to let me go for good.

June 15, 2003: Our thirtieth birthday. We gathered our respective friends at a beachside pub and celebrated together, with a huge carrot cake on the bar. He'd called me a few months earlier to see if I missed him as much as he missed me. I did. And I'd actually started a doctoral program while we were apart… in San Diego. We'd decided to meet for lunch, and that was it. We both knew we didn't want to lose what we had again. We were finally ready.

June 15, 2017: Our forty-fourth birthday. We celebrated with our two kids, ages eight and eleven, in our beachy townhouse of thirteen years. After those many seasons of letters and phone calls, laughs and tears, near-misses and disasters, here we were: eating carrot cake with our growing children, doing life together. We looked at each other and silently marveled that we had actually made it to this.

All that our kids really know about our love story is that we met when we were twelve, were friends for years, and married when we were thirty — *and don't all parents have the same birthday?*

~Megan Pincus Kajitani

My Bloody Lip

The simple act of caring is heroic.
~Edward Albert

I was thirty-eight and unmarried. My pastor said, "Every family needs an unmarried aunt to spoil the kids." That didn't make me feel better.

I am one of eight children, so I did have seventeen nieces and nephews. As the sibling without children, I flew in to babysit so the parents could have a weekend off. Every year, I flew home to help my mom host the extended family — eighty people — for Thanksgiving dinner. I came at Christmas and wrapped a mountain of gifts (hard for my siblings to do with their children around) and fed the hordes. My church had an active single adults' group that I coordinated. I started a business and had clients who depended on me.

My life was rich with people, events, friends, family, work, and church. Everyone counted on me, and I delivered. Singleness didn't bother me. Not that much, anyway.

When commiserating with friends, I always said, "There's one thing that's true in the history of every relationship in the world. One day, those two people didn't know each other, and the next day they did. Tomorrow could be the next day for you."

Not long before Christmas, I sat on the couch in my cozy little Washington, D.C., rowhouse, drinking coffee. My friend Steven called. Without preamble, he said, "I gave someone your phone number."

That someone was Tom, who had been living in a religious community.

At a Christmas party, Tom announced that religious life was not his calling. He was starting graduate school to become a psychotherapist.

"So, I told him," Steven said, "I always thought that if he left his community, I'd introduce him to you."

Tom and I met in February and dated for seven months. Business was slow for me that summer, and he was between semesters. We hiked, went to the beach, lay in the grass on the National Mall, and talked about our dreams. Sometimes literally. For years, Tom, once a land surveyor, had had a recurring dream. In his dream, he surveyed an empty field and could find three property corners, but not the fourth.

My sister and her family came to visit, and Tom put netting on my open banisters so the kids wouldn't fall through. I cooked dinners. We watched movies and ate hot-fudge sundaes. We fell in love.

In September, Tom got nervous. People kept telling him that he shouldn't get serious with the first person he dated after leaving religious life. He said he wanted a "time out." I agreed. (A veteran of the D.C. dating scene, I knew we had something special, but I also knew he had to learn that for himself.)

We still saw each other. He told me about his dates. (He seemed miserable.) I bided my time. He decided to stay in D.C. for Christmas, not go to his family or come to mine. I worried about him.

Christmas Eve, he called. "I'm lonely," he said. "But I'm not lonely for just anyone; I'm lonely for you."

New Year's Eve, we discussed getting married. Tom was leaving the next day for a weeklong silent retreat. He was "almost positive" that he was ready for marriage. He wanted the retreat to meditate about it, to be sure.

The days dragged. I could not wait to hear what he decided, and I surprised myself by fretting about it. Did I want to give up the life I had? I liked my life. A lot. Did I want to share my house with someone? I'd lived there alone for fourteen years. Did I want to share my life? I'd been single for a long time. If Tom came home and asked me to marry him, was I ready?

The week ended, and I drove to pick him up. Tom grinned and kissed me, and held me in a great bear hug. As I drove home, he told me about the retreat, about how he wandered along the beach and found sharks' teeth, about the books he read.

I let him talk, working up my nerve. "What about us?"

"Us?"

"You said you were using the retreat to decide about us."

He put his hand over mine and grinned. "Sorry, I'm so sure about it that I forgot you didn't know. The first night there, I had a dream — that one I always have about surveying a piece of property. This time, I found the fourth corner. I have no doubts at all."

I got all shaky and incoherent, so we stopped for lunch. Thirty seconds after we ordered, I bit my lip, and it started to bleed. It wouldn't stop. In the ladies' room, I applied pressure with a cold compress of paper towels. No matter how hard I pressed, my lip still bled — down my chin, onto my blouse, into the sink. I couldn't go back to the table like this.

The bathroom door opened a crack after a gentle knock, and Tom in poked his head. "Are you okay?"

"It won't stop bleeding," I told him, near tears.

"Hang on." Minutes later, he knocked again and handed in a teabag. "There's something in tea that stops bleeding. Hold it to your lip. Do you need me to come in?"

I once witnessed a man walk into a ladies' room to help his wheelchair-bound wife. Someone called security, and an ugly scene ensued. Tom was offering to do that for me.

I told him I'd be okay, and the bleeding stopped shortly after I applied the teabag. When I got back to the table, our order was wrapped and ready to take home.

"I figured you wouldn't want to eat here with a sore lip and blood all over. I'll drive."

Something felt strange. Uncomfortable. Wrong. Then I understood. Instead of me taking charge and caring for everyone else, someone was caring for me. I couldn't remember that happening before in my adult life. When Tom proposed, I said, "Yes." I had no doubts at all.

~Kathy Joyce

The List

*So, I love you because the entire universe conspired
to help me find you.*
~Paulo Coelho, The Alchemist

One Friday night in the spring of 1999, my girlfriend and I went to Ladies' Night at the local bar to see an all-male dance troupe. The building was a converted barn, with wide, hand-hewn beams and rough siding. The main stage was at one end of the cavernous room, while in the loft a balcony with a wide, wooden railing circled the outside walls. A large, dusty disco ball hung in the centre of the ceiling. Several older pool tables were tucked in the back upstairs, and each floor had a long bar up against the side wall. The servers wove through the crowds of women like salmon swimming upstream.

It had been a few months since we had been out together, so we were soon deep in conversation. When the entertainers came on stage dressed like the Village People, the packed audience whistled and catcalled loudly. A cowboy, a cop, an Indian, a soldier, a biker and a handyman — they wore next to nothing by the time the first song ended.

Beer goes right through me, so I joined the long line at the washroom. Standing next to me was Sadie, a tall blonde with tight jeans and a jacket with fringes that matched her boots. We struck up a conversation about guys, joking about how the dancers didn't represent the men we usually met.

She showed me her ring: a gold band with two pear-cut diamonds set on either side of a heart-shaped one in the middle. Shouting so that she could be heard, she confided that she had met her dream guy and had married recently. I bemoaned the fact that there weren't any nice, unattached guys in our small town. The ones out there had been thrown back, like fish that were too small or out of season.

"Write a list," Sadie said. "My girlfriend told me about it. I thought she was kidding, but she convinced me to try it."

She said that one night she sat in her kitchen and wrote a list of everything she wanted in a partner. With rugged good looks, a friendly personality, and a wonderful sense of humour, he would be kind, generous and loving. She described how he would treat her and care for her; she literally asked for a shining knight on a white horse. Summoning up his image, she sent the wish out into the universe.

Unbelievably, it worked. She had created such a firm vision that when she first saw him, she was sure they had met before. They fell in love. The day he proposed, he came to her on a white horse.

Sure, I thought. *I just met you, and we've been drinking. Nice if it worked, but…*

All week long, the idea niggled at my brain. Listing exactly what I wanted felt like a strange thing to do, but I figured I had nothing to lose.

That Friday night, after giving my two small, wiggly boys their bath, tucking them in and reading *Goodnight Moon* twice, I went downstairs into the quiet kitchen. I sat at the head of the table and looked around me at the command central of our lives. The crayon drawings on the fridge and the snapshots of family and friends reminded me how hard it had been to get us to this place of safety and freedom. Then I thought about the days when I longed to have someone to share it with, to talk and laugh about the day.

I lit a white candle and poured a glass of wine. Opening my favorite journal, I carefully thought about the men I'd dated: the losers, the tough guys, the sweet talkers, the crazies, and the handsome narcissists. I realized that I'd been admiring the wrong guys, the inappropriate ones, the flashy ones. Somehow, I thought they would be good life mates and good fathers. *No wonder,* I thought. *I've been paying attention to the wrong things.*

I wrote my list: a wide and ready smile, a great sense of humour, a lot of patience, a loving father, a kind person, a generous lover, a hardworking man with a steady income, not too flashy but handsome, good with pets, not obsessed with sports, warm hands, likes dancing and camping, laughs often and can laugh at himself. I focused on the person I described and held the image in my heart. Then I sent it out into the universe.

In early September, I took my youngest son to kindergarten for his first day. John was quivering with excitement when I kissed him goodbye, and he ran over to the LEGO table, his favorite. Blinking back unexpected tears, I met the teacher, a smiling woman with dark hair and wire-framed glasses. As I left, I noticed a man in a gray uniform and work boots talking to his son. He was crouched down low so they were face-to-face, and he spoke carefully and intently. The little blond boy with blue eyes watched his father closely. They gave each other a giant bear hug before parting.

Damn, I thought to myself. *Would you look at that? Another good one taken. He even brings the little guy to school. What a great dad he must be.*

In October, there was a field trip to the local pumpkin patch, and we met. He was a widower; his wife had died that spring, leaving him with two small children, a son and a daughter. We had a lot in common; he understood exactly what it was like to be a single parent.

The next year on Mother's Day, while we celebrated with our four children and my mother, he got down on one knee and proposed. And he is everything I had written, right down to the small details.

He has the warmest hands.

~Tree Langdon

13

The Perfect Dress

It's delightful when your imaginations come true,
isn't it?
~L.M. Montgomery, Anne of Green Gables

It was too ridiculous to consider. I couldn't even remember when I had my last date. But there I was, admiring the wedding gown and veil draped over my arm.

My friend Sharon and I had hurried to the secondhand store on our lunch hour. She knew I often stopped by resale shops to look for tatting shuttles to add to my collection.

In the shop's entryway, Sharon glanced around the one room. "I'll look by myself," she said. I nodded and headed toward a rack of long dresses near the back. I always checked for new additions for my singing-on-the side wardrobe.

I spied a wedding gown with matching veil in the middle of the rack. Curious, I gently took it down. The princess-style dress was simple yet elegant, with one wide panel of lace down the front and lace banding the short sleeves and neckline. Even though I'd day-dreamed about Mr. Right and our wedding, I'd never thought about the dress I'd wear. Even without trying it on, I knew I wanted to wear this dress on my wedding day.

My reverie broke as Sharon stopped to look at the gown. I could tell she was as impressed as I was. To my surprise, she urged me to try it on. I needed little encouragement and hurried to the dressing room. To my astonishment, the dress fit perfectly. I stepped back against the wall for a better view in the full-length mirror.

Then I remembered Sharon. I opened the curtain and took a model's stance. She gasped. "That dress was made for you, Joyce. Buy it."

As I debated, I heard my mother's voice in my ears. "Be prepared," the Boy Scout motto she'd drilled into us over the years, told me it wasn't silly. I would be preparing. That clinched it. I'd buy it. I hurriedly put on my office suit and rushed to the checkout counter before I chickened out.

On the ride back to work, we giggled about what I'd done. It was so uncharacteristic of me. My lightheartedness waned as we neared the office. Not wanting to be the laughingstock of the office, I begged Sharon not tell our co-workers. To my relief, she agreed it would be our secret.

That night as I taped two large garbage bags together to keep the dress clean, I smiled and chuckled again at my impetuousness.

Two years passed. Then three. Then four. During those mostly dateless years, I'd occasionally push back the clothes in front of the dress and envision myself in it. I wanted to try it on, but thought it too much work to fit the bags together again and re-tape them.

Meanwhile, no one at work teased me about the gown, so I knew Sharon had kept her word. I worried she would let it slip. I bid her goodbye with relief when she left for another job.

Two more years passed. Work, church activities, singing commitments, hobbies, travel, and family filled those years, and they flew by.

A few months after my thirty-sixth birthday, I began to get discouraged. My biological clock was ticking.

Several months later, a friend mentioned her new co-worker. "His name is Dennis, and even though I don't know him well because he works in another department, he seems very nice. Interested in a blind date?" she asked.

Like most people, I wasn't too fond of blind dates, but I agreed. It wasn't like I was busy.

Saturday night, Dennis arrived. I opened the door for him to come in and meet my mother, and I sized him up as we sat and talked. I liked what I saw.

Soon, we headed to the restaurant. With many common interests, we talked for several hours over coffee. Three more dates followed that week, and we became engaged the following Saturday night.

Sunday morning, I asked myself if I'd lost my mind. First, I had bought a dress many years before meeting Mr. Right, and then I had become engaged within seven days of meeting a man! Again, I'd set aside my usual common sense — for the man I already knew I loved.

We set our wedding date for mid-November, three and a half months later. At the top of my to-do list was to try on my dress. Would it fit? Fearfully, I pulled up the zipper. To my relief, it was a bit large.

The seamstress assured me she could take in the dress. My aunt had suggested that long sleeves could be added. She thought they would be more appropriate for a late fall wedding. The seamstress agreed and added that the lace from the short sleeves could be used to make a band encircling my wrists. It would add the finishing touch. I agreed.

When I picked up the dress the day before the wedding, I saw that the seamstress had outdone herself. The dress was perfect.

The next morning, I awoke to sunshine. I stretched, chuckled, and smiled, realizing that I'd be married in a few hours.

Later, waiting for the wedding march to begin, I straightened my dress before picking up my bouquet. Once again, Mom's "be prepared" admonition echoed in my ears. I chuckled softly, thinking of my gown, waiting all those years for this moment — to be worn when I married my Mr. Right.

~Joyce Ermeling Heiser

The New Girl

*The most precious possession that ever comes to a man
in this world is a woman's heart.*
~J.G. Holland

I grew up in a small, rural town where everyone knew everyone's name. There were fewer than seventy students in my high-school freshman class, and I'd known almost all of them since preschool.

Teenagers in the town of La Vernia, Texas could choose to participate in sports or raise an animal to show in the local 4-H stock show. My sister and I did both. Our summers were spent at the ballpark. My buddies and I played baseball, while my sister joined her friends on the girls' softball team.

The summer before my sophomore year, I arrived at the ballpark to watch my sister practice. Immediately, I noticed the new girl on the team. I did some investigating and discovered she was from nearby San Antonio. Her family had just moved to town. She was a freshman, and she would be attending high school with us in the upcoming year.

I'd always been pretty shy when it came to girls, but this girl made me want to break out of my shell. Melissa was different from any of the girls I'd ever known. She didn't dress like the girls at our school, and her hair was shorter on one side than the other. She was beautiful, and I had an instant crush on her. Unfortunately, so did all of my friends.

It wasn't long before my sister began inviting Melissa to our house for swimming. As soon as I'd find out Melissa was on her way, I'd call the guys. "She's coming. Hurry up and get over here." They all knew exactly who "she" was, and they usually arrived in record time.

I played it cool for the most part, relying on what I hoped was my charm and natural singing ability to set me aside from the pack. I'd love to say it worked, but I'd be lying. Melissa wouldn't give me the time of day. No matter what I did or how hard I tried, she didn't seem to want anything to do with me.

The summer came to an end, and Melissa's visits to our home became fewer and farther between. Over the next three years, I'd see her occasionally in the halls at school. I was excited when I learned we had a class together my junior year. I still got butterflies anytime she so much as offered a polite nod in my direction, but that's about as much interaction as we had.

I didn't understand it. As an All-District football player, I was popular, even securing the title of "Most Friendly" by a vote of my senior class. Melissa stood in the crowd and watched as I was crowned prom king, but she still didn't seem impressed.

And just like that, I was out of time. I graduated, leaving my high-school crush behind to begin her own senior year. I joined the workforce, accepting a job in the city. And while I no longer saw Melissa, I never forgot about her.

I'd been out of school nearly two years when I was invited to a friend's birthday party. I was leaning against my truck, surrounded by old friends, when she came walking up the driveway. We locked eyes, and every feeling I'd ever felt for her returned in an instant. Melissa walked through the crowd toward me.

"Joey!" she said, as she wrapped her arms around me for a hug. "It's been forever."

She was still beautiful. Everyone else seemed to melt away as we stood there talking. The conversation flowed freely.

As the end of the night neared, I knew it was the moment of truth. I looked up at the night sky for a little reassurance. Had the stars finally aligned for me? I'd had a serious crush on this girl for five years. My mind raced. I didn't want to get shut down again, but I also knew there was no way I could let her go without taking a chance. I took a deep breath and asked for her number.

Melissa gave me her number that night, and her heart shortly thereafter. One year later, we were married. Like any married couple, we've had our ups and downs, but through it all, Melissa has remained the one true love of my life.

I'm glad I put my fear and insecurity aside and took a chance all those years ago. That girl who wouldn't give me the time of day has given me her every day for the last twenty-five years. And I still have a crush on her.

~Joey Wootan

The Cute Diamond

Gratitude is the healthiest of all human emotions.
The more you express gratitude for what you have,
the more likely you will have even more
to express gratitude for.
~Zig Ziglar

I was in the market for a new car. My husband Joey surprised me when he offered to splurge on the high-end, luxury SUV I'd had my eye on. We arrived at the car dealership and spent more than three hours test-driving vehicles, going over options, and filling out the paperwork.

"Why don't I give you a tour of our service department?" our salesman offered. "Our café offers a complimentary continental breakfast and made-to-order drinks for you to enjoy while you're getting your oil changed. You can even have a massage in one of our private massage rooms while your car is being serviced."

Wow, I thought. *My old dealership had a Coke machine and a bowl of peppermints on the check-in desk. I could really get used to being a luxury car owner.*

Joey and our salesman left me at the café to order a fancy drink while they talked service plans. I stepped up to the bar and smiled at the attendant.

"What can I get you?" she asked.

I studied the seemingly never-ending menu of organic flavors that could be added to my custom-blended soda. Couldn't a girl just get a Diet Coke?

"Cute diamond."

I turned my attention back to the attendant, who had commented on the small diamond pendant I wore on a thin chain around my neck. Her tone confused me.

"My husband bought this for me when we were nineteen years old. I've worn it for twenty-five years," I answered somewhat defensively while studying her expression.

"Isn't that nice?" she said dismissively.

Now I knew I wasn't imagining it. There was no doubt this woman was being condescending. Instinctively, I raised my hand to my chest and touched my necklace.

"Well, he did a good job on your ring, at least," she offered while nodding to the wedding set my husband had presented me on our twentieth wedding anniversary.

I stood there too shocked to say anything. I could not believe that the woman who served drinks at the dealership's coffee bar had just thrown shade at my diamond necklace.

A little girl walked up to the bar next to me and grabbed on with both hands while attempting to peer over the counter on her tiptoes. Her mother apologized before explaining to the child that she needed to wait her turn.

"No, it's okay." I looked from the little girl to the attendant. "There isn't anything here I want, after all," I said before walking away.

I held the delicate pendant between my fingers on the drive home. The diamond was small, no question, but what it represented was anything but. That's exactly why I had continued to wear it, even after my husband gave me a much larger diamond that was intended to take its place. I couldn't bring myself to take this one off, though. It was a sweet reminder of the kids we once were, young and in love, with dreams so big they could only be fulfilled together.

I was twenty when I walked down the aisle wearing the small diamond pendant my groom had given me while we were dating. Joey had just started working for the local utility company, and I was a new college student with a baby girl. There was no time (or money) for a honeymoon as I attended school during the day and waitressed at a Mexican restaurant in the evenings.

What we lacked in material possessions in those early days, we made up for in love and commitment. We were in this thing called marriage for the long haul, and we were in it together. I graduated from college and took a job doing nuclear medicine at a local imaging center. Joey stayed with the same utility company, eventually working his way up to become an executive. We added a son to our family, and a few years later, we built our dream home.

It wasn't all smooth sailing. It never is when love is involved, but that was one more reason this necklace was so precious to me. It represented the journey — our journey together.

"I'll take you to another dealership. Don't worry, we can buy that same make and model somewhere else," my husband offered sympathetically.

I'd left the luxury SUV and our salesman on the showroom floor. I shrugged my shoulders and told Joey I'd think about it. The next morning, I woke up and knew exactly what I wanted to do. I had my husband drive me to a nearby Chevrolet dealership where I purchased a beautiful, brand-new Tahoe. It wasn't a difficult decision, and I certainly didn't feel like I was settling. My husband and I had been the happy owners of several Chevys through the years. They had proven to be comfortable, dependable, unpretentious, and long-lasting — much like our love.

~Melissa Wootan

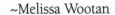

16

Romance Therapy

Have enough courage to trust love one more time and
always one more time.
~Maya Angelou

I was at college in Arizona when two of my girlfriends and I decided to delve into the occult. We went to "Madam Rosa's Palmistry" in hopes that our palms would reveal a future of fame, fortune, and hot guys.

Madam Rosa's place of business — a small, pink stucco house — was in a rundown section of Phoenix and had the décor you would expect. The customer waiting area was portioned off from Madam Rosa's realm by a curtain of colorful plastic beads. Small wisps of perfumed smoke emanated from a bronze incense burner placed on a velvet-covered countertop located in a corner near the mysterious Rosa's perch. Her glass orb was at the ready, sitting on a rickety, aluminum-legged, vinyl-covered card table.

It was a lot of fun for three giggling teenage girls, but we knew it was a sham, especially once we disclosed our fortunes to each other and discovered we all received the exact same ones.

After that palm-reading debacle, I avoided psychics for decades. But then my girlfriend started raving about a psychic she had used, who did readings over the phone. "He was amazing," she told me. "Everything he said was right on."

I was intrigued, and after having lost my husband to cancer, I thought I'd give a psychic reading a try. Being thirty years older, I was not looking for fame or fortune — and certainly no hot guys. I made the appointment, but as the day approached, I decided I was an idiot.

I did it anyway, and I was impressed with the man's ability to dive into my past and present, actually getting a lot of it correct. But then he said something that shocked me: "You will be in a romantic relationship sometime within the year."

I broke into a sweat when he said that. I moaned into the phone.

"What?" he said, with incredulity creeping into his voice. "Are you afraid of romance?" He chuckled.

"Yes!" I almost screamed.

He assured me that whether I was afraid of it or not, romance was more than just a possibility. "Love is definitely in your future."

I knew it wasn't possible, but I was wrong. I ended up reconnecting with a man I had met twenty years earlier. He was my physical therapist when I went into a rehab facility after losing three limbs to a vicious life-threatening bacterial infection commonly known as "flesh-eating bacteria."

I had liked him at first sight the day I met him at the rehab center. We had an instant rapport, which led to playful banter about every topic imaginable. But even more importantly, I knew that he was someone I could trust. He was strong, holding my body in an upright position as I struggled to reclaim my balance on knees that were no longer supported by legs. He never let me fall, providing me assistance to become adept at standing, walking, and even dancing on my knees.

As I worked hard, struggling to build the balance and muscles I needed to stand upright and walk on prosthetic legs, he would regale me with his family stories — and there were plenty as he came from a large Irish family. He would tell me jokes, distracting me from the pain and grueling physical therapy I had to endure.

I have spoken to groups of physical therapists about my personal story and rehab experience for years, and I always tell them about my physical therapist, Bob, and how having a physical therapist who is committed to the same goals, dreams, and aspirations as the patient can produce an excellent outcome. I am walking proof of that.

So when I met Bob again a few months ago, I did so simply with the intention of expressing the gratitude that I have held for him all these years. I wanted him to know how thankful I was for all he had done for me. I wanted him to see that I had become successful in my recovery, and that I'm capable and independent — all due to his work.

"I may be a person with disabilities," I told him, "but not much stops me from accomplishing anything I put my mind to."

Our fateful lunch date left me equally spellbound and startled by my feelings of attraction, which went well past a nice friendship. Our relationship quickly turned into the psychic prediction that I had run from, hidden from, and adamantly denied would ever happen.

Romance has happened as predicted. The hand I was dealt has turned into a winning one that I've finally figured out how to play — one I'm so glad I chose to never fold.

There are times when I think about my feelings surrounding my predicted romance. The thought that filled me with dread for so long now fills me with joy. My old friend, gratitude, has come back to me in full measure.

I have thought about Madam Rosa from time to time, too, and I think that maybe she wasn't so wrong after all. I certainly have not acquired fame or found my fortune, but somehow I've ended up with the hot guy after all.

~Cindy Charlton

The
Miracle
of Love

———— ⦿ ————

Love at First Sight

———— ⦿ ————

17

Nothing in Common

*The meeting of two personalities is like the contact of
two chemical substances; if there is any reaction,
both are transformed.*
~Carl Gustav Jung

My friend Daisy urged me to go to a Fourth of July picnic at Trout Lake. Everybody was welcome, and the fishing was free. The last thing I wanted to do was go fishing on that hot day in July.

It sounded like a horrible idea. I wouldn't know anyone there other than Daisy and her family, and I'd never been fishing. I wanted to stay home and spend the weekend reading a book.

I finally gave in and went to the picnic. Soon, I got bored, so I picked up a fishing pole and walked down to the lake. Although I'd never been fishing before, I figured all I had to do was get the line into the water and wait for a fish to bite the hook. But when I moved the pole backward in order to get some momentum to throw the line forward, I managed to get the line tangled in a tree instead. I jerked at it a few times, but it wasn't going to let go. I knew I'd have to walk back to the picnic and ask someone to cut the line.

A fisherman who had been standing nearby saw my problem and walked over.

"There aren't any fish in the tree. You have to get the hook in the water," he teased. It made me laugh. He climbed up the tree and untangled my line.

He was young and strong, and had a beautiful smile. He sat down on the grass, and I sat down a few feet from him.

He told me his name was Don. He'd just gotten out of the Marines and had come to Colorado to visit his parents before he went to Alaska where a job on a crab boat was waiting for him. His parents had dragged him to the picnic, and he hadn't wanted to come because he didn't know anyone except his parents. But the food was good, he enjoyed fishing, and he'd met someone nice.

"Who did you meet?" I asked, clueless that he was flirting with me.

"You," he said.

I blushed so red I probably glowed like Rudolph's nose.

He reached out, picked a yellow dandelion and handed it to me.

"A man is supposed to give flowers to a pretty lady. Don't think of this as a dandelion; think of this as a sunshine flower," he said.

I stuck the dandelion in the top buttonhole of my blouse. I decided that no flowers I would get for the rest of my life would mean as much as that sunshine flower. I wondered if it was possible to fall in love in five minutes.

We spent the afternoon walking around the lake and talking. We discovered we didn't have one single thing in common. In fact, we were complete opposites.

Don and I stayed to watch the fireworks, and then he did the most outrageous thing: He kissed me! I felt that kiss all the way from my lips to my toes and back again.

"I'll always remember your kiss and fireworks exploding in the sky," I told him.

He said he was only going to be in town for eight more days, and then he was leaving for Alaska. I got tears in my eyes. It wasn't fair that I'd finally met someone so special, and we'd only have eight days together. We'd never see each other again.

Don showed up at my house the next day wearing the ugliest shirt I'd ever seen. It was blue with little yellow flowers. It was too long, and the buttons were on the wrong side of the shirt — it buttoned like a woman's blouse.

"My mother likes to sew," he said. "She's not very good at it, but she made this for me, and it would hurt her feelings if I didn't wear it a couple of times while I'm home." I liked him even more than before. It couldn't have been easy for him to be seen in that shirt, but he was willing to sacrifice his own pride to spare his mother's feelings.

"I'm leaving for Alaska on Sunday. Alaska is the most beautiful place you can imagine, and I have a good job waiting for me. I know we just met two days ago, but I love you. If I leave without you, we'll never see each other again, and I think we'll both be sorry. Marry me and come to Alaska," he said.

He was strong and gentle. And there was that kiss during the fireworks that almost made my heart explode.

"Yes, I'll marry you!" I said.

We'd known each other two-and-a-half days, and we had nothing in common. We were getting married on Saturday and leaving for Alaska on Sunday — nine days after meeting.

I'd never had a serious boyfriend and had rarely even dated. My family had been convinced I was going to be an "old maid," and I was urged to get a good, steady job so I could support myself. But now, my family was shocked and horrified, and so was his. We received warnings of doom and disaster.

Both our mothers cried throughout the entire wedding ceremony. At times, their sobbing was so loud that people couldn't hear us exchanging our vows. It was a small, simple wedding. I wore a borrowed wedding gown that was too large for me, and Don wore a borrowed suit that was too small for him. The wedding photos show a bride and groom in clothes that didn't fit, two mothers with red, puffy eyes, and two grim-looking fathers. The next day, we were on a plane headed for Alaska. It was either the best thing — or the worst thing — I'd ever done in my life.

We continued to be opposites in every way. We didn't like the same music, food or movies. We had different religions, and our political views were as opposite as the North and South Poles.

Strangely enough, we never really had an argument. The extent of a disagreement was a sigh, a shrug and some eye rolling, but we never raised our voices. The disagreement usually ended with one of us making the other laugh. It was okay to be different. We loved each other, and we didn't try to change each other.

We were married for twenty-seven years when Don passed away. We have four grown children and four grandchildren. Except for the children and grandchildren, we still didn't have anything in common — and that's okay.

~April Knight

18

When Lightning Strikes

*Thunder is good, thunder is impressive, but it is
lightning that does all the work.*
~Sarah Mlynowski

It was the year of the great wake-up call. An article had been published in a national magazine stating that women over thirty had a better chance of being struck by lightning than finding a husband... and it was all anybody I knew was talking about.

Especially because they were talking about me.

Thirty-three and never married, I was working as an elementary-school teacher in the inner city. I was surrounded by women during the day and I was too tired at the end of the workday to do anything but curl up in bed with my lesson plans. I'd given up on love, moved in with my brother and considered my first-graders "my kids." As far as I could peer into my future, this was the scene before me.

I'd told myself that it was okay. My brother was a good companion, and my kids filled my heart with joy despite the fact they were rumored to be the "worst" kids on campus. They had, in fact, been labeled "Susan's Squirrels." Maybe even more because of this, I found my work fulfilling and my success at turning kids' attitudes around to be exciting.

Nevertheless, the article seemed to pour salt into the wound.

I wasn't sure how I'd gotten to that place. My mom had married at seventeen. I'd always thought I'd follow in her footsteps. But, as it happened, my high-school sweetheart wasn't "the one." Nor was the next guy. Nor the next.

Along the way, I earned two college degrees and a teaching credential while working two jobs to pay for tuition. When I finally looked up, I was thirty.

And then came the article.

"It's just not true," Joanne assured me one day at school as we discussed the article for the hundredth time. "I know in my bones that you'll find someone and soon. In fact, I predict you'll find your true love by spring."

Yeah. Right.

Weeks later, a consultant was scheduled to come to the school to teach us how to use music and movement to teach core subjects to our students. The mandatory workshops would be once a week per group for two weeks, and substitutes would take over our classes. Lower elementary was on Fridays. Workshops would be held in the empty classroom next door to my room.

The truth was I didn't want to go. I already had a strong music-and-movement program in my room and didn't need an outsider to teach me. But it didn't matter. The school had paid for Steven Traugh to consult, and I was to attend. Then, just as workshops were to begin, the flu struck the school. Kids and teachers dropped like flies as the bug spread its web over a third of the school. I was hit hard.

For three days, I was too sick to care. When I called in on Thursday, the office staff buzzed with tales of how badly my kids were behaving with the substitutes. Earlier that day, they had dumped all the crayons out on the floor and turned the desks upside-down on top of the mess to "draw" on the tiles. I was dismayed. I'd worked so hard to manage my class, and now this illness had undone all that hard work.

"I need to get back to my class," I said, still hoarse from the flu.

"You can't," countered the office staff. "You're scheduled for the workshop with Mr. Traugh tomorrow. We've booked a sub for your room."

The thought of sitting next door and being instructed on a program I didn't need while my kids tore my room and my program apart was more than I could handle. I called in sick and used the day to nurse my voice.

When I returned on Monday, the whole school was atwitter about Mr. Traugh.

"I never thought I could do so much with music."

"He is so adorable! We all had so much fun!"

"He's so smart and clever!"

"He's utterly amazing."

Even Joanne got on the bandwagon. "You have to meet him. You both teach in such a similar fashion. I know you'd love each other's approach. He just does everything with music — it's fabulous."

The problem was I'd missed my grade-level workshop, and I was scheduled for a different training the next week and would miss Mr. Traugh again. And while I could hear his music through the wall, our schedules during the day were so different that I never saw this mysterious man about whom everyone was squealing. I decided it just wasn't meant to be. Besides, I was sort of relieved to miss his workshop.

Joanne, on the other hand, decided that wouldn't work. She interceded with the principal and arranged to have me do the workshop the next day with another grade level if Mr. Traugh would agree. So, she grabbed me after class and took me to find him before he left the parking lot.

As we approached, I saw him bending over the trunk of his car. Draped in a black overcoat and deeply concentrating on his packing, Mr. Traugh didn't notice us as we hurried up to the back of his car.

Joanne called his name and began explaining that I'd missed the workshop. Could I attend tomorrow with the upper-grade teachers? He stood up and turned around to look at me.

Joanne swears that the electricity between Mr. Traugh and me was so intense that it knocked her back a step. Maybe so. I only know that the second I saw his face, a voice in my heart said, *Oh, there you are.* I knew, then and there, that I would marry that man.

He was slower.

In his workshop the next day, ten grown women giggled and elbowed each other like schoolgirls as they, each in turn, winked at me and gestured to Mr. Traugh behind his back. The electricity between us was palpable, but Mr. Traugh was so focused on his workshop that I began to doubt the feeling was mutual.

But the teachers knew. When it came time for everyone to stand to do a circle dance, those women ran to the far side of the circle and grabbed hands in a vice grip. The only open space was next to Mr. Traugh. As I tried to discreetly break one grip or another, Mr. Traugh admonished us for dawdling.

"Come on," he cajoled. "Even kindergarteners can make a circle faster than this!"

So, as ten women flashed silly grins at me, I slipped my hand into Mr. Traugh's. Instantly, his head snapped up, and he looked me in the eye. Later, he'd tell me that was the moment he knew he'd marry me.

So, maybe that article was right. I was struck by lightning. He was struck by lightning. And now, thirty years later, his wedding band wears the inscription: "Worth waiting for."

~Susan Traugh

19

The Heart of the Matter

*If you don't follow your heart, you might spend the rest
of your life wishing you had.*
~Brigitte Nicole

"Mom, do you know what makes a good marriage?" my twenty-year-old son, Jon, asked as he burst into the kitchen holding a freshly baked chocolate-chip cookie in one hand and a tall glass of milk in the other.

I glanced up from the pasta sauce that I set on simmer and responded, "No, Jon, please enlighten me!"

"Well," Jon said, as he cleared his throat, "it's all about compromise."

I didn't know whether to laugh or cry as Jon expounded on what he had learned in his Sociology of Marriage and the Family class at Grove City College in Pennsylvania. Jon's professor had been married for five years, and at the ripe old age of thirty-five, the best advice he could offer his students on marriage was compromise.

Jon was always right, so I knew better than to argue with him, but I wanted to say, "Your professor really hasn't gotten to the heart of the matter, has he? What if you run out of compromises? What if one of you wants a church wedding and the other one wants to get married in the back yard? Do you get married in the parking lot instead?"

As Jon bounded upstairs to get ready for his date with Kim — his college sweetheart — I mumbled a few words under my breath.

"What did you say, Mom?" Jon asked.

"Oh, nothing," I answered.

What I really wanted to do was share our love story. Jon had heard it at least a hundred times, but I never tired of telling it.

Mark and I met during our freshman year at Whitworth University in Spokane, Washington, in 1973. My roommate, Misty, was in charge of student orientation, and she asked if I wanted to go with her to pick up one of the new freshmen coming to take the college tour.

It was a Friday evening in November, and Misty convinced me that I had to ride along with her because there was black ice on the roadways, and she was afraid to travel alone. During our slow and cautious drive to the Spokane International Airport, Misty announced that she and her boyfriend, John, had already discussed marriage.

I shook my head in disbelief and blurted out, "How do you know that John's the one?"

With twinkling eyes and a warm smile, she whispered, "The heart never lies."

What kind of nonsense is that? I thought. It sounded almost Shakespearean — lacking in empirical data (as if love needed a reason).

When we arrived at the airport, the plane from San Francisco — carrying our new student — had already landed. Misty and I scurried up to the gate and waited for him.

As soon as the passengers journeyed down the ramp, I spotted a guy with long, wavy black hair and a contagious smile. He looked slightly lost. Without hesitation, I ran up the ramp and wrapped my arms around him, leaving my roommate gasping in astonishment.

"Are you Mark Pombo?" I asked, hesitantly.

"Yes, indeed, I am," he confessed.

Misty quickly offered her apologies for my erratic behavior and then said, "On behalf of Whitworth College and its representatives, welcome!"

On the other hand, I had already found the man of my dreams… the one my heart yearned for. It was love at first sight.

By the time we got to the car, we were already holding hands, and I was crying — almost hysterically — out of pure joy and disbelief.

Misty pulled me aside and reprimanded me. "What's gotten into you? We're here on official business," she warned.

Yes, it was official, all right. Two years later, Mark and I were married in my home church in Concord, California. There's no plausible explanation for what happened; it was as if two hearts became one the moment we met. Misty and John were married six months before us, and they've been married for forty-two years. We celebrated our forty-second anniversary on November 15, 2017.

Misty gave me the best advice I've ever received and thankfully just at the right moment. Although I never believed in love at first sight — until it happened to me — I know that a good marriage is more than just compromise and commitment. It takes all those things and more — because the heart never lies.

~Connie K. Pombo

20

Rocky Mountain Dream

*Your own words are the bricks and mortar of the
dreams you want to realize.*
~Sonia Choquette

"I'm going to get married in the mountains and honey-moon here!" I told my classmate on a starry night in 1980 while on a high-school band trip. Thirty years later, I exchanged wedding vows with the love of my life on a mountaintop in the Colorado Rockies, high above the YMCA camp where my dream was born.

I met my husband the same way — by declaring it. Strolling along the beach one afternoon in February while vacationing in Navarre, Florida, I was snapping pictures of my shadow and flinging seashells into the waves. Pausing, I smiled at the sky and yelled out: "I'm having too much fun for one person. Someone really needs to enjoy this with me!"

The next day, I drove forty-five miles to Rosemary Beach. And I met Tim.

It wasn't love at first sight. When I first saw him on the cross-over, where I intended to enjoy a peaceful evening alone, my first thoughts were: *Dang it! There's a guy here!* Slowly, I climbed the steps up to the platform and said, "Hey, how's it going?" Tim told me cheerfully that the dolphins had just started to jump out of the water. "Dolphins?" I was surprised. "I didn't know there were going to be dolphins here!" I'd only seen them at Sea World and was thrilled!

In an instant, we became friends. We played well together with our cameras and had fun observing the dolphins. I pulled out a bottle of Chardonnay from my backpack and commented, "I'd offer you some wine, but I've only got one glass." Tim replied simply, "I'll go get one," and he was gone.

I continued to photograph the dolphins, hoping he would return soon. The sun continued descending, and the dolphins moved on. Puffy clouds were forming, the sand was glowing orange and pink, and Tim finally returned — glass in hand — just in time to catch the blazing farewell to an enchanting day. We shared wine and conversation and discovered shared interests beyond our photography passion as, side by side, we awaited the arrival of stars.

The sole reason for Tim's driving twenty-five miles west from his vacation spot to this particular beach was because Venus was supposed to create a pillar effect on the water after the sun disappeared on this very night. Soon, our vigilance was rewarded with twinkling stars overhead. And then Venus arrived. Shining brightly in the night sky, the Goddess of Love skipped her light atop the waves and cast her strong gaze upon us. We never did see the pillar, but we did feel an effect that night as if we were touched by something beyond our sight.

Dining in the village together, we traded questions, and continued easy conversation through dessert and coffee. And then we were asked to leave. Shocked, we sat silently. "The restaurant has been closed for forty-five minutes. Come back next year when you celebrate your anniversary and spend the night upstairs," our waitress suggested. We paid the tab quickly, clarifying that we'd only just met earlier that day.

At our cars, we finally exchanged phone numbers and decided to meet again in two days. We hugged and said goodnight.

A cold, cloudy Sunday welcomed our return to Rosemary Beach. There weren't fireworks when we hugged or rockets shooting overhead. Rather, we experienced a calm sense of familiarity — a powerful feeling of belonging, as if we'd always been.

Over champagne and chocolates, we revealed more about our lives as the temperature continued dropping. Eventually, the sun appeared, and we wandered slowly through the town, winding our way back down to the sugar-white sands. A vibrant sky accented by glittering sunlight tinged with shades of gold was beautiful to behold and photograph. Sparkling waves and crimson sky entertained us until the last sliver of light disappeared below the horizon. Huddled next to each other on the damp sand, with a pink glow remaining over the soft hush of the waves, we sat quietly.

I knew he'd try to kiss me. And my mind started to race. *I have a date on Wednesday. I have to tell him.* He looked at me. I looked into his eyes. And before I could speak, he kissed me.

I didn't kiss him back. I wanted to. I gazed down, then back into those sparkling blue eyes. My heart pounding, I blurted, "I have a date on Valentine's Day! I thought you should know. That's why I didn't kiss you back!"

His eyes held me captive as he grabbed my hand. "Of course, you have a date. Why wouldn't you? You're amazing!" Blue eyes twinkling, he leaned closer and whispered, "Kiss me once as if you don't have a date." And I did! He fell over onto his back in the sand. "Wow, I'm glad I asked," he teased as I giggled, and he sat upright. Holding hands on the dark beach, shivering in the cold, we grew still once more, quivering from our first kiss.

We found a steakhouse down the road and warmed up with a hot drink. Our incandescence attracted attention. A bar patron bought us a drink. "Did you two just get married or something?" He was curious. "You two are as bright as a Christmas tree. Everyone can feel it," he insisted. We thanked him and confessed we were newly acquainted.

Soon thereafter, we settled our tab and headed toward the exit where I spied a bowl full of packaged candy hearts with love messages. I took two. "Here, take one. I'm not sure if we'll see each other again in Florida, but I do know we'll see each other again. When we do, let's exchange these." He agreed. Realizing we might not see each other again in Florida, our goodbye kiss spoke volumes about us. At last, we said farewell.

On Tuesday, we met one last time for two hours. My Florida vacation was over, and soon Tim would return home to New Jersey. We knew only that we needed to trust in our future's unfolding. I declared, "I'll see you again. I know I will," before I quickly kissed him goodbye.

"You will see me again," he assured me.

St. Valentine delivered a blizzard to the East Coast the following day, allowing me to fly home to Wisconsin, and preventing that date I was to have from catching a flight. I called Tim with the good news. "Happy Valentine's Day, darlin'," he said, answering my call. And happy it was as I ordered take-out, talked to Tim across the miles on the phone, and spent my favorite-of-all-time Valentine's Day alone.

We celebrate both anniversaries every year. Whenever we tell our story, our hearts beat a little faster and overflow with gratitude for the divine timing that brought our soul connection into being, and to Venus, the Goddess of Love, who holds a special place in our hearts.

~Sharon Kay Beyer

21

Romance between the Stacks

It is only with the heart that one can see rightly;
what is essential is invisible to the eye.
~Antoine de Saint-Exupéry, The Little Prince

I had been working in a bookstore for over a year with no romantic prospects, but then a particular girl was hired to do the same job as me. We both vividly remember the first words I spoke to her, even though we had different interpretations of those words.

"Oh, so you're Jennifer," I said upon meeting her on her first day of work.

All I meant was that I had heard about her from a mutual friend before she started. Jennifer still thinks my statement had more negative overtones than I intended, but those were the only words I could come up with while being struck by love at first sight. It is true that for a moment in time upon first meeting someone, we can be distracted by physical beauty — long, red hair; smooth, porcelain skin; the greatest smile I had ever seen — but it gradually takes on a more spiritual connection. Upon getting to know her better, she became even more beautiful. Her inner charm radiated. Her attractiveness snowballed. I wasn't looking for Jennifer, and she wasn't looking for me, but love at first sight is a hard feeling to shake.

When our shifts coincided, we worked alongside each other in the bookstore. We shelved books. We helped customers find titles they couldn't find on their own. We snuck secret glances at each other from across the store. We bonded over discussions about the works of authors that we both admired and made fun of what we thought were each other's guilty pleasures (hers — Nora Roberts; mine — Stephen King). After two months of this, we went on our first date and continued seeing each other amongst the stacks while working and hanging out a fair bit in our spare time.

Three months after that first date, I was scheduled to embark on a four-week backpacking trip to Chile that I had planned before meeting Jennifer. The night before my departure, Jennifer gave me a plate of homemade chocolate-chip cookies, which touched me beyond anything else — as if there was nothing else she could do to impress me more. But then she did impress me more — she gave me her copy of *The Little Prince* by Antoine de Saint-Exupéry. The book was one of her favourites, and she knew I had never read it. She wanted me to take it on my trip to remember her.

I was going to be absent for a while, wandering carefree out in the world, but those cookies and that book changed how I felt about what I would be coming home to. We had not reached the point of saying that we loved each other yet, but we both sensed it was coming. As a booklover myself, I knew she was taking a big step by trusting me with her favourite book, and this told me all I needed to know about how she felt about me.

On my overnight flight to Santiago, I read *The Little Prince* cover to cover. The story is about flying away from grown-up responsibilities, getting lost, inter-planetary travel, acquiring knowledge, and finding one's way home. I could not stop thinking about Jennifer as I held the book in my lap and read the words of this fabulously imaginative story. Just as I could not shake the sense of being cast under the spell of love at first sight when we first met, I was not able to shake the urge to see her again when I returned home. To cut a long story short, two weeks into my trip, my feelings of homesickness intensified. I had never abandoned a trip before, but I was seriously considering going home early. I missed the familiarity of my life back home, of working in the bookstore and mingling with the people with whom I worked (especially one person), so I booked a ticket home. After a twelve-hour flight back to Canada, I called Jennifer.

When she answered the phone, I said, "Oh, so you're Jennifer."

I was hoping it had a different tone than the first time I used that line. At least, she knew it was me on the other end of the phone and expressed surprise about me being home early.

"Being so far away, I learned that 'what is essential is invisible to the eye.'"

"I see you read my book," she said.

It was a quote from *The Little Prince* that I had committed to memory to impress her. In my heart, it had become obvious that our dating would continue when I returned home. It could very well be that by having a physical piece of her with me — in the form of her favourite book — I was urged to get home sooner than expected. After I slept off my jet lag, we met the next day, and the first thing I did was hand her back *The Little Prince*. It had accompanied me for thousands of kilometers, and its wise words had given me plenty to think about. But from one booklover to another, I knew I needed to return it straight away.

"Now that I've read it, I see why it's your favourite. Thank you for trusting me with it."

"I needed a reason for you to come home," she smirked. "I knew you would return it."

We went back to our routine of shelving and selling books, not so secretly enjoying each other's company again in the ambiance of the bookstore. We were engaged eight months later and married six months after that. We met because of books, and we connected over one particular book (even when separated by continents), but we have stayed together for thirteen years (and counting) because of the love story we continue to write ourselves.

~Darin Cook

22

The Art of Love

Meeting you was fate, becoming your friend
was a choice, but falling in love with you
I had no control over.
~Teresa Conroy

I trudged into my morning art class, one of my first classes of junior high. I was an anxious seventh-grader, gawky and gangly. I didn't know anyone in the room. I waited in the corner, nervous and unsure, while the art teacher exuberantly sang out our seating assignments.

I couldn't stop staring at a boy with blond hair who was leaning against the wall, hands in his pockets. I was twelve, so I didn't understand the funny feeling in the pit of my stomach.

The sound of my name snapped me out of it. The art teacher pointed to my seat. Once I settled in, she pointed to the seat across from me and announced the name that would forever change me.

The blond boy plopped into his seat across from me. He stared at me, his blue eyes making my stomach flop.

Over the months, we worked on art projects together and we were in several other classes together as well. I was the studious girl who sat in the front row and never got in trouble. He was the free-spirited rebel who was more concerned about making a joke than learning anything.

Somehow, though, from that first day in art class, something clicked. Despite our different personalities, there was a common thread between us — our humor. Even though that blond boy hated school and had all sorts of issues that almost scared me away, he could always make me laugh — often to the teacher's chagrin.

Over the years, we grew up together. That funny feeling I couldn't identify at age twelve turned into love. And even though so many naysayers teased us, saying we couldn't find true love in junior high, we proved them wrong.

Boy, did we prove them wrong.

Things weren't perfect, mind you. We fought, and we fought often. We thought about throwing in the towel, and that distant forever we sometimes talked about seemed impossible. Maybe everyone was right, we thought. Maybe it's just not possible to fall in love at twelve, to spend forever with the boy or girl seated across from you at the art table.

Even when we tried to walk away, though, we came back together. It was like we were magnetized. Or maybe, just maybe, even then we knew that the special thing we had between us didn't come around every day. Maybe we realized the bond we had was worth fighting for.

We stayed together through proms and school functions. We went on all sorts of trips and filled several scrapbooks before we graduated. We walked hand-in-hand into the "real world" and struggled to find our individual paths while staying together.

We fought to remember that boy and girl we once were, who fell in love over paintings and charcoal drawings. We fought to hang on to the best parts of our pasts while growing and changing. We fought to appreciate the love between us and the beautiful history we'd enjoyed.

And, despite all odds, we did it. Eleven years after we were the boy and girl at the art table, I found myself staring at that boy again — this time as I walked down the aisle in my white dress, my flowers trembling in my hands. There he was, the blond boy from my past, now a man who was my everything. We said our "I dos," and we smiled, thinking of the naysayers who swore we wouldn't last.

Because we certainly did.

At our wedding, we danced to Faith Hill's "Breathe," the first song he asked me to dance to in seventh grade. Wrapped around each other in the middle of the dance floor, I smiled as I looked into his familiar eyes, thinking about what a full-circle moment it was.

We weren't the same boy and girl from seventh grade. Life had dealt us quite a few blows. We were older, a little bit wiser, and a lot less carefree. Still, swaying in his arms on the dance floor on our wedding day, I knew in many ways we'd forever be those kids who fell in love thanks to an art teacher's seating chart.

It's been six years since our wedding now, and it's been seventeen years since I trudged into that classroom, unaware I was about to meet my best friend and soul mate. We've settled into married life. We've got a small house, a huge dog, and way too many cats. We've got routines and bills. We've got our struggles and issues.

But we've also got a life and a love bigger than those two kids at the art table could have ever imagined.

~Lindsay Detwiler

23

Two Thousand Miles for a Kiss

Every love story is beautiful, but ours is my favorite.
~Author Unknown

In early April 1993, I spent my twenty-sixth birthday on Emerald Isle, North Carolina. I waded through the surf meditating about my life, including past relationships, my fundamentalist upbringing, and how I'd finally subdued my extreme anxiety about college. I finally had my life together, but I was lonely. I picked up a seashell and threw it as hard and as far as I could into the ocean, letting it carry my hopes like a message in a bottle.

Two weeks later, after returning home to Johnson City, Tennessee, I was at work telling my friend Trish how much I enjoyed my Army ROTC physical-education class at East Tennessee State University. We had rappelled off of a tower and some buildings on campus, and I wanted to try it someplace else. Trish said she and her husband Kurt had a friend coming to visit the next weekend who was a rock climber. She invited me to go rock climbing and hiking with them.

"Great!" I said. "As long as you're not trying to fix me up or anything…"

She assured me she wasn't because Chuck was in the Navy. He was just passing through on his way from San Diego to Maine to participate in building and commissioning a new ship. She said they had been friends with Chuck for several years, having met him in the early 1980s when he was a Navy recruiter in Johnson City. He was going to be in town visiting them for a week.

The day before our hike, Kurt and Trish hosted a barbecue for Chuck. He and I hit it off instantly, chatting non-stop, amazed at the things we had in common. Not only did he enjoy reading science fiction and fantasy, as I did, but we shared a love of the outdoors.

Neither of us realized how exclusive our conversation had become, but when I got up to refill my drink, Kurt passed me in the hall and joked, "Hey! Chuck didn't come two thousand miles to see *you*, ya' know!"

The next day was exhilarating as we hiked and climbed in Linville Gorge and Table Rock, North Carolina, near where parts of the movie, *The Last of the Mohicans,* was filmed. Kurt and Trish hadn't seen the movie, so we convinced them to watch it with us after the hike.

During the movie, Chuck noticed that my feet were cold because I kept drawing them up under me. Without a word, he retrieved a blanket and tucked it around my feet. I was pleasantly shocked. No one had ever done anything like that for me.

After Kurt and Trish went to bed, Chuck and I continued talking into the wee hours of the morning, discussing everything imaginable. When the subject of music came up, we discovered that we both liked all kinds, from classical to heavy metal. I told him I'd love to discover the name of a song and the band I'd heard playing during a scene in the movie *Patriot Games* and during a Volkswagen commercial.

I was stunned when he said, "Hang on," and popped a CD into the stereo.

"Is this it?" he asked, playing "Harry's Game" by Clannad. He had a CD with the song I was asking about!

I recall thinking to myself, *Why can't I meet a guy like this here in Tennessee?* Then it occurred to me that I *had* just met this guy in Tennessee. The fact that he didn't live here didn't matter as much as I thought it would.

So, when he asked me out for the next night, I said, "Yes." He walked me to my car and asked if he could kiss me goodnight. Again, I said, "Yes."

Wow! What a kiss. We agreed that in my twenty-six years and his thirty-five years, we'd never had such a powerful first kiss.

Chuck was supposed to leave the next day, but he remained in Tennessee for another two weeks, exhausting the remainder of his leave. We dated every night and took another rock-climbing and hiking trip to North Carolina.

In May and June, we exchanged daily phone calls and frequent cards and letters. Chuck said he knew it was serious when I came to see him in Maine, and we visited Acadia National Park and Bar Harbor, where he bought me an expensive pair of rock-climbing shoes.

On the Fourth of July, I astonished my family by quitting my job and moving to Maine with a twice-divorced sailor nine years my senior whom I had known for two months. I wasn't worried because I knew he was "The One."

In December that same year, he surprised me with an engagement ring, but it came with the sad fact that we would soon face a six-month separation. His ship would be making its maiden voyage from Maine to San Diego, and would then have maneuvers in Hawaii. I couldn't join him in California until the following July. So, he moved me back to Tennessee, and we spent Christmas together with my family.

The night before he was due to return to Maine, he said, "You're going to forget all about me while I'm gone."

I said, "You're crazy. I'd marry you tomorrow." And we decided to do just that! But the next day it snowed, and the local courthouse was closed. We couldn't get married.

I said, "Call the Greene County Courthouse. It's the Federal courthouse. I bet it's open."

I was right. So, we eloped. He had a plane to catch, so there was no announcement, no pictures, no wedding dress. We just got married, and then I drove him to the airport.

In December 2018, we'll celebrate our twenty-fifth wedding anniversary. Sorry, Kurt, but it seems Chuck really did come two thousand miles to see me after all.

~Lorraine Furtner

24

The Proposal

All that is worth cherishing begins in the heart.
~Suzanne Chapin

Two of my girlfriends and I were sitting at a front table of a small jazz club called Presidios in downtown Tacoma, Washington. My girlfriends were country-western fans, and I could see they were not going to last long, so I had to plead with them to stay. Unexpectedly, I felt a tap on my shoulder and heard a deep voice asking me if I would like to dance. Without giving it a second thought, I sprang to my feet and proceeded to the dance floor. When our eyes first met, I found myself smiling, and I couldn't stop. It was as if my smile muscles became frozen. My cheeks began to ache as I fought to stop my reaction to this man.

Two weeks later, this deep-voiced, blue-eyed dancing man asked me to marry him as we were sitting in the front seat of his extremely rare 1962 split-window Sundial Volkswagen camper bus. I didn't hesitate for a moment because I had known he was my destiny from the first moment on the dance floor. We were married four weeks later, to all of our friends' surprise, as we were not the kind given to spontaneous anything, much less relationships. I am glad to report that we are still dancing after twenty-five years.

A short time after we were married, however, my husband decided to sell the Volkswagen camper without my knowledge. He liked to buy and sell cars frequently, so it wouldn't normally be any big deal. But when it came to the one in which he had proposed to me, I was suddenly struck with sadness that it was now in the hands of a stranger. Call me a romantic, but I couldn't seem to help myself.

"How could you sell the bus that you asked me to marry you in?" I cried, tears welling up in my eyes.

He stood before me in astonishment, not realizing the impact that selling this vehicle would have on me. I was devastated. He was shocked that I was devastated, but the bus was sold, and that was that. This loss eventually lessened, but every anniversary I reminded him of how much I wished we still owned the place where he had asked me to be his wife.

Ten years later, on a warm August evening, he called my name, insisting that I come outside. I was busy in my office at the time, but I finally conceded. Yelling, I stuck my head out the back door. "What do you want? Where are you anyway?"

No answer… I proceeded down our driveway, and there I saw it — the 1962 Volkswagen. The side door was open, and he was sitting inside with a candle flickering and a bottle of wine. He had searched all over the country until he found the same moss-green, sundial camper bus that he had unwittingly sold and he had bought it back for me! I was undone.

As we sat in each other's arms, sipping our Chardonnay, he whispered in my ear, "Will you marry me… again?"

~Miryam Howard

The Miracle of Love

How We Met

25

The Needle in the Haystack

How do I love thee? Let me count the ways. I love thee
to the depth and breadth and height my soul can reach.
~Elizabeth Barrett Browning

The odds were nothing less than finding a needle in a haystack. Richard was a forty-nine-year-old man. I was a forty-two-year-old woman. Across a dark, crowded room, Richard saw me first. I was on the dance floor. As the other dancers moved, making a slight opening, I saw him, too. He was smiling as our eyes met. I smiled back. The dancers again shifted their fluid form, and he was gone from view. It was just like the Frank Sinatra song; we were "strangers in the night exchanging glances."

When the dancing ended, I walked toward the man with the welcoming face. Standing in front of one another, we made our introductions and acknowledged the coincidences of our professions and educational backgrounds.

Richard joined me on the dance floor. Dancing was my passion, not his. Yet he kept up with me. We closed the club.

Two nights later, we shared a walk, talking about our pasts and our dreams of finding a needle in a haystack. We held hands and hoped our search had possibly ended.

Could we defy the odds of the singles world? Could one glance in a crowded dance club change the course of our lives? We were not singles in our twenties or thirties. I was one month into my forty-second year. Richard was four months away from turning fifty.

Richard visited me every night the week after we met. I had never felt like this about anyone before. He was comfortable in his own skin. There was nothing phony about him. His gentleness was so appealing to me.

As Richard tells it — and he tells it correctly — I made him wait two years before I agreed to marry him. It wasn't, however, the choice of *him* that I questioned. It was the decision to marry.

I was a professional woman with a dynamic and fulfilling career. My friends were loyal. My freedom was valued. It was difficult for me as a single woman in my forties to think of sharing my personal space with another. My thinking at the time went something like this: If I married, Richard would live with me. He would be there all the time. *All the time!* How and when would I have my cherished privacy?

It took me two years to work through this fear. During that time, Richard was not only my lover but my best friend. That was the key to our successful growth as a couple. When I felt closed in by our relationship, I talked to him about it. When I wondered what it would be like to share my space, I talked to him about it. When I hungered for my freedom, I talked to him about it.

One day, I told Richard that I was going to a singles party to once again experience what it was like. We had been dating for several months at that point, and I was restless. He looked at me for what seemed like a long time, and then he said that if I needed to do that, I should. He was not happy about it, but I was free to make that decision. I told him I would not do anything behind his back, but I intended to go.

A few nights later, I walked into the party. During my first hour there, a number of men asked if I would like a drink or wanted to dance. I continually refused. As I walked through the room, I started wondering why I was there. Then I started missing Richard. I missed the familiar ease and gentleness of our connection. I missed his face.

I missed him.

I left the party, which was downtown, and drove to Richard's house, which was in a Chicago suburb. I knocked on the door. He opened it and extended his arms toward me. "I was hoping and waiting," he said softly. We stood there hugging for what seemed like forever.

That night was a turning point in our relationship. I was beginning to realize that I wanted *us*. Yet I still wasn't sure how it would all work. We each had our own long-standing phone numbers, checkbooks and savings accounts. We each had treasured furniture and favorite colors and specific ways of doing things. In reality, as small as these issues may have been, we were two people with established lives. I was used to being single. If I wanted cereal for dinner, I would have it. If I wanted to take a bubble bath at one in the morning, I did it. I had been living my life in single mode for a very long time.

Once I admitted to myself that my life was more fulfilling because I shared it with Richard, we worked through the logistics of our separate lives and set our wedding date.

I married Richard the day before my forty-fourth birthday. We walked down the aisle together because that was a symbol of how we felt about our life as a couple. We had grown into a partnership of equality and sharing. It was all I ever wanted in a relationship. I took his last name and kept mine. My hyphenated name became an everyday reminder of my pride in being me *and* in being Richard's wife.

As the years have passed, Richard's arms have become my home. My space has become our space. If Richard is not in it with me, I miss him. When I need privacy, I take it, and my husband understands. What I feared disappeared long ago. The union of two souls has formed a oneness that retains the essence of who we are as individuals. We are a man and woman. We are a husband and wife.

We are a reality I was once afraid to dream.

Richard does not let me forget that I made him wait two years. However, I believe that one cannot be what one needs to be until one is ready. Richard refers to our relationship as timeless love.

We often tell each other the story of a man who saw a woman

dancing and wanted to meet her. We know that we both found the needle in the haystack.

~Elynne Chaplik-Aleskow

A Match Made in Music

Every heart sings a song, incomplete, until another
heart whispers back. Those who wish to sing always
find a song. At the touch of a lover,
everyone becomes a poet.
~Author Unknown

"Come on, Mommy," my children hollered with glee as they danced to the music blaring from the stereo. I clasped their hands as we circled around the front room, dancing well past their bedtime. Once they'd gone to bed and fallen asleep, I couldn't wait to stick the tape back in and listen again.

I was the keyboard player in a country-rock band. Our drummer had given me a cassette of original songs that his buddy, David (called "DB" by family and friends), had recorded. My band member had high hopes that DB's hot keyboard/piano licks might rub off on me. While I did glean a few tips, this musician's playing far exceeded my capabilities. However, the tape wasn't a complete bust. The kids and I now had some awe-inspiring dance music, and I enjoyed the magical way the songs boosted their spirits as well as my own.

Life hadn't been easy for me or the children. My husband and I shared an unhappy marriage, and the kids rarely saw their dad. He found someone else and, eventually, so did I. We should have called

How We Met | 9

it quits. Instead, my husband begged me to give our marriage another chance, which I foolishly did — only to have him ask for a divorce two years later.

During trying times, people often turn to alcohol or drugs, but I turned to DB's songs. Despite a desperate, confusing time in our lives, the children and I often consoled ourselves by dancing to our now-favorite music. After tucking the children in bed each evening, I'd sit on the floor, wiping my tears while DB's voice carried me to a brighter place. In fact, I'd fallen deeply in love with these songs and couldn't imagine my life without them.

As the years flew by, DB's music tagged along with me like a trustworthy friend, through a move, a second divorce, and some of the leanest, darkest times of my life.

DB's fresh, stirring voice sang of hope, joy, nature, love, and spirituality. When I listened, I believed in something better, not only for me, but especially for my children. And no matter what chaos ensued in my life, through heaven or hell, his music lifted me to a higher plane.

One day, while enjoying a day-trip in the mountains, I tucked DB's latest tape in my pack. As I listened to one of his newest songs, the opening lyrics got under my skin.

They were simple words: "Unwind — all's fine — sun shines inside me." And I wanted to know how it felt to have the sun shining in me. I considered how reassuring it must feel to know that all is fine — I could not imagine such peace.

It hit me — I had lived and breathed this music forever, yet I'd never thought much about the songwriter who had written these songs. There was no way this musician could write and sing with such rapture if these feelings didn't exist within him. And I knew in that second that I wanted what he had. I wanted to feel his bliss and know what he knew. His spirit, so clear in his songs, had seen me through so much that, at that moment, I felt as if I had known this gentle soul my entire life.

It was a milestone for me. I gathered my courage and phoned David. I explained who I was and told him, "I want what you've got. I want to be like you."

We talked for hours. After that call, we became pen pals, but didn't fall in love right away. I lived out west, and he lived in the east. More than six months later, we realized that we had fallen in love, and our lives ended up resembling a giant maze full of obstacles — each one a story in itself.

Even though David's agenda didn't include marriage, and I'd vowed to never wed again, almost seven years after hearing his songs for the first time, and a year and a half after making my phone call, we tied the knot. Last fall, we celebrated our twenty-eighth wedding anniversary.

I find it mind-blowing that I fell in love with my husband's music long before I fell in love with him, never suspecting that he was my soul mate. Even though I wished we'd met earlier and he'd been my only one, I always find it comforting to know that, through his music, David *had* always been with me, through the worst and best times of my life, supporting me all the way. To this day, his songs still make my heart sing.

~Jill Burns

27

Destiny on the Open Sea

When you let go, something magical happens.
You give God room to work.
~Mandy Hale

I t seems a lifetime ago that I was the drummer for the Salvation Army church band in Victoria, British Columbia. It was such a fulfilling time, especially in the summer months when we would go down to the waterfront to perform for all the tourists. I have a long-standing love affair with that grand, old city: the elegant Victorian architecture; the spectacular English gardens; the craggy bluffs topped by quaint, old homes nestled amongst stately oak and graceful arbutus trees; the heavenly scent of cherry blossoms lining the streets in a carpet of blush pink petals; and the familiar sound of horse and carriage, clip-clopping along the pavement. How I love driving along Dallas Road with my windows down, listening to the cries of seagulls soaring overhead while breathing in the scent of seaweed and salty air. I also love walking along the city streets. An electric energy comes with the hustle and bustle of visitors who arrive in droves from all over the world.

It seemed only natural to move to a city that held such a special place in my heart, especially after going through many years of emotional turmoil and transition. About a year after my divorce, I found myself in an unhealthy relationship that stripped away every last ounce of self-esteem I had. When I finally faced the fact that it was a hopeless situation, I moved away to give myself a fresh start. But it wasn't easy to let go. We were still seeing each other on occasion.

A few people at my church knew what I was struggling with. So one night, after band practice, one of the musicians prayed for me. "Dear God, please help Micki find the right man and keep all the wrong ones away. Amen." It was a simple prayer but to the point. That same week, a good friend came up to me and said, "Micki, I feel very strongly that if you would just let go of that man who is making you miserable, the right one will come along." Normally, I would be skeptical hearing something like this, but it was coming from someone I deeply respected. And I knew in my heart that hanging onto this toxic relationship was killing me inside. I needed to move forward with my life, so I took her advice, mustered up the courage and ended the relationship, once and for all.

Only a week or so after all this transpired, I was on my way back to Victoria from a visit with my dad and his wife on the mainland. The ferry terminal was being renovated, and everything had changed. I felt confused as to where I was supposed to go. I saw a slender man around my age, with sandy blond hair, walking ahead of me. I caught up to him and asked, "Do you mind me asking where you're going?"

He grinned and said, "Victoria."

I asked, "Do you mind if I follow you? I'm feeling a little lost."

Still smiling, he replied, "No, I don't mind at all." We walked onto the ferry together, and I found myself standing beside him in the cafeteria line. It suddenly occurred to me how awkward this was. So, although I was hungry, I excused myself, saying, "Thanks again. It was nice meeting you." I went outside to sit in the sunshine.

As I sat on the boat deck with my eyes closed, enjoying the sea breeze and the sun's warmth on my face, a thought came into my head as plain as day: *This is the man you are going to marry.* Naturally, I dismissed the thought, thinking it was silly. But it would not go away. So I had a private little chat with God....

If I've gone crazy, please ignore me. But if this is Your voice, then I need You to bring that man out here because I am not going in after him. As You well know, I am not adept at picking out men who are good for me, and I'm tired of being hurt. So if this is really You, I need You to bring him here.

After I spoke those words, I didn't give it another thought and continued basking blissfully in the sun.

Not long after, I felt a presence beside me. My eyes flew open, and there he was. He said his name was David, and he had been over to visit his parents on the mainland, which was why he was on the ferry. He had a kind face and a shy, gentle manner. I remember thinking how easy it was to talk to him, as if I had known him all my life. I forgot how hungry I was and just ate up every word of our conversation.

The ferry docked, and after exchanging e-mail addresses, we parted ways. It felt natural to give him a quick hug and a little peck on the cheek. It seemed as though neither of us wanted to say goodbye.

After a few days, I was genuinely pleased to find an e-mail from him. We wrote back and forth for a couple of weeks, and then he started calling. One day, he phoned to say he was coming to Victoria to visit his son and asked if we could meet. I agreed. We spent the day together driving along Dallas Road, enjoying the scenery and each other's company.

Just like before, it was so comfortable being with him. We parked the car along the shore and discovered a small inlet where we sat together and talked. Suddenly, his arm was around me, and I found myself snuggling into him as if we had been together forever. Then he caught me completely off guard and admitted that he loved me. In retrospect, this probably should have scared me to death, but it didn't. Everything just felt so natural, so right. David made me feel safe. And for the first time in a very long time, I felt like I was home.

We talked about getting together the following weekend, so I drove up island after work to be with him. By the time I arrived, it was late, and he had fallen asleep on the sofa. When my knock went unheard, I walked in and was greeted by a path of flower petals. It led me to a vase with more flowers and a little hand-written note that said, "These are all the flowers in my garden, but none of them compare to you." I have been given a lot of gifts in my lifetime, but none of them touched my heart quite like this.

We spent the weekend getting to know one another. I met his teenage daughter and liked her immediately. She was quiet and shy, like her dad, and seemed to welcome me without hesitation. When it came time for me to head home, somehow, unexpectedly, the topic of marriage came up. I was astonished to hear him say that he wanted to marry me. I was equally amazed to hear myself say, "Yes." It was as natural as anything we talked about whenever we were together.

On my way home, alone in the car, I was shaking my head and talking to myself. *Are you crazy? You barely know the man! What are you doing jumping into this so quickly, especially with your track record!* After a few minutes of verbally berating myself, I calmed down and said a prayer. *God, if this is really Your doing, please give me peace.* Suddenly, I was flooded with an overwhelming sense of tranquility and a comforting reminder: *It really was Me who spoke to you on the ferry that day.* And that was that. Who was I to argue with the Almighty?

David and I were married approximately a year later in a quaint, little historical church in Parksville, B.C. My co-workers thought I had lost my mind. I can't say I blamed them, but that was okay; I was so happy, I really didn't care what anyone thought. And as much as I loved living in Victoria, leaving to be with David was one of the best decisions I have ever made. Besides, I can always go back and visit, which I do from time to time.

I often think back to the day it all began. What if I hadn't stopped to ask for directions? What if David had given into his shyness and not approached me? It was clearly meant to be. Both of us had come out of long, unhappy relationships. Perhaps God had simply decided it was time for us both to experience some joy in our lives. And not a day goes by that I am not thankful.

I never did get to eat that day on the ferry. But I did get the man.

~Micki Findlay

28

Ireland, Love and Butterflies

*When you love someone, all your saved-up wishes
start coming out.*
~Elizabeth Bowen

On my first trip to Ireland, I was drawn to the magnificent scenery, as well as the greenness and the hospitality of the people. But it was more than that. I also felt a sense of belonging that I felt nowhere else, not even in my own hometown. When I left that island, I whispered a prayer: *Please show me a way to live here.*

Once home, I began planning for my next trip. At the same time, I was introduced to vision boards as a tool to bring about something in my life. Taking photos from my trip to Ireland, I created a vision board entitled "Irish love." I included pictures of the Irish countryside along with a tall, dark-haired Irishman. I chose an image of a butterfly as my personal symbol and placed it in the center of the vision board. The idea of both metamorphosis and beauty struck a chord within me.

At the time, I was in my mid-thirties, single with a nice career. I had never lived outside of a five-mile radius from where I was born. I traveled a lot, but I always came home. So this dream to live in Ireland was pretty big. I carried on with my life, but I continued to gaze at my vision board. It made me happy. Sometimes, when I looked at the images on the board, I would get excited as if it had actually happened.

I began to imagine myself living in the west of Ireland with the love of my life.

One year later, my friend and I returned to Ireland. Curiosity and perhaps a little bit of hope led us to the tiny town of Lisdoonvarna, County Clare, in mid-September 2001. We had heard about the traditional matchmaking festival that takes place there for the entire month — a remnant from years past when farmers came to town at the end of the harvest to choose a wife. Appropriately, we found ourselves in a pub called The Matchmaker early Sunday evening. My friend had been asked to dance, and I was left standing against the wall. I happened to turn around and noticed a very handsome man entering the pub. It was just like in a movie: He was tall and dark-haired with the golden light of the setting sun streaming in around him. He took my breath away; it was like being hit with a bolt of lightning.

Trying to shake it off, I turned back around to watch my friend being twirled around by an able Irishman. It wasn't long before I felt a tap on my shoulder and came face-to-face with the man himself — Mike. He asked me to dance. Eventually, we ended up in the lobby of the adjoining hotel sitting on wicker furniture while a ginger cat slept lazily on one of the chairs across from us — oblivious, as we were, that we were at the beginning of our relationship.

Through the course of the conversation, we discovered that we had both been to the Cliffs of Moher and the tiny village of Doolin that day at the same time, but we hadn't seen each other. Mike admitted that he had seen me in a restaurant earlier. Later, he saw me walking down the street and going into the pub, so he decided he was going to make my acquaintance. He was an Irishman who had spent many years living and working as a carpenter in New York City. I was from Buffalo, which is at the other end of New York State. He spoke of his love for America, and I told him about my love for Ireland.

I soon left, telling him that I was returning to the U.S. on the following Friday. He nodded in his quiet, thoughtful way and asked for my address and phone number. It had been a magical night. My friend and I left early the next morning for the next stop on our trip. The following day, as we made our way through the rain on the remote

Aran Islands, we heard about the terrorist attacks on New York City. We were one of the first flights out of Shannon to Toronto on Friday the 14th. Despite our wonderful trip, we were anxious to get home.

On Sunday night, Mike rang my house. He said he was worried about me, and we talked for hours. We spoke on the phone every night thereafter and wrote letters until he decided to move back to New York City in October 2001. With only an hour plane ride between us, the relationship became more manageable. Unlike other guys I had dated, I knew he was the one. I couldn't explain it, but I just knew there was no one else for me. We married in 2002.

We had two sons over the ensuing years. In January 2006, we made the decision to move to the southwest of Ireland where Mike still had his home. Things were a whirlwind after that, packing up and shipping things, and the time flew until the day we departed at the end of April. When the plane touched down, I was overcome with doubt. What had I just done? I had never lived away from my hometown, and here I was moving 3,000 miles away!

We arrived in Ireland and received a big welcome from Mike's family. They had been anxious to meet me and our little sons. Mike's sister took us over to the house. It was a typical Irish farmhouse, and it had been in Mike's family for ten generations. He had lovingly maintained and updated it before he left, and his sister had kept on eye on it for him during the past five years.

When she opened up the house, we carried our children into the place that was going to be our home for the foreseeable future. As I stepped into the sunlit hallway, I was greeted by three bright blue butterflies fluttering around. Immediately, I was reminded of the vision board from so many years ago depicting my dream to live in Ireland and marry an Irishman — with the image of a butterfly in the middle. My fears dissipated, and I knew that everything was going to be all right. And that house has become the home of many happy memories.

~Michele Brouder

29

In an Instant

There is never a time or place for true love.
It happens accidentally, in a heartbeat,
in a single flashing, throbbing moment.
~Sarah Dessen, The Truth About Forever

The first day of school was challenging for my daughter. I was newly separated, and the transition was hard for my daughter, son and me. We had recently moved into a new apartment, which meant that my daughter would be starting kindergarten at a new school.

The days leading up to the first day of school were full of anxiety for both of us, but there was no avoiding it. Once I took her to school, I stayed around as long as I could, even lingering in the class well after the other parents left. Eventually, after receiving a stern look from Ms. Smith, her new teacher, I knew it was time to leave. I planted as many kisses as I could on my daughter's face, and then left with a heavy heart. I would have stayed all day if I could. *She will have a great day!* I tried to convince myself. *She's going to love her new school.*

The day was long, and on more than one occasion I seriously thought about going to the school just to peek in on her, but the look from Ms. Smith kept coming to mind. School let out at 2:30, but I didn't see any harm in getting there at 2:00. I was the first parent there, peeking in the little glass window to see what they were doing, and how my daughter was adjusting to her new space. Eventually, other parents trickled in. Some of us made small talk, discussing the school, the teacher and how we thought our children were doing. Many of them were anxious as well. Most of the parents there were women, but a man whom I am now convinced was custom-made for me walked in.

He was more than handsome; he was beautiful. And he had intense eyes that took in everything he saw. They landed on me and stayed there long enough for me to blush. I didn't know what was going on, but I found myself wondering. *Is he really looking at me? Does he see me looking at him? Am I overthinking all of this?* I hadn't been in "the field" for nearly a decade. I wasn't sure how it worked anymore. My thoughts were interrupted when the door flung open, and the kids ran to their respective parents. My daughter's eyes lit up when she ran to me. I smiled. Other classes were dismissed, and the crowd thickened. I lost the guy whose eyes had caught mine. I wanted to see him once more to make sure he was real. That night, I thought about him. I was in love. Was that even possible?

How can we love someone whose name we have never uttered? Whose name we don't even know? I am a very logical person and certainly believe in science, but I wasn't sure if love at first sight had been proven. Whether it had or hadn't did not matter to me because I was sure I was in love.

The next day was a repeat of the day before. I was there early again to get my daughter from school. In my mind, if he felt what I felt, then he would have been there a little early too to talk to me or even flirt a bit. However, he wasn't there. *Had I imagined him the day before?* I wondered. Or perhaps it was just a chance encounter. Maybe his brother could not get off work and asked him to pick up his son, and he would not be returning to the school.

My daughter told me all about her day, and I said "Really" and "Oh, that's great, honey" at the appropriate times. It wasn't that I wasn't listening, but I was busy scanning the crowd, looking for the man who made me feel like a schoolgirl all over again. He was nowhere in sight. Finally, we made it outside. I had purposely parked my car far away because I didn't want to get caught up in the school traffic. On our walk to the car, I spotted someone moving quickly. It was him. He was just late. I was happy to see him, but I didn't want him to know it. We continued to walk toward each other, and I didn't know what to do the closer we got. *Should I speak and acknowledge him, or should I just keep walking?* Lucky for me, he had already thought all of that through.

"Hello. How are you doing?" he asked.

"I'm fine. How are you?" I replied.

"I'm doing okay. My name is Nathaniel," he offered.

"I'm Idella," I responded.

We shook hands, and when we did, he put a small piece of yellow paper in mine and closed my fingers around it.

I didn't call him that night. Or for a while after that. We continued to see one another at the school in passing, and gradually started making small talk. It took me a while to actually open myself up enough to call and initiate a conversation with him, but the connection via the phone was the same as the first time I laid eyes on him: instantaneous. We talked about everything — our recent failed relationships, moving on. There was a two-year lapse between when we first met and actually became romantically involved. We both had unfinished business. My ex-husband and I were legally separated when I met Nathaniel, but it took more than a year for the divorce to be finalized.

Nathaniel was not married, but he had built a life with his ex-partner. It was a process for them to move on as well. They did not have children together. The little boy he picked up from school was not his biological son, but they still had to decide how they wanted Nathaniel to navigate the relationship he had built with the kindergartener. There were other things they had to sort out as well. We did not rush these processes because our connection and union had always been natural and organic.

I knew that I loved my now husband the very first time I saw him. Because of him, I can attest that love at first sight is real. After twelve years and two more children we are still in love. And, honestly, every day feels like the first day. That's love.

~Idella M. Anderson

30

Our Little Town

There are no accidental meetings between souls.
~Sheila Burke

I was pushing forty and newly divorced. I had two kids in elementary school and was back to working nine-to-five, trying to make ends meet.

A few years before, my life had seemed picture perfect. I was living in sunny California working part-time just to stay busy. My days were full of tennis, swim meets and soccer outings. Weekends meant friends, barbecues and endless laughs.

One evening, my husband came home and announced we were moving back to New Jersey because he felt he had hit the ceiling at his current job. I had grown up there, but I was disappointed because now I was finally committed to my new home in Southern California. Reluctantly, I began to pack, and we moved again.

That was the beginning of the end.

He hated living in New Jersey, and we grew apart.

It was heartbreaking for all of us. My parents were married for over forty years. I felt it was so important to show my children what a happy marriage was. Clearly, we were doing a lousy job of it.

I was sad and exhausted for a long time after our split. We had bought a house in a beautiful country-club neighborhood and I made a few friends there. It was lovely, but I always envied my old friends who planted their roots in the town I had grown up in. They married their high-school sweethearts, bought their parents' homes and were all still connected. I was living about thirty minutes away from the place I once called home.

My hometown, Carlstadt, was a little German town that still preserved its old cobblestone streets. The downtown was tiny, splattered with little Italian delis, a firehouse and an old library. You couldn't go for a cup of coffee without running into someone you knew. It was an older town, and not much had changed since I grew up there in the 1970s. Perched on a hill, the little town of Carlstadt boasted tremendous views of New York City. It was a simple and sweet way of life, and in my heart it was home. I had the best memories growing up there.

One morning, I woke up and took a good look in the mirror. *Dear God,* I thought. *I need to do something with my hair.* Once very much concerned with my looks, I had totally given up. My hair looked dull. I looked lifeless.

I made an appointment, and the next Saturday I schlepped a half-hour away to a salon a friend had recommended. I spent two hours in that salon. Highlights, a good cut and a blowout transformed me from sad and solemn to sensational for a change. I was walking out of the salon when my girlfriend Nanci called. We had grown up across the street from one another in Carlstadt. We had remained the best of friends for over thirty years. Since she lived near the salon, she asked to meet me for lunch. I arrived at the restaurant she had recommended and discovered I was not exactly dressed for it. There was valet parking and people were dressed to the nines. I was in shorts and sandals, with no make-up. Honestly, the only thing I had going on that day was my hair. I felt intimidated, yet I gave the valet my keys and slithered into the restaurant.

Despite my casual appearance, it felt good to get out and see my old friend. We caught up, and the afternoon flew by. While we were getting ready to leave, my girlfriend started chatting with an older man on her way back from the restroom. The older man's younger, handsome friend stood next to him and glanced my way. He seemed awkward just standing there, and for a minute I thought he would come over and say "hello." The fact that he didn't sort of intrigued me. I was never interested in the men who threw themselves at me in my younger days.

The next thing I knew, my girlfriend and her friend were on the deck taking pictures of the view of New York City. I got up to kill time and went to the ladies' room. That's when the shy friend reached out his hand and said, "Hi, I'm Tom. Our friends really need to come out of their shells, right?" he said as he glanced over at Nanci and his pal, Tony. We laughed, and then we talked. He displayed a quiet confidence and, honestly, he had me at "hello." I was smitten.

"So, where are you from?" he asked. I told him I lived in the Ramsey Country Club neighborhood.

"Really?" he replied. "I live in Franklin Lakes."

Wow, I thought, *that's the next town.* While Ramsey was beautiful, Franklin Lakes was the Beverly Hills of Bergen County.

He had been divorced for many years and had yet to meet "the one." I looked at this man, and a chill ran down my spine. I literally had not felt this way in twenty-plus years. Just looking into his eyes, I felt alive again.

Then he knocked me off my feet. He looked at me and said, "Franklin Lakes is beautiful. It's a magical little place, and I'm blessed my business thrived and allowed me that lifestyle. I will never forget where I grew up, though. It's in my blood, and I treasure every minute I had living there."

"Where is that?" I asked.

"Oh, a little German town about forty minutes from here," he replied. "Have you ever heard of Carlstadt?"

"Seriously," I exclaimed. "No way!" Well, that was the start of my new beginning. He sat down and we talked — and talked and talked. My friend Nanci had left, and we were still talking hours later.

I was unsure how to deal with my children and a new man in my life. We dated for several years, and every date was better than the next. Sometimes, all we had time for was a cup of coffee, but it didn't matter. When my guy walked into the room, my heart fluttered. A simple smile from him would send me to cloud nine. It does to this day. I honestly thought these feelings only existed in fairy tales.

He loved me and my kids. He swooped me off to Italy, France

and so many other places I had never seen. He was waiting for years to find the one and, lucky for me, I became his.

I learned at a young age that one must always show appreciation by reciprocation. Scale means nothing as long as the love and thought are there. I couldn't plan trips to exotic, amazing places like he did, but once a year I planned a mystery trip for him. I told him what to pack, and that's about it. I took him to many amazing spots that he had never been, and they were all within driving distance, too! I loved listening to him beg for hints.

After five years, when my children were a bit older, he popped the question. Naturally, all of our wedding photos were taken in the beautiful, little town where we grew up. We were in our forties and sixties, yet transformed into kids, laughing and running up and down those old cobblestone hills. Our frazzled photographer followed along patiently. We posed for pictures in our old baseball field. We had come to find out that we both played ball for many, many years in that old ballpark. We took pictures in front of the old Lindbergh School, too. Although we were more than fifteen years apart in age, we came to realize that we had both sat at different times in the same kindergarten class.

We have been together now for over ten years. Our family has grown bigger, and so have our hearts. I've grown to believe one should never give up on love. If we open up our hearts, love is out there, especially when we least expect it.

~Mary Ellen Flaherty Langbein

Making Melody on eHarmony

*A partner is someone who makes you more than you
are, simply by being by your side.*
~Albert Kim

After my divorce in 2003, it didn't take long to figure out that I sucked at being single. Having gotten married right out of college, I didn't really have any practice at living on my own. The thought of learning how to date all over again while in my thirties was scary as well.

As a result, I didn't leave the house much. Fortunately, 21st-century technology came to my aid. A guy doesn't have to figure out where to go to meet women when he only needs to go as far as his computer! But which dating site should I choose?

I didn't choose well at first. I had a date with a gal who put up multiple profiles on the same site to see who would date her. I had a date with a former co-worker who seemed to want a marriage proposal on the first date. I chatted with a nurse online until she sent me a picture of her tattoo — in a place that I normally wouldn't have seen on a person I had not yet met. She broke off that awkwardness by saying that I was too short for her. (She was six feet tall and liked to wear high heels.)

I tried another dating site. I figured the site wasn't asking the right questions, or enough of them, when my first 100-percent compatibility match was a dominatrix. I still had my sad results page up on my computer when my ex-wife came to drop off the kids for weekend visitation. She looked at it and actually felt sorry for me. She suggested I try a site that I had not heard of called eHarmony.com.

I gave it a look a couple of nights later and saw that it was $49.95 a month to join. I said "nope" to myself and went to bed. After sleeping on it, however, I reasoned that on the Internet, as with many other areas of life, we get what we pay for. Since "free" wasn't getting me anywhere, I plunked down the $49.95 for a single month. I put my kids in my profile picture because I wanted to be up front about the package deal involved with dating me.

After a few days, eHarmony matched me with a "community college educator" from a town about an hour away. Her name was Diana, and we seemed to have a lot in common. I began the multi-step process of communication on eHarmony, which progresses from multiple-choice questions through the list of "must haves" and "can't stands" to open-ended questions and eventually the opportunity to take communication offsite if things are going well.

Just a couple of days after being matched, however, Diana "fast-tracked" me. This is a feature eHarmony had whereby, with mutual agreement, a couple could bypass some of these get-to-know-each-other steps and go straight to open communication.

I was a little freaked out by this at first. Fast tracking to me was a red-flag warning for "black hole of emotional need." For some reason, though, I didn't run away screaming. I couldn't say exactly why, but something made me feel that it was all right to accept the fast-track request. As it turned out, Diana was in her last couple of weeks of a six-month trial, and she just wanted to be sure that she had an adequate chance to communicate with me before her membership expired.

It didn't take much open communication for us to figure out that we were very good at making each other laugh. I told her that the word "soul mate," so prevalent on eHarmony, just gave me a rash. She said she had three criteria for deciding whether she wanted to meet me in person. She asked if I was an axe murderer, a cross-dresser and if I had all my teeth. I responded, "I'm not an axe murderer, I still have all my teeth (except for the wisdom teeth), and that incident with the black negligee was blown completely out of proportion." Apparently, that was a good answer because she agreed that we should meet in person.

Now it was my turn to ask a critical question. We were going to meet for dinner, but I wanted to be sure that we were food-compatible. Growing up in an Italian family (on my mother's side), food was an integral part of our identity and culture. So when I asked her what kind of restaurant she wanted to go to, she said, "The Italians can do no wrong with food as far as I'm concerned." Good answer.

Then she addressed a common first-date issue — the nervous stomach. She said she wasn't one of these girls who would just order a salad and ice water on the first date and then eat two bites because she had a problem with eating in front of a man. I told her, "Good, because I like to cook, so what good to me is a girlfriend who won't eat?"

She responded, "I think I like you."

I liked where this was going.

Our first date was at Tuscany, a small Italian restaurant in Springfield, Illinois. We discovered quickly that one of the greatest benefits of eHarmony's multi-step getting-acquainted process (fast track notwithstanding) is that it almost completely does away with first-date jitters. There are no awkward questions or lapses in conversation because by the time you meet in person, you're already past that stage. I had only known Diana for about two and a half weeks, but it felt like I had known her much longer.

I had one rule for first dates: Never touch my date at our first meeting because it is disrespectful and sends the wrong message. Well, that rule went out the door fairly expediently as we held hands across the table and talked into the night. We had arrived when the restaurant opened, and were still talking when it closed. So we took it out to the parking lot and talked for another hour after that.

Finally, when we decided that we really ought to call it a night, Diana asked me, "What's next?" She was probably just asking about the potential for a second date, but even then, there seemed to be so much more meaning to the question. I found that I couldn't answer it without thinking about what was next for the rest of my life. Deep down, I knew, even then, that this was going to be the last first date I would ever have.

And it was. Diana and I have been married twelve years now. We've been through a lot, but just writing this down makes me relive the excitement and anticipation of that first date.

And yes, I do still get a little itchy when I hear the word "soul mate."

~M. Scott Coffman

32

New Beginnings

You may have a fresh start any moment you choose,
for this thing that we call "failure" is not the falling
down, but the staying down.
~Mary Pickford

When the phone rang, I was expecting a call from my florist. Instead, it was my old friend, Sister Jean, looking for a favour. "We have a large group of sad people who need help!" she told me. "One of the regular team leaders had an emergency and can't make it this weekend. Can you fill in?"

Sister Jean ran weekend retreats for New Beginnings, a group dedicated to helping the separated, divorced and widowed. It was Valentine's Day, which is always hard on people who have lost their partner. But as it happened, I had nothing on my calendar because I, too, was single.

"Sure, I can help. I'll be at the convent house tonight with all my talks for the group. Ink me in wherever you need me."

New Beginnings had helped me after my stressful divorce several years before. I likened the weekend retreat to a short stop at a station en route to my destination of getting my life back together. At that station, I threw my unwanted baggage of anger, hurt, disappointment and fear out the train window and moved on. It was very therapeutic, and I learned about grieving. I also learned that I was not alone in this experience and, most importantly, I discovered hope. Now that I was feeling more confident and happy again, I wanted to give back and share that magical hope with others.

A few hours later, I entered the meeting room. I recognized most of the team members except one — a tall, distinguished man with thick, wavy, white hair, who was looking a bit overwhelmed. As fate would have it, the only vacant seat was next to him. Upon introducing myself, he told me it was his first weekend as a team leader, and he had no idea what was going on. Sister Jean had called him with an SOS, too, and he didn't have the heart to turn her down. I reassured him that I'd walk him through it, and he would be surprised at the rewards he received from helping others. How prophetic those words turned out to be!

As team leaders, we took turns addressing the group with stories of our own divorces and spousal deaths. One has to be truthful and vulnerable in this situation. I learned that my new friend, Luis, was widowed, having lost his wife to cancer. My story entailed discovering my husband on television at a ballgame with his mistress. It always added a bit of comic relief to an otherwise somber weekend. By now, even I could find the humour in it.

By Sunday evening, the participants had all headed home with newfound faith in their hearts. There is nothing like hearing other people's stories to buoy your spirits and make you realize that you can get through your own challenges. Sister Jean hosted her team leaders with a glass of wine and pizza as we debriefed. After all, this had been Valentine's Day weekend, and a difficult time for broken-hearted, lonely people. The team leaders tidied up, and each of us headed off to our cars.

As I turned the key in the ignition, I heard the ominous click, and my heart sank. Now what was I going to do? It was dusk, and bitterly cold. Most of the team leaders had already left the parking lot. I got out of my car as Luis was driving by. He stopped and asked if I needed help.

"Yes," I replied, "my battery is dead."

"No problem. I can give you a boost."

Within a matter of minutes, my hood was up, cables were connected, and my motor was purring. This elegant gentleman was my knight in shining armour!

I met Luis at several more New Beginnings weekends and events. We continued to share our stories with others. We started our friendship by knowing intimate details about each other's past lives. I was impressed to find a man who was willing to share his feelings and be emotionally vulnerable. We started to date and slowly got to know each other. It was a friendship based on trust and truth. We found that we always had meaningful conversations and enjoyed many of the same interests. Both of us had a curiosity about life and wanted to share new experiences.

Two years later, we invited Sister Jean and many of her team leaders to our wedding. At our wedding lunch, we related the story of our meeting to our guests.

Luis opened his speech by saying, "I had no idea that I would find my beautiful wife in a setting where I was helping others deal with their pain. What a reward I received."

For my part, I quipped, "Luis boosted my battery, and he's been boosting it ever since."

The guests' laughter brought down the house. What a joyful life's journey it has been.

~Linda A. Mikus

33

A Mystical Meeting

Knowledge is the soil, and intuitions are the flowers
which grow up out of it.
~Henry Ward Beecher

I grew up an only child and spent most of my free time reading and creating imaginary kingdoms in the yard. My dad encouraged my imagination. While he read to me at night long past the age when I could read myself, he also made up stories about fairy realms and mysterious creatures. I was always the fairy princess charged with keeping my subjects safe.

As I grew older, it was comforting to imagine I was somehow still protecting the mystic creatures from a cold, disbelieving world. I always left acorn caps filled with sugar in the violet beds where my subjects dwelled. I believed they thanked me by guiding me whenever I was searching for something I had lost, or even when I wasn't, such as when I felt an urge to look down and I found money on the ground.

I learned to listen to my inner voice. It wasn't constant, but when I felt a hunch, it was always right. Most people laughed it off as luck, but I could tell the difference whenever I felt the internal push. It never let me down, even though the rewards were sometimes small. Still, I won more than a normal share of raffles and contests — not every time I entered, but every time I listened to the inner urging.

Life passed, and I found myself a divorced mother of three, struggling to raise my family. I worked as a substitute schoolteacher, taking every assignment offered — even after having surgery on my foot, which required crutches for several weeks. One rainy November morning, I was called out, and I dressed for work in a dress and one good shoe. I hobbled to the car and made my way to the intersection where I always turned left. Then I felt something I hadn't experienced for some time.

Something deep in my heart whispered *go the long way today*. I had been struggling with depression over the way things had turned out so I told myself it was time to grow up — I wasn't going to listen to some silly hunch. I put on my left-turn signal to go the normal way, but the feeling inside grew more insistent. *Go the other way.*

I glanced at the dashboard clock and saw I had ample time for a detour. Shrugging my shoulders, I changed my signal and turned right. I got about two blocks when my car stalled. I put on my flashers, hobbled to the front and lifted the hood. Trying to balance on my one good foot and keep my rain-drenched hair out of my eyes, I willed the thing to start. This was years before cell phones were common, and I was frantic to get to the school. I wiggled wires and jostled parts, but the car wouldn't start.

Now I was faced with two choices: I could hobble the mile home on crutches, in a downpour; or I could sit in the car and wait for help. I was on the verge of tears. I reached up to close the hood just as a car pulled around and parked ahead of me. The man driving it was tall, dark and handsome. In less than five minutes, he had my car running. In exchange for his help, he asked for my phone number. I had been on exactly two dates since my divorce four years earlier. My focus was my children, and I had dismissed any thoughts of having a man in my future.

Then came the nudge in my heart again, a solid little poke. *Trust your inner voice. Take a chance.* So I agreed to meet for coffee that evening, insisting I buy. All day, I told myself he wouldn't show and I needed to stop acting like a schoolgirl. Still, his eyes were so green, his smile so mischievous. If ever I had imagined a prince, he looked like the mystery man who appeared out of the storm to rescue this bedraggled maiden.

That evening, I entered the restaurant, expecting to sit alone and relax. But there he stood, waiting by the door. We sat for hours and learned our interests were mutual. Books, movies, hobbies and foods all matched up. That night led to dinner, then dinner and a movie. In time, he met my children, and they approved.

It is now twenty-three years later. A year after that meeting, we were married. I set out acorn caps on our wedding day, and after our daughter was born, I taught her about the fairy folk and how we had to protect them. Even if I never hear the soft whisper again, I won't mind. The wee folk have given their princess her prince. Who could ask for more?

~Anna M. Lowther

Chapter
5

The
Miracle
of **Love**

Divine Intervention

Come Here

Grow old along with me! The best is yet to be.
~Robert Browning

It was a beautiful summer day in July. I had cleaned the house, bought the groceries and run the errands. Now I had time to walk the beach and unwind before the relatives arrived for Jim's anniversary mass.

I pulled on my bathing suit, shirt and shorts and headed for Cold Storage Beach, my favorite at low tide, because I could walk all the way to Brewster on smooth, hard sand with a view of the entire arm of the Cape.

A year had passed since the morning when I found Jim on the floor, struggling to tell me what happened. I called 911, and he was dead six hours later at Cape Cod Hospital. He'd had a massive brain hemorrhage.

It was a long and lonely year for me. I completed a bereavement group therapy course and cried a thousand rivers, yet I felt no relief. Despair was my daily companion, and life seemed so meaningless without my soul mate.

We had been married for forty-eight years! He was my anchor. Our four children were grown, and it was time for us to complete our bucket lists. He was my happy-go-lucky side and balanced my seriousness perfectly. Friends with good intentions tried matchmaking, but I was not looking.

"Damn you, Jim!" I cried out to the vast ocean in front of me. The

Divine Intervention | 121

surf splashed against my legs, sending my protests straight to heaven, but no comfort came. I followed the edge of the sea and walked until the incoming tide surrounded me and I was on an island far from shore. But I was oblivious to where I was and kept on complaining. I was purging myself of feelings I had kept locked inside, and it felt good to let them go. The water seemed deeper, and I realized I had to head for shore or swim. I took off my shirt and shorts and made it to shore before the tide overcame me.

How fast the tide came in, I thought, *and how foolish of me not to pay attention.* The late afternoon sun felt like a warm blanket. I stretched out and soaked it up. "God help me," I sputtered.

Looking to the west, I saw a man coming in my direction. We seemed to be the only two people way out on the flats. My friends always warned me about walking the beach alone. I walked into the water to avoid him.

"Nice day!" he shouted out to me. Then he said something else that I didn't hear.

"Excuse me?" I asked, not really wanting to engage in conversation with this man. I was too engulfed in my own misery.

"It's kind of spooky. You are standing where I threw her ashes."

Oh, my God, I thought. Then I faced him.

He was tall and thin with a graying beard. A golf cap and sunglasses obscured his face, but his body language was loud and clear. He was kind and not to be feared.

"I'm so sorry," I called out against the sounds of the surf. We looked at each other.

"Are you all right?"

"My husband died, too."

Then he opened his arms with such sympathy. "Come here," he said softly.

In a haunting fog, I walked from the water onto the sand and into his arms, and we shared a moment that changed us forever. It was a warm hug that said, "I'm sorry for your heartache. I know how you feel."

He took hold of my hand and led me to a rock where he had engraved his wife's initials.

"She died a long time ago when I was a lot younger," he said. "I live in South Carolina now. I'm here visiting a friend in a nursing home. He's not doing well, and I wanted to see him before he dies. I always come here and visit before I head back."

Then he told me how his wife had died of cancer and of his fulfilling her desire to be cremated. "The bay was our favorite place. We brought up a family here."

I asked about his friend, and when he told me the name of the nursing home, I realized that my employer, a doctor, was the director.

"I'm the secretary for your friend's doctor! What a small world it is," I said.

"I married again, but I learned the hard way that you just can't replace someone you loved. It didn't work, and I sold our house in Brewster and moved to South Carolina."

It felt weird being so close to him in such a secluded area. I took my cue to leave after revealing very little about myself.

How could I have just walked into his arms like that? I thought. *He could have been a serial killer.* Yet I felt something… a spark that both excited and scared me as I walked faster back to my car.

Weeks later, he called me at work. He had found the doctor's name and did some investigating.

"I'm the man you met on the beach. Do you remember me?" he asked.

"Of course, I remember you. How could I forget you? I thought you were an angel. And if I looked back, you would be gone — and I didn't want you to be gone."

"No one has ever called me an angel before," he said. "Can I call you at home?"

I gave him my number, and he called that night. We talked every day after that, realizing how much we had in common.

One night, he called as I was falling asleep.

"How old are you?" he asked in a panic.

"What?" I said in a sleepy fog. "How old am I? A gentleman never asks a woman her age!"

"I don't want to be arrested for courting a minor. I'm seventy-eight years old."

"Wow. You don't look seventy-eight at all. Do you have a pacemaker?"

"No. I'm very healthy. So how old are you?"

"Well, you're the math teacher." He had told me he was retired from teaching high-school math.

"I was married at nineteen in 1962. Figure it out."

"Sixty-nine," he shot back in an instant. "I thought you were much younger."

"Hooray!" I laughed again. "We're both old."

"I can't stand it any longer. Can we meet on the beach again at that same spot? I'm making plans to fly up."

In September, my phone rang. "I'm at the beach. Are you coming?"

I made sandwiches, packed them into a backpack and threw in a bottle of champagne. I was off in a whirlwind.

As he came into view, he walked toward me, arms outstretched.

"Come here," he sang, and I flew into them. When I pulled out the champagne, his smile turned to laughter.

As we sat on the rock toasting each other, three women walked by.

"Congratulations!" they called.

He hadn't proposed, but those women were prophets. We were two lonely people led to that remote area of beach by fate, but we were destined to spend the rest of our lives together.

~Sandra Bakun

35

A Dream Come True

Isn't that how falling in love so often works?
Some stranger appears out of nowhere and becomes
a fixed star in your universe.
~Kate Bolick

I looked down the petal-strewn gauntlet. It occurred to me that this was either the dumbest thing I'd ever done or the smartest. Either way, it was certain to be the most memorable. This was my wedding day.

At the other end of the aisle stood the man who had asked me to marry him. He looked terrified. I could see sweat glistening above his eyebrows. Then it occurred to me that perhaps it wasn't terror he was feeling as much as the humidity in the sanctuary. This was unquestionably the hottest, most humid day Missouri had seen this year.

The church was one of the most breathtaking places in town, primarily because it was one of the oldest. I suppose it shouldn't have surprised me that the cooling system hadn't been updated. However, I didn't know that it still relied on a swamp cooler. I learned that day that swamp coolers take a great deal of time to cool the room, and this particular swamp cooler had not been given enough time to compete with the miserable heat and humidity of the day.

So there I stood, sweating in a wedding gown that cost more than my first car and high heels that I never would have worn any other time and would never wear again. Those sitting on the left were complete strangers to me and were undoubtedly concerned about the groom's mental capacity to enter into legal contracts such as marriage. And those on the right were good friends of mine, most of whom were already quite confident that my mental capacity was questionable.

They weren't the only ones who were concerned. They couldn't be thinking anything I hadn't already considered. *Will he be able to settle down with a family after being a bachelor all these years? What will happen to my daughter and me if this turns out to be a mistake? Are we insane?* I pondered that last question the most.

There wasn't much about our courtship that was ordinary.

My four-year-old daughter Sophie and I lived in Kansas, and we were pretty much on our own. She'd begun to ask when she would get a daddy and insisted that he would drive a truck because that's what the father of every other child in daycare drove.

My groom, on the other hand, had always been the single uncle who played with his nieces and nephews while their parents enjoyed adult conversations. In Minnesota, 415 miles away, John had been alone for a long time. He'd never been married and he had no children.

We had only two things in common. First, we each felt we were missing something without a spouse. Second, we both knew Rob and Tracy. I had gone to high school with Rob, and John had gotten to know the couple in college. And it was those relationships that would be key to the future of John, Sophie and me.

In Minnesota, summer had finally given way to fall. John lay in his bed and prayed, "Lord, will I always be this lonely? Isn't there someone out there for me?" This prayer played over and over in his head as he fell asleep. Once asleep, he had three separate but connected dreams.

In his first dream, he was dating a woman with a little girl. In his second dream, he was standing at the altar with Rob as his best man. In his last dream, he was opening wedding gifts with his wife on one side and one of his sisters on the other.

Later in the week, John called his former college roommate.

"Rob, I had the weirdest dream, and you were in it. I was dating a woman with a little girl. We got married, and you were my best man!"

"Well," Rob grinned, "I happen to know a woman with a little girl, and she's looking for someone."

The next time I saw Rob, he mentioned casually that he had a friend who was single and might like to meet me. At the risk of inflating my ego, he left out the details of the dream. After all, who needs a prima donna who thinks she may be someone's dream-come-true?

"Seriously, Rob! He's in Minnesota, and I'm in Kansas. What are we supposed to do?"

Rob wasn't worried. "Oh, you meet, you fall in love, and you get married."

Nine months later, John and I stood on opposite ends of the aisle at the beginning of a new life together. And my daughter would have a father — the first man to tell her how incredible and beautiful she was.

In less than twenty-four hours, the three of us would drive to Minnesota, where I had no job and knew no one except John. I took a deep breath and began my walk down the aisle. I knew only one thing with relative confidence: I would agree to absolutely anything if it got me out of this dress and these heels!

Twenty years later, I'm happy to say that God planned a successful marriage. It hasn't been a simple marriage — certainly not one without many challenges — but those challenges have strengthened our love and appreciation for each other.

~LaRonda Bourn

36

Father Knows Best

For it was not into my ear you whispered, but into my heart. It was not my lips you kissed, but my soul.
~Judy Garland

The snowdrift halfway up the driver's side of my tan Pontiac Grand Am surprised me. How could three inches of snow do this? I guess this explained why it was so easy to claim the last carport slot at our townhome complex. Choosing the end space when I moved in seemed like a wise choice for fewer door dings from other cars, but the longer-term residents knew something I did not — the Wichita snowdrifts can bury one's car.

I decided to walk to a nearby neighborhood church instead of driving to my downtown church. I added a pale blue sweater under my coat and a matching scarf to protect my head and neck. The wind had died down, the trees sparkled in their snowy winter coats, and the pristine snow crunched under my boots. I took my time and admired the wintry scene. Very few cars were out and the world felt fresh and full of promise for a pleasant day. Idly, I wondered about how to make snow ice cream until a noisy crow trying to chase several finches away from a bird feeder interrupted my thoughts.

Soon, I arrived at the little church during their Sunday school hour and introduced myself to a few people who were already sitting in the small but slightly chilly sanctuary. The pastor talked casually with several other people, and then eventually came to greet me.

"Hello, I'm Ted. What brings you to our little congregation today?"

"I live in one of the nearby townhome complexes and decided to walk here instead of digging my car out to drive to my downtown church, where I'm an active member." I added that so he would not think I was a prospect.

With a little more chitchat, he learned I was single, forty, and a preacher's daughter.

"Oh, my dear!" he exclaimed. "You have to meet my son. He's a fine man, and you have so much in common."

I took a step backwards and mumbled something about being tired after my walk and needing to sit down. *No more blind dates*, I reminded myself. I'd decided dating at forty was generally disappointing, and I was happy with my life.

Recognizing my reluctance, he added, "Of course, he lives in Seattle, so it could be a while."

I relaxed and enjoyed the service. Ted kept in touch, inviting me to eat meals with him and his wife on occasion. We became friendly neighbors during the winter and early spring. Sometimes, he would mention his son again. I was careful to be merely polite until the day Ted showed me a picture of his son. I'm sure my eyes widened in appreciation. I know my pulse quickened.

"I'm sure the Seattle ladies feel very lucky," I said in a feigned attempt to dismiss my interest. He didn't bring up his son again, to my disappointment.

A few months later, Ted called me for a favor.

"My son is flying in tomorrow to spend a week for my birthday, but his flight arrives late, and I don't drive after dark. Would you please pick him up at the airport and bring him to my house?"

How could I say no to a sweet couple who had become friends? Besides, I had become intensely curious about Ted's son Keith. The next night, I drove across town to the airport. It was getting dark as I left my car in short-term parking. The airport smelled of coffee and sweet baked goods. Tempting, but I was on a mission. While I dutifully waited to spot someone who looked like the handsome face I remembered from his father's photograph, I wondered why I hadn't thought to bring a sign. That's what they do in the movies. A tall, handsome man with bits of gray hair at his temples approached me. He looked at least ten years older than in his dad's photo.

"Are you Jeanetta?" he asked.

"Yes, and your name is…" I left the sentence unfinished, just in case.

"I'm Keith, and I'm delighted to finally meet you."

Finally? Had he been looking forward to it? What had Ted been telling him about me?

Keith stared at me with a silly grin on his face during the entire drive from the airport to his dad's house. When we arrived, Keith unloaded his suitcase from my car, and we walked up the gravel driveway to the door of his folks' house. I noticed someone had planted spring bulbs, which were starting to add yellow and purple buds to the greenery. Several planters lined the edges of the small porch, but there were no clues as to what would sprout in any of them. Before we could knock, the front door flung open with a loud bang, and the screen door screeched its need for oil.

"We've already eaten our supper," Ted said, reaching for the suitcase. "Why don't you take him to your favorite restaurant?"

What could I do? I drove Keith to a favorite 1950s diner. It was a busy Friday night, but we found an empty table in the far back section. We both ordered large, meaty salads and their signature cherry limeade sodas. I added a mint-chocolate-chip specialty milkshake, so Keith added a French vanilla. The jukebox played music from the 1950s and early 1960s. Bright red-and-aqua décor and 1950s memorabilia surrounded us. We tinkered with selecting songs from the little jukebox controllers at our table. Our conversation flowed easily as we discovered more about each other's lives, pasts, and goals. Eventually, I yawned, and we were both surprised to discover more than five hours had passed. All the tables around us were empty. We were the last people to leave, and they locked the doors behind us.

After that, we spent every evening together for the next ten days until Keith had to go home.

Hundreds of e-mails and phone calls, and several flights later, Keith proposed.

When Keith announced our plans, my future father-in-law said, "What took you so long? I knew you were right for each other when I first met her!"

I discovered that sometimes God works through a string of unusual events: a bothersome snowdrift, five hours disappearing over cherry limeade sodas, and two separate lives ready for a nudge to find each other.

~Jeanetta Chrystie

37

The Three Signs

Don't find love; let love find you. That's why it's called
falling in love, because you don't force yourself to fall,
you just fall.
~Jack Kerouac

My thoughts roiled. *What's wrong with this guy? Doesn't he know how to make dinner conversation? Did I accidentally drop a hair in his tacos?*

My roommate Wendy and I had invited our friend Chris and his new apartment mate for dinner. David, we learned, was a computer programmer who happened to have striking blue eyes and a deep Barry White voice. But throughout the night, he barely talked and he looked pale, like he had seen a ghost.

"What's up with David?" I asked Wendy after they left. "The social awkwardness is a real turn-off."

"I don't know," she replied, tying up her running shoes and zooming off. Wendy wasn't into "girlfriend talk."

A week later, David called. "I've got this essay assignment at Rutgers. Would you mind helping me with it?"

"Sure," I answered promptly. As a high-school English teacher, how could I resist?

As I sat in his bare bachelor apartment, he spoke buoyantly, inquiring about my high-school students. I learned that he had a deep faith, played guitar, liked Pink Floyd and Kurt Vonnegut, and loved the ocean. Then I plodded through one of the tritest essays I had ever read. All the while, his eyes studied my face. I willed myself not to redden, gave him a few kind suggestions, and then rose to leave. As I zipped my jacket, he asked, "Would you like to see the new Pacino movie on Friday?"

"Not really. Thanks anyway." I was still remembering our awkward taco dinner and his lack of sophistication. Besides, I had always imagined marrying another educator, some dark-eyed Mediterranean type. I know, I know, the fantasies of a twenty-something...

His confidence was unperturbed, and his smile was unflinching. "Okay," he responded. "Maybe another time."

He walked me to my car, his feet keeping up with my swift exit. As I turned the ignition, he leaned playfully into my window, his azure eyes swimming with Rhett Butler confidence — so different from the reticent man a week ago. Now he was coming across as a bit cocky. "Have a great week."

"I will," I vowed primly, pulling away. So that's what the essay help was about: a ruse.

Back in my kitchen, I unloaded on Wendy. "Can you believe it? He pretended he needed help so he could ask me out."

A Mona Lisa smile curved across her lips. "Maybe I shouldn't tell you this, but he told Chris — who told me — that you filled the signs."

"What signs?"

She shrugged. "I don't know. Just that he broke up with some girl — Annie, I think — and he didn't want to make the same mistake again. So he asked God for signs."

"Well, I'm never going to date him anyway," I declared. "He's not my type."

Over the course of a month, David organized bowling parties, lasagna dinners, and game nights. We exchanged small talk and enjoyed mutual friends, and he respectfully kept the unspoken boundary between us.

Thanksgiving came, and I visited my sister Margaret and her family in Virginia. That's what I needed: a toddling niece and their easygoing home to distract me from my restless singlehood and ennui.

In Margaret's guest room, I mulled things over. My curiosity grew. *What were these signs, anyway?* Then I argued with myself. *No, don't change your mind about David. You're just feeling desperate to find "the one." Hold out for...*

But something was creeping like soft cat feet into my heart. *How do you know this isn't meant to be? Why not find out?*

To my surprise, I knelt and prayed — yes, a bit dramatic, I know — like a trope-filled Hallmark movie. "Lord, if you want me to date David, have him ask me out again."

When I returned to New Jersey, I found a foil-wrapped African violet on my doorstep. The card read: *Welcome back. Hope you had a good trip. ~David*

I called to thank him. "Guess I'll hear from you again," I said, signing off.

"You bet," he rejoined. I could detect the knowing grin across the miles. But this time, I was not jangled by it.

A week later, I consented to our first date. Opening the door of his black Mustang, his eyes danced with feigned mischief. "It's a full moon. Sure you want to go out with me?"

Sitting with him in a candlelit pub felt strangely peaceful. First dates with other men had always felt contrived, the conversations forced and postured. But the man sitting across from me was at ease. He did not try to impress me. He was sincerely interested in what I had to say.

At my door, our eyes studied one another. And then we kissed. At that moment, I knew I would love him. Being with him felt like coming home from a weary journey.

I did not want to ask him about the signs until we were engaged. I did not want that knowledge to influence any part of our journey. One night as we sat on my stoop, he opened his journal.

"A few months before we met, I spent a lot of time praying and journaling," he said, "asking God to point me to the right woman. Sounds flaky, but I've been known to be a fool at times."

Laughing, I poked his ribs. "You? Never."

"This is what came to me: One — she will invite me to dinner."

"My, you're a presumptuous guy, aren't you?" I teased.

"Well, you did. Check One."

"Sign Two: that verse from Psalms — 'The joy of the Lord is your strength.' I had no idea how that would fit in — not until I walked through your door and saw the wall calligraphy with the exact same verse."

"So that's why you asked which one of us made it."

"You — Check Two."

"And then?"

"Three — one of my favorite verses: 'For now we see through a glass, darkly; but then face to face.' You and Chris were talking about discouragement. Suddenly, you said, 'That reminds me of the verse from First Corinthians: 'For now we see through a glass, darkly; but then face to face.'"

"Incredible — three signs in one night. So what were you thinking?"

"Thinking? I wasn't. I was in a state of shock."

"Your mouth was hanging open," I razzed. "You looked scared to death."

He smiled. "Actually, I thought, *Her? Really, God? She's a prim and proper English teacher. Can she even rock the dance floor?*"

"Oh, you did, did you? So if it wasn't for the signs, you'd have passed me by!" Sniggering, I tried to swat his arm, but he pre-empted, clasping my hand in his. He brought it to his lips and held it there, his eyes full of emotion.

"Signs or no signs," he said finally, "I love you, Sandra."

~Sandra Croft

Change of Plans

*Faith is what makes life bearable, with all its tragedies
and ambiguities and sudden, startling joys.*
~Madeleine L'Engle

"How did you two meet?" Our new friends, Mike and Jacqui, sat back in their chairs on the other side of the dinner table. I cringed inside as I looked over at Michael. He gave me the "your turn" nod.

"We met online."

It still rankled me to say those words. I had never wanted online dating to be my love story. I had wanted something romantic and organic — like, he stopped to help me change a flat tire in the rain, sat next to me on an airplane, or joined my small group at church. I wanted a special story, and online dating lacked surprise and spontaneity. Even though it no longer carried the stigma it once had, for me, it still carried a residue of social failure.

When I was younger, I thought I'd have to be desperate to try online dating. But then I turned twenty-eight and was still single. I faced the reality that my social circle didn't include a potential husband. I worked full-time with all-female co-workers. The singles' population at my church was nonexistent. And as an introvert, partying on a Friday night wasn't my idea of fun.

So I gave online dating a try.

I swiftly weeded out the profiles that contained selfie photos taken in the bathroom mirror. I wanted a guy who made the time to take a decent photo. When I came across the profile for "Jack of All Bikes," I was intrigued. This dark-haired, lanky widower seemed to have a lot of the qualities I was looking for. I sent him a smiley face.

He wrote back right away, and we started a conversation. I swooned over his thoughtful, well-written e-mails. After just a few weeks, he asked if he could call me. I smiled at the screen as I typed my reply, "I'd like that."

That night, I was housesitting for my boss and heard the faint jingle of my cell phone in the bedroom as I walked past the doorway. I would have missed it otherwise. When I saw the area code, I knew it must be him. I hadn't expected him to call so quickly.

"Hi, it's Michael."

I sat on the floor, staring at my reflection in the mirrored closet door, twirling a strand of hair around my finger. We talked for two hours. After every awkward pause, he came back with another thread of conversation. Before we hung up, we made arrangements to meet at a café halfway between our homes, which were an hour and a half apart in the San Francisco Bay area.

The day arrived, and I told my roommate where I was going in case Michael turned out to be an axe murderer. Waiting for him at a wrought-iron table outside the café, I pulled my jacket tighter against the January wind and scanned the people walking by for a face I knew only from photos. Then I saw him—looking handsome in a brown button-down shirt. He stuffed the keys to his motorcycle in the pocket of his jeans as he walked in my direction. We made eye contact.

"Sarah?"

I nodded and stuck out my hand, heart pounding.

He ordered tea, and I fingered the yellow sleeve on my cup of hot chocolate. It had a small saying printed next to the logo: "Enjoy the little things because some day you may look back and realize they were big things."

What if I have just met my future husband? I thought of the journal I'd been writing in since I was eighteen. Throughout the years, I'd faithfully written letters to and prayers for my future husband, trusting

God to bring the right man at the right time. It hadn't been easy to wait through a decade of singleness — watching all my friends get married, questioning my worth, and feeling invisible.

In the few weeks we'd been writing, Michael had already started to make me feel visible. Online dating created this strange situation where we were meeting for the first time, but were already past the small talk. We talked for real — about his late wife, about the mistakes we'd made, and about our common faith. It wasn't love at first sight, but I felt excited. I wanted to know more.

Afterward, Michael walked me back to my car and said, "I had a nice time. Do you want to do this again?"

Soon, we were driving back and forth every weekend. It was difficult building a relationship from scratch, with no overlap in our lives, and long distance, too. But we walked through the awkwardness together, and I just kept saying "yes" as we journeyed through unknown territory.

The day after Valentine's Day, Michael asked me to be his girlfriend. In March, I ran out of pages in my journal. That summer, I told him I loved him. In September, he moved to my town. I knew our relationship was racing toward engagement, but I was still scared. Was I sure he was "the one"?

Then, one night shortly after he moved to my town, I woke up around 3:00 a.m. with a single, piercing prompt: *Ask Michael when he renewed his relationship with God.* Michael had shared that though he'd grown up in the church, during his early twenties he'd walked away from his faith for a season and made some poor decisions.

I asked him the next day.

"It was January 2005," he replied. "I went to a Wednesday night Bible study."

After he left, I pulled out my journal, tracing the gold cross embossed in the burgundy leather cover. Michael didn't know anything about this. I flipped to the front page. My first entry was dated Wednesday, January 19, 2005. I felt chills run up my spine. The month I'd started praying for him ten years ago was the very month he renewed his faith and began a journey that transformed him into the man I could marry. I knew it wasn't coincidence — this was the love story that I'd longed for and the confirmation I needed. Online dating hadn't been part of my plan, but it was part of God's.

I looked back at Mike and Jacqui and twisted the ring on my finger under the table. Even though I had to admit to online dating every time Michael and I told our story, I couldn't complain. I married him!

~Sarah Barnum

39

Saved

The golden moments in the stream of life rush past us
and we see nothing but sand; the angels come to visit
us and we only know them when they are gone.
~George Eliot

"Trees were doing 'enders' in the Guadalupe River after the rain last night, and the man at the gas station says the Medina is at flood stage, too," said our paddle-trip leader, Leonard. "But it doesn't look bad to me — a few haystack rapids. I think we can make this trip. It's up to you if you want to run it, but I'd hate to drive five hours to make a paddle and not do one."

The five men on this trip were not about to have their whitewater adventure thwarted. So, after some discussion, they agreed with Leonard that we could manage the haystacks. We'd just have to be extra vigilant as it was early spring, and an unexpected dunk in the frigid Medina River would steal one's breath.

I was the neophyte and the only woman on the trip. After having had no sleep the night before due to the rain pouring off the tent and a tornado threat conveyed to us by the flashlight-toting campground host, the little voice in my head screamed to just go back to the campground. But if I didn't paddle, neither could my partner. If the group was up for this, so was I.

I didn't know it at the time, but one of the reasons Leonard arranged the trip was to introduce my paddling partner, Roy, and me.

We had each been dating other people in the canoe club, but those relationships were failing. So, when this canoe trip started, Roy and I did not know what our strengths on the water — or otherwise — were.

The first couple of miles were easy, with stimulating haystacks and pushy water but no obstructions. At this rate, it would be a fast trip with hardly any paddling. Then, around the next sweeping bend at Enchanted Estates, there was a low-water crossing.

The six intrepid paddlers pulled out to scout the conditions at the crossing. The river was at flood stage. Six inches of water flowed over the top of the bridge. We would have to portage — or… maybe not. The guys devised an alternate plan. Put the lighter person in the bow of the boat and the heavier person in the stern, then power up and let physics pop the boats on top of the bridge. Not a great idea, but better than an exceedingly difficult portage.

The first boat attempted the plan — and it worked. Then the second canoe powered up, popped up on top of the bridge and skidded to a stop. So, Roy and I thought, okay — we could do that. We got in Roy's canoe, pushed off, turned the corner and powered the boat toward the center of the bridge. Although we reached the bridge with breakneck speed, our boat did not "pop" up on top of the bridge. Instead, we hit the center piling, and the boat came to a sudden, violent standstill. My body was almost thrown on top of the bridge by the force of the sudden halt.

Leonard grabbed my life jacket to pull me onto the bridge and safety. At that moment, the boat shifted and started to "wrap" the bridge center piling. The rush of water going under it caught my feet and sucked both of us under the bridge — and underwater. The velocity of the stop threw Roy forward in the canoe. He broke two oak thwarts with his rib cage before he, too, was swept into the river and under the bridge. Now all three of us were in the rushing waters — our leader Leonard, my canoeing partner Roy, and me.

I remember feeling the gravel at the bottom of the river and my head hitting the bottom of the bridge. There was no air space. During the tumbling underwater, I never knew that Leonard was still holding my life jacket. I remember thinking, *Oh, this is what it feels like to drown.* And then I saw light over my head and heard Leonard's voice: "Don't fight me, Jan. I have you." The next moment, I was bobbing in the river, breathing precious air, and Roy popped up behind us. Even though the river was at flood stage, we managed to walk to the edge of the river where the other paddlers helped us out.

The trip was over. The guys tried to pry Roy's canoe out of the river, but the strength of the floodwaters wouldn't release it from its death grip around the piling. Some divine power kept us from being caught between the boat and the bridge piling — and from continuing downstream. Just around the next bend, a tree was down across the entire river. The river was pushy there with no take-out in sight. Had we made it past the bridge, all of us would have been casualties of the river. Maybe the mishap at the bridge had saved the entire group.

But it was two weeks later, when the river went down enough for the boys to retrieve what was left of Roy's boat, that we learned the extent of our godsend. Even after the water had receded, a tow-truck winch had to pry the boat from the bridge. There were four chutes under the bridge we could have washed through. Leonard and I were flushed through chute 2, while Roy negotiated chute 3. Chute 1 was filled with barbed wire — we would have been ripped to shreds as we drowned. A huge cypress stump completely filled chute 4 — we would have been flattened against it with no way out.

This near death experience definitely bonded Roy and me. We became friends and started dating. Nine months later, we married.

We believe some divine power was at play that fateful day we washed under the bridge and into each other's lives. A force took over and protected us when we had no choice but to let go and let it take us. To this day, thirty years after our miracle, we are still together.

~Janice R. Edwards

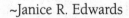

40

Grandma Introduced Us

Grandmothers hold their grandchildren
in a special place in their hearts.
~Catherine Pulsifer

It all started when I was a teenager, and the white in my grandmother's hair was just beginning to weave itself among her chestnut curls. She'd put her face close to mine and whisper, "When I die, I'm going to send you a sign from heaven. If it's allowed, I'll do it. So, be on the lookout."

My mother's laughter would always intervene, telling me to ignore Grandma's strange words. I'd go back to my homework, and the two ladies would return to the kitchen, their conversation mixing with the sounds of cooking.

Years later, shortly after my college graduation, I held my grandma's hand in her nursing home. Her hair was pure white now. Her legs had lost their muscle tone from months spent in a wheelchair. She'd lower her voice and say, "Remember to look for the signs."

This time, my mother didn't intervene. We just sat in the silence, knowing.

I didn't believe it then. Of course, I didn't. I was busy developing a career and enjoying my social life. Grandma had lived into her eighties. She had seen me grow into a woman. I knew I was lucky to have her watch over me all of those years.

Little did I know that it wouldn't end there.

Several years later, I was a young, single teacher spending most of my weekends correcting spelling tests. I had grown tired of the crazy social scene and had settled into a calmer life. Many of my dreams had been realized, but there was still one unfulfilled: a family to call my own.

One afternoon, my mother told me about a friend who visited a psychic. "She said she was very accurate. Wanna go?"

I was disinterested and turned the conversation to another topic.

A week passed, and I dropped by my mother's home to take her to dinner. She stood in the doorway with her hand behind her back.

Her face was bright as if she were a child holding a secret. She leaned close to me and said, "Guess what?"

She told me she had had a conversation with another friend that day about a psychic.

"What's with all the hocus-pocus stuff?" I was growing suspicious.

She shrugged her shoulders. "Not so sure myself. She brought up the subject, not me."

She whispered the next words. "Apparently, she goes quite regularly."

She showed me what she had hidden behind her back. In one hand, she had a business card of a psychic; in the other was a number scrawled on a napkin.

"This is the psychic my first friend recommended to me." She waved the napkin in the air. "This is the business card my second friend gave me."

She waved them both, and said, "*Two* different people gave me the same psychic's number in the same week. The *same* psychic."

The friends didn't know each other and the psychic lived an hour away. We also happened to live in Los Angeles, with psychics aplenty nearby.

I jumped at the opportunity. "Let's call."

We scheduled back-to-back appointments. On the day of our scheduled readings, we made our way down the freeway. I was in an unfamiliar area of Los Angeles. However, as I took the exit, things began to look more familiar to me.

We passed a nursing home, and realization came to me.

"Mom, that's Grandma's nursing home." I pointed to the small building on the right. I shook when I said the next words. "That is where Grandma died."

And my directions ended just a few yards away. The psychic literally lived a stone's throw from the nursing home.

I don't know what we expected when we rang the woman's doorbell. Surely, we hadn't expected my grandma to be standing there with her curlers and bathrobe. But when the little woman opened the door to two nervous women, wringing their hands and talking about their dead relative, she took it in stride.

"People always tell me stories like that," she said.

She proceeded to read me first. I was quickly disappointed. She saw me in a serious romantic relationship and was wondering why I was reluctant to have a baby. Apparently, a spirit child had been following me around.

I proceeded to cross my arms over my chest and informed her she was incorrect. There was no man in my life. And if there was a spirit child, that child needed to go bug his or her father. Clearly, the man was not looking for me as feverishly as I had looked for him.

She sensed the consternation in my voice and backpedaled a bit. "Well, sometimes a partner enters your life spiritually just before he enters in the physical world. Six months. Give it six months. He'll be wearing blue."

She paused and reached across the table to touch my hand gently. "And as for your daughter… Find a quiet moment and tell her to go bug her dad. Might work."

Needless to say, I left unimpressed.

However, I did circle April 2002 on my calendar. *Six months? Hmmph. We'll see.* That night I had a warm bath and said a silent prayer to my ghost daughter, asking her to go haunt her dad, wherever he might be. I figured it wouldn't hurt.

I had almost forgotten everything by April 2002. But when a handsome man with a broad smile met me for lunch one Sunday, I started to wonder. He was kind and attentive. Well-spoken. But it was his blue shirt that hit me the hardest. He wore blue at almost every date for the first month. It was as if my grandmother was screaming across the table, "Marry this one!"

We slid into an easy, happy romance and were married a year and a half later. Today, we have enjoyed sixteen years together and have three daughters. It took me a year of knowing him before I shared the story of the psychic. He was most interested in the date of my reading. I had taped it and showed him the date I had scrawled on the cassette. It had taken place a couple weeks before Thanksgiving 2001.

My husband smiled when I shared it with him. "I remember that Thanksgiving. My parents and some longtime friends had staged an intervention of sorts — cornering me and urging me to give love a try again. I had given up looking after a bout of bad luck." He smirked. "Completely thrown in the towel."

One friend had specifically told my husband to date a teacher. She felt someone in a helping profession would be a good match for him. He had such a helpful nature himself.

So he did. And here we are.

Today, when people ask how I met my husband, I always pause and say, "My grandma introduced us." Then I point to my young daughter playing in the corner and say, "And that one assisted."

~Michele M. Boom

41

Treasure in the Rafters

A mom's hug lasts long after she lets go.
~Author Unknown

My mom died when I was in my twenties. The loss was devastating. Although time has softened the pain, it hasn't stopped me from wanting to pick up the phone and share special moments with her. I've thought about how nice it would be to talk with her so many times over the years, like when I fell in love, had my first child, and bought my first house. I expect I'll never stop feeling that way.

I really wanted to talk to her when I met my husband. James and I dated on and off for a few years before getting married. During that period, I thought so many times how nice it would have been to call my mom, get her wisdom, and know what she thought of him. My dad and stepmother were great throughout that time, but I still missed my mom.

One day, my dad called to let us know that he and my stepmother were preparing their house to sell it. He had a few boxes of my mom's possessions still stored for my sisters and me, so he invited us over to go through them and choose items we'd like to keep. It was an emotional night for the whole family.

The boxes contained everything from clothes to pictures and jewelry. One large box was full of pottery. My mother had always loved pottery made by local artists, so I had grown up with it adorning shelves around the house. Some of the pieces were pretty, but pottery really wasn't my thing, so I moved on to another box.

James, on the other hand, was fascinated by it. He'd taken ceramics classes in high school and college, so hand-thrown pottery always appealed to him. As he dug through the box, one piece in particular stood out because the style was so similar to his own.

One feature on the pot that really caught his eye was the thumb indentations pressed into the sides. In college, one of his ceramics professors had pointed out that many of his pieces looked alike. In an effort to branch out, James had employed that same thumb-press technique on some of his pots.

Riveted by the similarities, he turned the pot over to see the signature of the artist. To his surprise, the artist had the same initials — J.O. Then James noticed something else that was distinctive. When James signed his pottery, he not only carved his signature into the clay, but he also glazed it on. This piece was done in that exact manner.

And then it happened. As James later described it, it was like the whole room went dark until all he could see was the pot. His heart started racing, and the realization hit him like a tidal wave. The pot looked so much like one of his own because it *was* one of his own. That pot, which I clearly remember seeing on the living room shelf in my younger years, had been thrown by my husband and bought by my mom at a college street fair around seventeen years before we even started dating.

The serendipity of the encounter astonished us all that night. It felt like a loving embrace from my mom — a confirmation that, had she lived long enough to know James, she would have chosen him just like she chose that piece of his pottery. That pot gives me peace. Although my mother may or may not have met him when she bought that pot, I feel strongly that if she were here, she'd be holding that pot, smiling and telling me, "Well done."

~Whitney Owens

The Miracle of Love

Happily Ever Laughter

42

Incident at Elk Lake

I think the next best thing to solving a problem
is finding some humor in it.
~Frank A. Clark

I double-checked my reflection as I waited for my date to arrive on that bright Sunday afternoon in May 1989. I'd worked hard to put together just the right outfit: a pretty scarf, crisp white blouse, neatly ironed capris, and new leather flats. At eighteen years old, I was still self-conscious about my fashion sense, but what I saw in the mirror reassured me.

My date arrived and held open the passenger door of his sports car. Our plan was to go for a drive in the country just north of Victoria, British Columbia, and then to find a little restaurant to have afternoon tea. We chatted comfortably as we cruised down the Pat Bay Highway.

"Look," I said, as I spied the sign for Elk/Beaver Lake Regional Park. Neither of us had ever been to the park, and we decided on impulse to check it out. The beach was packed thanks to the beautiful weather, but we managed to find a parking place. A pleasant trail took us away from the noise, first through a forest, then briefly past a residential area, and finally alongside a series of small ponds. We'd been walking for about twenty minutes when, for the sake of my new shoes, I suggested it was time to head back. Instead of simply turning around, however, we decided that we would explore the faint path that led through the field on our right, in the hope that it would let us make a circuit around the far side of the ponds.

To our frustration, the "path" petered out quickly. But we could see water through the bushes in front of us, and we were certain that if we could just get through a few waist-high weeds and brambles, we'd be at the pond. From there, it would be an easy stroll around the shoreline.

The brush was considerably denser than we realized, but the deeper we got, the more determined we were to keep going. We were convinced that the way forward had to be easier than the way back. A good twenty minutes later, we finally reached the water's edge, only to be greeted by an even denser thicket on our left and an unstable bank on our right. To test it, we took a few tentative steps along the shore — and were instantly ankle-deep in oozing muck.

Wiser people probably would have retreated at this point, but we were young and didn't know the meaning of the word "defeat." There were bulrushes in the pond in front of us, but through them we could see freshly mown grass on the far side. It was less than a stone's throw away. We conferred briefly and came up with a plan: All we had to do was leap from one mini-bulrush-island to the next mini-bulrush-island, and in a few hops we'd be across.

There was one problem with this strategy: The bulrush "islands" weren't islands at all — they were floating clumps of vegetation. The first hop put us in slime up to our thighs. A few more awkward leaps, and we were both submerged to our waists.

By now, we were too invested to turn back. We gritted our teeth and pushed on. After several more minutes, we reached the edge of the bulrushes — only to discover that twenty feet of the muddiest water imaginable still separated us from the far shore.

Our moment of reckoning had arrived. We could go back the way we'd come — guaranteeing us another miserable half-hour — or we could commit ourselves fully and dog-paddle across.

We dog-paddled.

If everything we'd suffered so far wasn't bad enough, we had an audience that afternoon: Three men were training their dogs to retrieve decoys from the pond. Later, we learned that the pond was — and still is — an official Retriever training area. Imagine how those men's mouths hung open as two fully dressed young people swam out of the rushes past their dogs and climbed up onto the bank beside them.

My lovely outfit was now covered in brown slime — we were both dripping from the neck down — and we still had to make our way back to the parking lot. We passed a number of people on the trail that afternoon, and not one of them had the nerve to ask us what had happened.

Finally, we reached the parking lot, and my date graciously asked if I wouldn't mind changing into one of the pairs of paper coveralls he just happened to have in his trunk, before getting into his sports car. I took the folded pair he handed me and set out for the women's restroom. But for some incomprehensible reason (given how crowded the beach was that afternoon), the women's restroom was locked, which meant that I had to find a spot in the bushes to wriggle out of my clothes. And if that wasn't bad enough, there was one final humiliation. My date hadn't handed me just any pair of coveralls. The ones he'd given me had been used as part of an astronaut costume the previous Halloween. I had to walk the entire length of the parking lot in a white paper suit that said NASA down the side.

My date and I had only been seeing each other for a few months at this point, and our misadventure at Elk Lake could have been the end of our brief relationship. It wasn't. In spite of the space suit he made me wear, I fell in love with my fellow dog-paddler that afternoon. I can still remember the precise moment it happened — as I was swimming through the slime beside him. *This is the one,* I thought. He had an appetite for adventure and a great sense of humour. We climbed into his car that afternoon, and we both laughed until we were in tears.

I married Bern the following summer, at the tender age of nineteen. It's been twenty-eight years since our impromptu swim in a Retriever pond, but five kids, three grandchildren, and many adventures later, we're still laughing.

~Rachel Dunstan Muller

Some Men Run

I swear I couldn't love you more than I do right now,
and yet I know I will tomorrow.
~Leo Christopher, Sleeping in Chairs

There was so much of me missing. It felt strange and awkward lying beside my husband. It had been six weeks since I'd had my entire right leg, hip and pelvis amputated in a last-ditch attempt to rid my body of aggressive bone cancer. The surgeon told me it was a very rare amputation. At thirty-two, I was young and strong, and he expected me to make a full recovery — but with a big part of me missing. I was most definitely *not* the woman my husband Rick had married.

Rick and I were already an oddly matched couple by most people's standards. I was big-boned and tall at 5 feet, 9 inches, and he was short and slight at 5 feet, 7 inches. I was a voracious reader, and he hadn't picked up a book in years. But he was honest and hard-working, and he made me laugh. Of all the men I'd dated, I knew Rick was the one I wanted to spend my happily-ever-after with. But I wonder if he would have included the words "in sickness and in health" in his wedding vows if he'd known.

We had been married for five years when I was diagnosed. We loved each other very much, and had a perfect and beautiful three-year-old son. It was time to add to our family, but my hip had been bothering me. I wanted to be sure there was nothing seriously wrong before becoming pregnant. During the course of a very tumultuous year, from an initial suspicion of simple bursitis to the devastating diagnosis of cancer, I spent months trying to be strong and denied the growing pain in my hip. During that year preceding my amputation, I underwent biopsies and surgeries and rehabilitation, but the cancer won out. Because it wouldn't respond to radiation or chemotherapy, surgery was the only option to save my life.

On January 6, 1988, I became a member of the elite group of amputees known as hemipelvectomies. I was reluctant to join, but I knew it was my only option if I wanted to live.

My husband stood behind me when the surgeon told us the news. Rick was being brave, but I could feel his grip tightening on my shoulders as the doctor's words sunk in. The cancer would move quickly to my lungs. They wanted to do the surgery the next day — December 23rd. I was surprisingly calm when I heard the news. Somehow, I knew I was going to be okay, but the doctor said he could not guarantee that I would see Christmas the next year. So, if this was going to be my last Christmas and New Year's with my family, I wanted to spend it on two legs! I told my wonderful surgeon that I was free on January 6th, and he agreed to do the surgery after the holidays.

We had a wonderful family Christmas with our three-year-old son, Kevin. He was thankfully oblivious to the drama about to unfold. My husband and I went dancing at a friend's wedding. My hip hurt, but my husband held me tight as we danced the night away, enjoying every magical moment on the dance floor together. We celebrated New Year's with our extended family, laughing, sharing and making memories. Every face and smile etched into my heart, but none more deeply engraved than my husband's. We made love and clung to each other with hope and fear in equal measure. January 6th came all too soon.

Rick held my hand until they wheeled me through the operating-room doors, and he was holding my hand when I woke up in recovery. I looked down at the bed and saw the outline of one leg under the sheet where there should have been two. My eyes told me that the leg was gone, but my brain told me it was still there. Something was terribly wrong. The pain was unbearable. How could something that was not there hurt so much? No one had warned me about phantom pain.

Throughout my hospital stay, my darling Rick was there when I opened my eyes in the morning and closed them at night. He held my hand, spoke loving words of affirmation, and massaged the bed where my leg "should" have been. Some men run when their spouses are sick. They see themselves as "fixers," and if they can't fix something that's broken, they feel like failures. A marriage often crumbles when a spouse is seriously ill. It's not always because they don't love each other anymore, but sometimes because men feel they've failed somehow. Rick never considered leaving me when I lost my leg. He didn't see me as broken, so he didn't see the need to fix me.

We had always enjoyed making love, and showing affection came easily to both of us, but I was surprisingly nervous and shy lying in my husband's arms. The surgeon had said I needed six weeks of healing before attempting intimate relations, but intimacy was the furthest thing from my mind. I didn't feel beautiful anymore. I didn't think my husband would desire me like he did when I was whole and had two legs. Terrified he might find my new body repugnant and turn away from me, I started to cry as he held me in his arms. He kissed my face and traced my tears with his finger. "What's wrong, honey? Are you in pain?" How could I explain to this sweet man that the pain from my missing limb was a far cry from the pain I was feeling in my heart over the thought of losing him?

I sobbed in his arms and told him, "I wouldn't blame you if you left me. I'm not the same girl you married five years ago, Rick." I choked on the words. "You didn't sign up for this, and it's okay if you can't love me. I understand."

He pulled me close to his chest and whispered soft words I'll never forget: "Glenda, I didn't marry you for your legs." He paused for effect and kissed me softly as I began to relax in his loving arms. "Don't you know by now that I'm a boob man?"

We both broke out into fits of laughter, and I knew right then that we would be okay. I never again doubted his love for me, and I never doubted his ability to take away my fear with love and laughter.

In November 1990, less than three years after my amputation, we did indeed add another baby to our family. In a documented delivery, I gave birth to a perfect seven-pound, fourteen-ounce baby boy, Andrew. Rick and I continue to love and laugh often.

~Glenda Standeven

44

No Room for Stubborn

To keep your marriage brimming with love in the
loving cup, whenever you're wrong, admit it;
whenever you're right, shut up.
~Ogden Nash

The first time Neil and I met was in the emergency department. He was a local restaurant owner who cut his face when a bottle broke; I was the physician who sewed up his injury. I was intrigued by his smile and sense of humor, but nothing came of it that day. The second time we met, however, makes for a much more entertaining story.

It was a beautiful outdoor wedding, and after the ceremony, while the bridal party took pictures, I wandered over to where Neil sat in the bright sunshine. I said hello and asked if he remembered me, and he admitted that he didn't. His version of the story is that I asked next, "Would a hypodermic needle of Novocain up your nose remind you?" I don't think I've ever said the phrase "hypodermic needle" in my life — only TV doctors do — so I am sure he was wrong. My version of the story is that the bright sun was in his eyes, and he didn't recognize me at first, so I politely re-introduced myself. Even then, I'm not sure he knew who I was, but we talked pleasantries for a few minutes until his ride was ready to leave. "I'm working at the restaurant tonight if you want to come by," he said as he wandered off with his friend.

What did that mean? I wondered. *Was that an invitation or a casual remark made to a potential customer?* It left me oddly disquieted, and since I already told a girlfriend I would go to a party with her that evening, I tried to put it out of my mind.

Unfortunately, even though the party was fun, I was too distracted by Neil's words to enjoy it. "Are you okay?" my friend asked.

"I really want to go to his restaurant," I told her. Kathryn was a great friend, so without a second thought, she said with enthusiasm, "Me too. Let's go!"

Once we got to the restaurant, Kathryn and I found a table and sat down. Within two minutes, Neil showed up to take our order. *Is this a coincidence?* I wondered. *Is he actually waiting tables, or is this his way of getting to talk to me?* Like a crazy middle-schooler, the questions jumped around in my head.

When our food was ready, Neil brought it to the table and sat down to join us. Kathryn kindly wandered off, while Neil and I talked about the beach — we both loved the ocean. We debated about books — we both loved to read. We also discussed exciting things about which I knew nothing, like kayaking, spelunking and waterskiing. I was hooked.

In an uncharacteristic moment of bravery, I asked if he wanted to get lunch sometime — someplace besides his restaurant, so he could relax. "I'd like that," he said, flashing his lopsided grin. We made plans to meet at another local restaurant two days later.

"Oh, girl, you've got it bad!" I remember Kathryn laughing as we left. And she was right, but I almost let my stubborn streak ruin everything. You see, there's another part of the story Neil and I disagree on.

To this day, I know we decided to meet at Harb's Bistro at noon. I got there right on time, excited to see him again, and told the waitress I would wait to order until he arrived. I waited. And waited. The clock ticked by as the first hour slowly passed. Embarrassed, I ordered a cup of coffee and a glass of water. *Did I get the time wrong?* I wondered. The waitress was sympathetic and checked periodically to see if I needed another coffee, but otherwise left me alone.

Gradually, I started to get angry. *I have plenty of other things I could be doing!* I stewed and steamed through the second hour, but I didn't even want to go to the bathroom for fear I would miss him. Finally, at 2:30 p.m., after two-and-a-half hours, I gave up. Marching back to the car, I mumbled all sorts of things to myself. *How dare he waste my time like this! How rude and inconsiderate — what a jerk!*

By the time I got home, I was ready to tell him a thing or two, so I called the restaurant to complain. "Sorry, he's out for the afternoon," said the waitress who answered the phone. "Actually, I think he's on a date."

Furious now, I retorted, "Well, tell him he missed his doctor's appointment, and I require twenty-four hours' notice for cancellation!" As soon as the words blurted out of my mouth, I was mortified. I slammed down the phone, as much embarrassed as mad.

Meanwhile, around the corner from Harb's, Neil sat waiting at Travelers. Also angry, but more patient than me, he finally left after three hours. When he got back to work, his manager said, "Your doctor called. You missed an appointment."

Neil was confused for a second, until he remembered I was a doctor. "What is she talking about?" he yelled. "I waited for three hours!"

Still thinking he was talking about a medical appointment, Jamie said, "Wow, that is a long wait. I wouldn't go to that doctor again."

That could have been the end of the story. Anger, embarrassment and pride make us do all sorts of things we later regret. For the first week, I held on to my righteous indignation. In the second week, the questions kicked in. *Did he stand me up on purpose? How cruel to go on a date with someone else when we already had plans. Or did he forget he was supposed to meet me?* Finally, my heart took over. I really enjoyed his sense of humor. I liked that he read books, and was brave enough to go spelunking and waterskiing. So, in the third week, with a little gentle encouragement from Kathryn and a few deep breaths, I called the restaurant and asked for him.

This time, he knew who I was right away. "Why did you stand me up?" he asked as soon as he came to the phone. "And why did you leave me that obnoxious message?"

"What are you talking about? You stood me up!" I exclaimed.

Within a few seconds, we realized what had happened. We agreed to disagree about who had the restaurant right and decided to meet at a completely different place the very next day. This time, we both showed up early, and the rest, as they say, is history.

That wasn't the last time I swallowed my pride, nor was it the last misunderstanding Neil and I ever had, but it taught me a good lesson. Imagine what I could have lost if I hadn't given in and called that day. Relationships don't work well when stubbornness and self-importance get in the way of compromise and compassion. Fortunately, we got better at apologizing and being humble, which is a very good thing. In a marriage, there is no room for a stubborn streak!

~Colleen Arnold

45

Pass the Magic, Please

If I get married, I want to be very married.
~Audrey Hepburn

I don't know why my study-abroad semester ended the week it did in 1994, nor why my mother back in Michigan chose the particular tour through Italy she signed us up for when my classes were over. I don't know why we ended up sitting on the tour bus where we did, nor why a couple my mother's age from Los Angeles — Richard and Roberta — ended up sitting across the aisle from us the first day of the tour.

What I do know is that when I first noticed them, they were tossing Hershey's Kisses to everyone on the bus to celebrate Richard's birthday. And I understood, with a clarity I've almost never experienced since, that they were, without question, the happiest couple I'd ever seen. I was twenty-two at the time, about to return home to Michigan and a college boyfriend who mostly made me miserable. It seemed inevitable that I would marry him and settle down, simply because that was what everyone my age was doing.

I watched Richard and Roberta that first day like a spy, trying to figure out what it was about them that just seemed to work. It wasn't just that they were a naturally gregarious pair. Even when it was just the two of them talking, Richard would say something, and Roberta would throw her head back and laugh with a kind of joy I didn't know anyone — let alone a couple my parents' age — ever seemed to feel in each other's presence. Watching them, I only knew that they had exactly the kind of relationship I wanted for myself.

I stared for so long that my mother said, "What are you looking at?"

I said, "There's something really special about those two."

On the second day of the tour, we had dinner together at an open-air café in Florence, and I asked how they met. They told me that Roberta had placed a personal ad in the newspaper six years earlier. Richard had responded to it after her subscription had expired, but some kind, anonymous person working for the newspaper sent his response to her anyway. She called his number when he wasn't home, but he called her back, and they talked for three hours. And when she opened her front door the next night, and they saw each other for the first time, it was magic.

Tears had filled their eyes by the time they finished telling the story. There were tears in my eyes, too. I knew I couldn't possibly marry my boyfriend back home, not after knowing that what Richard and Roberta had together was really possible. Richard was forty-four and Roberta was thirty-eight when they got married. I realized that waiting for the right person was what mattered, no matter how long it took.

As it turns out, I had to wait a long time. I didn't marry that college boyfriend after all, nor the next one, nor the one after that. This was in part because a card would arrive every Christmas with a picture of Richard and Roberta on vacation somewhere, grinning happily at each other. Each year, I'd study it closely, and — no matter who I was dating — think, *I don't have that.*

Which is why, well into my thirties, I was still single when a friend introduced me to my now husband, Matt. He makes me throw my head back and laugh with the kind of joy I saw on Roberta's face all those years before. He makes me so obviously happy that one night my friend Monique, who was in her thirties and struggling romantically, said of my husband and me, "I watch a lot of couples, and I've never wanted what they have. But there's something special about you two."

I told her the story of meeting Richard and Roberta twenty years earlier. And I realized how easily I might have missed them had we taken different tours or been seated in a different place on the bus. Those three days I spent with them changed my life. A year after I told

Monique the story of Richard and Roberta, she married a man who makes her throw back her head and laugh just like I do with my own husband. I know because I've seen them when they think no one is watching, and as Richard and Roberta would say, it's magic.

~Mary Elizabeth Pope

46

The Smell of Love

The rate at which a person can mature is directly
proportional to the embarrassment he can tolerate.
~Douglas C. Engelbart

I wanted to look my best, and it's hard to look one's best when it is thirty-three degrees outside. Stiff, insulated jackets are never elegant — at least, none of the ones I owned. And so it was with a martyr's heart that I bravely pushed aside my warmest jackets and selected a thinner, brown coat. Also, the color made my eyes look nice.

I was stuffing my purse with my cell phone and wallet when I heard a knock on the door. It rang through the small dorm room like church bells. Tim was here already? I checked my hair in the mirror and opened the door.

And there he was. My heart sputtered as Tim smiled at me. He was looking as nervous as I felt, and was dressed just as inappropriately for the cold December weather. Tim was a diehard summer fan and refused to wear anything other than a Hawaiian shirt. So here we were, me in my thin coat and him in his endearingly optimistic floral shirt, ready for our first date.

As freshmen college students living on campus, we didn't have cars. Instead, I had my trusty, hand-me-down mountain bike named Pegasus, and Tim had a gray street bike. We pedaled quickly through the streets to the movie theater. Our breath steamed behind us as we hurried. Once we were in the warmth of the theater, things would be different. At that moment, though, I was so nervous, it took all my concentration just to make my numb fingers grip the handlebars.

"It's a little muddy over here," Tim said as we approached the bicycle rack outside the theater. "You can take the far end. I'll park here." Like a true gentleman, he parked his bike in the dirt and let me take the clean space. I watched him dismount and step gingerly around in the mud. It was a very dark night, and the stars were bright in the sky despite the golden glow of the street lamps. He laughed as he slipped a bit in the sludge, throwing his hands out for balance.

During the movie, Tim put his arm around me for the first time. The thrill of it! It would have been perfect except that, in the enclosed space of the theater, a child's dirty diaper began to flood the aisles with an unpleasant odor. Tim seemed unperturbed. (I learned later he had very little sense of smell.) I ignored it as best I could, breathing through my sleeve when a draft spread the smell too much.

After the movie, Tim took me out to eat at a burrito shop. The air was heavy with the smell of spices. Being a Friday, it was a full house, and so we were relegated to the corner by the bathroom. It wasn't long before the gentle stench of the lavatory began to creep its way over to join us at our table. I had to laugh to myself. This was the smelliest date I'd ever been on!

We rode back to our dorm rooms after dinner, and Tim walked me to my room and wished me good night. Just like that, our wonderful first date was over.

The next day, as I was walking through the halls to visit some friends, Tim's roommate Brian stopped me in the hall. "How could you stand it?" he said. "You must really like Tim to sit through all that."

"Sit through what?" I didn't understand. Not a single moment of the previous night had been a chore.

"The smell," he prompted. When I still showed no sign of comprehension, he laughed, long and hard. "When Tim came home last night," Brian told me, still wiping the tears from his eyes, "we had to kick him out and make him wash his shoes. He smelled like an open sewer. You had to have noticed. He had poop all over his shoes. He said he must have stepped in it while parking his bike last night. He thought it was mud at the time."

Looking very embarrassed, and with only socks on his feet, Tim came out of his room. He'd no doubt heard Brian and me talking about the date.

"I'm sorry you had to go through that," Tim apologized. "I really thought it was only mud. I couldn't tell the difference."

"Really, I didn't even notice it was you," I said truthfully.

Six years later, my husband still avoids suspicious mud patches for fear of recreating our first date.

~Rae Mitchell

47

Opening My Heart Again

Because of you, I laugh a little harder, cry a little less,
and smile a lot more.
~Author Unknown

I'd seen Winston from a distance a few times before we met, his long hair pulled back in a ponytail and capped by a forest-green beret. Tie-dyed tights covered stocky, muscular legs shod with rugged, brown hiking boots. He'd throw on a loose T-shirt or pea coat, depending on the season.

Mutual friends introduced us, and I found him just as interesting in person as he'd looked from a distance. In the days that followed, we talked for hours, sharing ideas, beliefs, and dreams for the future. When I left for college in Utah, eight hours away, I left a part of myself with him.

Every chance I could, I drove back to my hometown in Montana. We got serious fast, and he soon visited. He worked at whatever temporary jobs he could find, but his real love was rock climbing in Montana, Utah, California, and everywhere in between.

He told me once that I made him think about things he hadn't seriously considered before. Our roundabout way of talking about marriage came up in a conversation at REI, surrounded by carabiners, ropes, and cams. He snatched a piece of metal with a spring-loaded, tube-chock design that expanded inside a wide crack, creating a place to clip in a rope, shortening a potential fall. A Trango Big Bro.

"If you buy this for me, I'll marry you," he said, a wide grin revealing the small gap between his two front teeth.

I pondered the proposition. "If you marry me, I'll buy it for you," I countered.

We walked out of the store empty-handed but holding hands.

Weeks turned into months while he travelled to California and I dropped out of school. In April, we returned to Montana. We didn't know where this next adventure would take us, but we'd find out together. By June, I'd found a job at a clothing store. He landed a job driving for a rafting guide company.

The road to the river was winding and dangerous — the type of road where people drive too fast. He and a co-worker were heading to work late one morning when she made the fatal error of passing on a blind curve. Her small Honda was no match for the wide and sturdy Cadillac they hit. He died instantly; she, a few hours later.

In one second, my future — my heart — was crushed along with that car.

My parents delivered the news after my shift at the store.

For the next two-and-a-half years, I avoided the pain and my future that never happened. I spent my time smashed, single, and stuck in inescapable grief. Alcohol was the only way to turn it off temporarily.

Rock bottom came one January night, when I stood on the porch smoking in twenty-below-zero cold. I planned to sneak around to the side of the house, hit my head against the brick wall to knock myself out, and then freeze to death before anyone found me the next morning.

I wasn't drunk enough to go through with it, so I smeared the cigarette butt under my foot, went inside for another glass of tequila, and passed out.

The next morning, I enrolled myself in an outpatient treatment program.

One requirement of the program included AA meetings. I didn't talk much in those first meetings, just listened. And observed. I watched a man named Scott from across the room. His almost black, curly hair was cut short above a pair of twinkling, deep brown eyes and a baby-faced smile. Loose jeans and rugby shirts matched the casual comfort he exuded. He spoke with confidence, demonstrating a level of ease generally reserved for those with a few more years of life experience. He'd gotten sober young, a broken spirit who'd found a way out, a sense of self, and a way to move on after his girlfriend — to whom he'd planned on proposing — had cheated on him, leaving him lost without the future he thought he'd known.

Two years my junior, he'd already earned several yearly sobriety chips. He carried himself with self-reliance, displayed a boyish charm, and made others laugh with his goofy sense of humor.

Following a few weeks of casual conversation after meetings, he finally asked me out, ignoring the unspoken "13th Step" of not dating anyone during their first year of sobriety.

On our first date, we stayed up all night talking and laughing. We shared our first kiss as I left in the morning, leaving me with a lighthearted giddiness I hadn't experienced in years.

Early into the relationship, on an evening walk, we stopped in a park. "So, what is this?" he asked, wrapping his arms around me to ward off the crisp air.

"What's what?"

"This. Us." He paused. "What are we?" He pulled back just a little to gauge my reaction.

"Oh," I said.

I'd been warned to avoid a relationship only ten months into my sobriety, but he was a keeper. He sensed my hesitation.

"How about cuddling companions," he suggested.

I laughed. He had a way of making me laugh, which was something I commented on several months later when we found ourselves giggling after one of his silly, off-handed remarks.

"I like making you laugh," he replied.

Despite the laughter and the relationship heading in an obvious direction, neither of us wanted to get hurt again. But we didn't want to lose what we had, either. And he understood my previous loss. While others I'd dated before him had said that they were competing with a ghost, he reasoned, "If I died, I wouldn't want you to forget me."

He knelt before me one summer evening while we were walking our two dogs. We married the following June.

Unsure about having children, we put it off a few years. We said we weren't ready, but honestly, we were both afraid — not only of our ability to be parents, but of what we could lose. That kind of grief is inescapable. I'd witnessed it in Winston's parents. My loss felt unbearable; theirs was indescribable.

Our first daughter was born in June, six years after we said "I do." Our second daughter arrived two years later.

One morning, a friend asked me, "How do you divide your love?" He and his wife had one child, with no immediate plans for more.

"You don't," I answered. "Your love just gets bigger."

And that, I finally understood, applies to lovers and spouses, too.

I hadn't lost love. It simply expanded, just like that spring-loaded Trango Big Bro.

And I'm clipped in for the adventure.

~Maurene Janiece

48

Surviving the Honeymoon

If happiness is the goal — and it should be — then
adventures should be top priority.
~Richard Branson

"We don't have any film left," I called out to my husband Steve, who had stopped the car and was standing in the open door, the better to see down the road.

He shook his head and sputtered, too angry to speak.

I had used the last frame of film a while back to snap a shot of the road sign: "Jupiter — 12 Miles."

"But when would we ever be this close to Jupiter again?" I asked.

"When would we ever be this close to an alligator?" he countered, gesturing to the twelve-foot moving log in the middle of the road.

We were on our honeymoon, and had just spent four days in Orlando. Now we were driving toward the Everglades at midnight, testing the boundaries of our tolerance for nature and for each other.

After the alligator slithered away, Steve opened the trunk to grab a can of mosquito spray. Mosquitoes swirled in the headlight beams, but we had no idea how thick they would be at the campsite.

I heard *pfft* and then an inhuman yowl and *clank* as the can hit the asphalt.

Moments later, Steve reassured me he was okay even though he had just sprayed DEET in his eyes.

When we reached the campground, we found a kiosk still occupied by a ranger. He unrolled the screen and leaned out. "Are you aware that the 'skeeter' is the official bird of the Everglades?" Steve chortled and passed him a few dollars to pay for the campsite.

The ranger paused before offering this tidbit: "When you've had enough, there is a lodge just a mile down from here." He looked us each in the eye before retreating behind the screen.

Steve and I sighed and continued forward, though slowly.

"What an adventure we're having," I said meekly.

"All my life, I've wanted to see the Everglades in person!" Steve crowed. "It took finding the love of my life to give me a chance to come here," he continued. "Thank you for being my wife!"

Then we stopped and opened the door.

An audible buzz immediately surrounded us. We hurried to grab the tarp and the tent, and rushed to unfurl them both at the same time, struggling to coordinate our efforts as the mosquitoes began to dive-bomb, biting our lips and eyelids. We coughed as they flew into our noses and throats. Steve flailed his arms while he tried to assemble the tent, and there was a sickening crack as the main pole broke in half.

"Just unzip! It doesn't matter!" I yelled, cinching my hoodie around my face until only my nose and eyes were open. Moments later, I said, "Never mind! Go back to the car!"

"The car has been compromised!" he shouted back.

Gallantly, he held the tent high while I ducked into safety, pulling in the air mattress and sleeping bags. I fumbled with the pump while Steve jerry-rigged the tent.

Once inside, we didn't even bother with sleeping bags, but simply lay face down on the air mattress.

After a moment of silence, I heard the *hisssss*. My souvenir "Just Married" pin had punctured the mattress. My body was covered in welts from mosquito bites. The tent was ready to collapse on us. I lay quietly next to my new husband, wondering how we had gotten ourselves into this mess.

Once we settled down, we could hear the many sounds of wildlife around us. There were buzzing things and chirping things. We heard the trickle of water not far away, and a kind of sniffing sound that I didn't want to consider. Moonlight cast moving shadows on every side of the tent. And then the growling started.

It was a deep sound, like a belch that sometimes continued into a low moan. Something was walking through the grass around our tent. A twig snapped. I heard breathing outside.

I began to weep softly.

"What's wrong?" Steve whispered.

"Alligators," I answered.

Steve snorted and turned over. "I'm sorry for bringing you here," he spoke to the tent.

"No," I sniffled. "I agreed to come. I wanted to have an adventure for our honeymoon." I said these words, but what I thought about was our wedding vow: "until death do us part." I figured this might be a very short marriage. All through the night, that grunting sound kept me awake, believing a gory death was just on the other side of the flimsy nylon membrane.

In the morning, we opened our eyes to an incredible scene, like a world far beyond earth, full of strange mangrove trees and spindly white herons. Birds with brilliant plumage swooped from branch to branch. There were butterflies in jewel tones, and spider webs glistening in the summer sun.

We cinched up our hoodies and rushed to the car, which we drove out to the visitor center. A professional photographer and his wife were there to walk the wooden path far out into the swamp; they were both dressed in head-to-toe screening, just as we should have been. The ranger advised us to rid our car of mosquitoes by driving at exactly thirty miles per hour, and then opening both doors to let the wind suck them out.

But by far the best feature of the center was a large diorama of Everglades wildlife. We could push a button next to a label to hear that animal and see it light up. Steve was fascinated with this display. He pushed every button, and suddenly I heard it — the growl that had me saying the rosary at 2:00 in the morning.

Steve pulled me close to him and said, "Isn't that the animal you heard last night?"

"Yes, that's it! I guess the alligator light isn't working."

Steve pointed into the corner at a flashing toad.

"Bullfrog," he clarified.

"But… what about the shadow walking by?"

"I dunno," he shrugged. "Raccoon?"

Also not likely to eat us alive, I realized.

When I look back on our honeymoon, I remember the amusement park, the lovely dinners, and piña coladas in the Keys. But I also vividly remember that moment, standing next to Steve, when I realized we had survived an adventure together. If someone ever asks me why in the world I agreed to go to the Everglades in June, I would have to answer, "Why ever not? It was my husband's lifelong wish to see the place in person, and my lifelong wish to stay alive."

~Robin Jankiewicz

49

Breaking the Rules

List, list, O, list!
~William Shakespeare, Hamlet

Mom and I had our arms up to our elbows in warm, sudsy water, washing dishes from our Thanksgiving dinner. Mom had just shared how much she liked my boyfriend, John. It was the first time my family had met him, and Mom had beamed when John presented her with a bouquet of freshly cut flowers. Dad had taken such an instant liking that he asked John to help carve the golden brown roast turkey. All had gone better than expected, but now my mom had a puzzled look on her face because I had just told her that I had to break up with him.

"But why?"

"He's six years older than me, and your rule is no more than five."

My mom had a list of rules for how to find the right marriage partner, and the rule of no more than five years' difference was on the list. After carefully studying successful and failed marriages, Mom had determined an age difference larger than five years could well lead to incompatibility later in life.

I had already ignored Rule #1: "A relative or close friend should introduce you." Mom felt that my family and friends would know if the guy had good character and would be a good match. How could I explain that John and I had met in a bar on Singles Wednesday? He smiled and introduced himself, and we started talking every Wednesday after that until he finally asked for my phone number. Mom hadn't asked how we met, and I wasn't volunteering.

While my former boyfriends had been from North Carolina, and my parents often knew the boyfriend's family, John had been born and raised in Los Angeles. His favorite foods included sweet corn tamales and chicken enchiladas with mole verde sauce. He needed me to explain Southern sayings like "if the creek don't rise." As a Duke professor, he traveled all over the U.S. and Europe to attend conferences, while I explored the East Coast.

I was my parents' only daughter, born and raised in Greensboro, North Carolina, a graduate of East Carolina University, and an elementary-school teacher. I had moved an hour away to Durham, but in many ways it was a world away. I lived near two major universities — UNC-Chapel Hill and Duke. UNC has always been our state's pride and joy, and one brother, two uncles, and several cousins were UNC grads. We all cheered for the Carolina Tarheels. Dean Smith, the UNC men's basketball coach, was often quoted in our home. Barely ten miles from UNC, that other university, Duke, with its impressive gothic architecture, was a nice place to visit, but we Tarheels considered Duke to be the devil, just like its mascot. Every year when the UNC men's basketball team played the Duke Blue Devils, the rivalry between the two teams and their fans became even more intense.

"What religion is he?" my dad asked. Yes, another rule for a spouse. My parents felt that marriages worked best when both persons worshipped alike, and both my mom and dad came from a long line of Methodists, including several ministers. John, however, did not identify with one denomination, and he felt no need to go to any church — an answer that did not sit well with my parents. How could I get them to see that he lived life in the way that churches hoped their parishioners would? I saw the way he treated others with respect, taking the time to thank a person for a job well done — from the short-order cook who prepared his omelet to the volunteer firefighters at their annual fundraiser. I knew that he spoke well of a person or said nothing at all, just like my dad had taught me. I knew that he was as good as his word. I knew, without a doubt, that he was a good man with a strong moral compass.

I loved John with all my heart, even if he didn't fit Mom's list of rules. I noticed the way he listened to opposing viewpoints, stating that he had definite opinions, but that good evidence could convince him to reconsider. He seldom offered his opinions unless asked, but when he spoke, I never second-guessed what he meant. Underneath his quiet reserve, he had a passion for his research, and when I asked a question, he would draw diagrams and explain the concept, without ever making me feel less intelligent.

He worked long hours, and his research was often cited, but he always acknowledged that his work built on the ideas and research of his mentors. He appreciated my passion for teaching remedial reading to kids who needed successful school experiences. He understood the importance of my family and friends in my life. Most of all, I loved the way he made me feel about myself. With John, I could be myself — my *best* self.

My parents wanted to get to know him better. John joined our family for Christmas, several Sunday dinners, and Mom's family reunion the following June. John and I visited his California family in July, and I enjoyed getting to know his mom, sisters, aunt and uncle, cousins, and best friends from high school. The two of us drove north on the Pacific Coast Highway from Los Angeles to San Francisco, and John showed me places he loved in his home state.

In late July, we visited my family to announce our engagement. My brothers and dad welcomed John with firm handshakes, and one niece gave him a bear hug, but I could tell that Mom still had reservations behind her smile. Which rule still worried her?

"Mom, I thought you'd be thrilled. I'm in love with him, and he is with me."

Still trying to understand Mom's hesitation, I added, "And you said that the six years didn't make a difference, that he looks young for his age."

As I held my breath, waiting for her answer, I realized how desperately I wanted my mother's blessing. I wanted more than an acceptance of John as my future husband. My hope was that John would be welcomed with open hearts as a member of our family.

"I'm not worried about his age, or that he's from California. I love how he looks at you, the way he treats you. I love the way he laughs when you are sharing your stories. He loves you for who you are, just as you are. You two should be married. But my team is UNC, and John's team is Duke. All I ask is that I never have to watch the UNC-Duke basketball game in the same room with him."

For the man of my dreams, love of my life, the one who didn't fit Mom's checklist of rules for how to select the right mate, this was Mom's only concern? No problem.

~Suzanne Garner Payne

The Miracle of Love

In Sickness and In Happiness

50

Wrong Number, Right Man

Being deeply loved by someone gives you strength,
while loving someone deeply gives you courage.
~Lao Tzu

The day we got married, Eddie included one unique promise in his vows to me: "Linda, I will take care of you, no matter what. You'll never have to worry about a thing."

In tears, I said, "I do" to the most caring man I had ever known. Twenty-one years later, I still feel the same way.

At thirty-four, my hopes of ever finding a good man were diminished. I was divorced, with two young children, little or no child support, and a recent diagnosis of rheumatoid arthritis. Who would want to marry me with all my problems?

I grew more pessimistic as time went on. The disease that destroyed my joints was relentless. Within five years, my hands showed major signs of deformity, and my knees swelled so badly I could hardly walk. The same type of arthritis that had crippled my uncle and grandfather had hit me hard.

When medications failed to work as they should, my doctor made a very simple suggestion: "Try taking stress out of your life."

I knew he was right, but it seemed impossible. Still, I tried to follow his advice. I quit focusing on what I couldn't do and started looking for what I could. I pushed myself to stay busy by going back to college and working part-time for my church. That's when I met Eddie.

It started with a wrong number. Eddie explained that he was trying to call my ex-husband about a truck he had for sale. His number was listed in the phone book right after mine, so Eddie accidentally called me — a mistake I would later chalk up to fate. That began a nightly phone ritual that would last for weeks.

I looked forward to hearing his enthusiastic, optimistic voice. His positive attitude and love for life were contagious. His years as Chief of Police in our small town left him with a million real-life stories to tell. One was personal — a near-fatal gunshot wound. I had heard about it when it happened five years earlier, but I assumed he had made a full recovery. Instead, he told me he nearly lost his arm and was still dealing with the repercussions. His honesty made it easier to talk to him about my own life experiences.

So, I told him all about my life, painful divorce and the dreadful disease that followed on its heels. I explained how I was the "lucky" one — the only family member in my generation to inherit RA. He didn't seem too bothered by the prognosis. *He doesn't realize I could end up in a wheelchair,* I told myself. *I will save that for later.*

Sometimes, he failed to call at the usual time. That brought on a million doubts. *He's had second thoughts,* I surmised. Realizing I might be headed for a big disappointment, the time came to end the waiting game. Meeting him face-to-face would be the ultimate test. One of us had to break the ice.

The next day, I asked him to come over for supper. He hesitated and then agreed. I was so nervous. I spent all afternoon preparing a meal for a man who had a reputation for the best barbecue in town. It had to be perfect.

He arrived on time, dressed casually. He had a nice smile and a clean, manly scent. My heart thumped out of my chest for the first thirty minutes. Since we had gotten to know each other over the phone, our conversation picked up where it had left off. Being in his company reminded me how much I missed having a man in my life, but I cautioned myself not to get too excited. There were lots of perfectly healthy single women out there.

I was used to hiding my hands under the dining table, forcing myself not to limp, and pushing myself up out of a chair with my hands. He seemed not to notice the things that made me insecure, and instead he complimented my looks. He also couldn't quit praising the chicken casserole and coleslaw. I had found the way to this man's heart!

I listened patiently as he told me the story of the night he was shot and nearly died. "I've got an ugly scar," he said, "and a lot of pain."

Now, it was my turn to come clean. "I may end up in a wheelchair."

"So?" he said. He took my small, disfigured hands in his. "I believe in taking life one day at a time and living it like it's my last."

I took a deep breath and felt relief wash over me. "Me, too." I had spent far too much time worrying about the future.

Two years later, Eddie is my husband, best friend, and caregiver. Together, we face the future with optimism, knowing there will always be highs and lows. I am thankful for brief periods of remission between my lengthy flare-ups. Surgeries to correct joint damage plus a hip and knee replacement have become part of the battle. One surgeon told my husband, "Rheumatoid arthritis is terminal. She'll live and die with it." To that, my husband responded, "So what? Life is terminal, too."

When I am at my worst, Eddie keeps up my spirits. There's no time for pity parties at our house. We always have a plan and new goals. Even when I can't participate in a project, I'm his cheerleader. I sit on the sidelines whether we're planting a garden or building a barn — slow to give orders, but quick to inspire.

He never complains about helping me with things I used to take for granted: dressing, showering, shampooing, brushing my hair. In fact, he loves it when my hair turns out just right or the tennis shoes he bought me give me more balance. He laughs and tells our friends he never knew he would run a beauty shop or do the job of a shoe salesman. His sense of humor makes a bad situation not so bad.

Due to the crippling in my hands, I'm always dropping things throughout the house. He responds in a lighthearted way, "I know where you've been, sugar," he says as he enters the room and starts picking up. "All I've got to do is follow your trail."

He knows what it's like to suffer and he understands how hard it is to keep on keeping on. He pushes me to be the best I can be and asks no more of me than he asks of himself. Because of that, I try to make his life easier by giving it all I've got.

So far, my trips in a wheelchair have been few. Sometimes, a walker or a cane has come in handy, but most of the time, when I'm unsure of the next step, I just hold on to Eddie's outstretched arm. It's always there. When I'm by his side, he's the strongest man I've ever known. And, without a doubt, I'm a stronger woman because of him.

~Linda C. Defew

51

All the Right Things

Timing is everything. If it's meant to happen, it will,
at the right time for the right reasons.
~Author Unknown

In 2010, I had been using Internet dating sites for some years. I'd had a certain amount of success with these sites — I'd been on a few dates, and even made a couple of good friends — but that was all. I was sixty-one, and to be honest I felt I was wasting my time. Most men wanted someone younger, and I was getting tired of meeting new people. My subscription to the website I was using had just run out, and I decided not to renew it. Money was tight, and this was one way I could cut back a little.

However, it was winter, I was snowed in, and I had little to do. One day, I started idly flipping through "profiles" on the site, just to kill time. That was when I came upon David's profile. It was slightly unusual in that it purported to be written by his cat, Cookie. Now I'm a big cat lover, but most attempts at writing a quirky and eye-catching profile simply don't work. However, David's wasn't hokey or silly; in fact, it was rather clever and amusing. It was also correctly spelled and punctuated, and misspelled profiles were instantly consigned to my personal dating junk pile. He loved cats, which was a must with me. He lived on a canal boat, which sounded interesting. And he was basically happy alone but looking for friends, so he probably wasn't needy.

In Sickness and In Happiness | 189

There was only one problem: To contact someone, I'd have to pay and re-join. And I had no intention of wasting my money yet again. What to do?

Then the first coincidence happened. The very next day, I got an e-mail from the website offering me a half-price subscription. I'm a sucker for bargains, so I joined — just for three months. And I wrote to David — or rather, my cat Magnus answered Cookie's letter! Cookie replied, and our cats soon agreed that their humans needed company other than cats. David and I began writing to each other. And eventually, when his boat was fairly close to my home, we met up. Although it wasn't love at first sight, and bells didn't ring, we got on rather well. So, we met again, and again, and again....

The next winter, David moored the boat as close to my house as the canal goes. Then the weather became totally horrendous, with the worst snow we'd had for many years. The boat was iced in, and he couldn't empty the toilet or get any water, so he moved into my house with Cookie. At first, it was just temporary, and he went back to the boat now and then so that we could both have our own space for a while. Then he stayed for longer, and longer, and longer. Then we went on holiday together, and it went so well that as soon as we got back, we started planning another trip abroad. We realised we had fallen in love. Eventually, he sold the boat and moved in permanently.

So far, this looks like a simple happily-ever-after love story, perhaps unusual enough for two people of our fairly advanced age. But there is much more to it than that. Soon after we met, David confessed that he had terminal prostate cancer. He had only been expected to live a few months, and that had already been a couple of years earlier. Now he hoped he had a couple more years, but realistically that would probably be all.

I was taken aback to say the least, but I decided to carry on with the relationship. After all, two years with someone I loved was better than nothing. So after David moved in with me, he naturally needed to find a doctor and hospital in my area. David had originally been told that his cancer had spread, but the new consultant suspected the original diagnosis had been wrong. He repeated all the tests and said he could find no evidence of secondary tumours. So he recommended radiotherapy, which the original doctors had never even suggested, thinking it would have been of no use. Of course, David did as the doctor suggested.

It has been over three years since David's radiotherapy treatment. His cancer isn't "cured," and he still has treatment and regular check-ups. But now, more than ten years after the original diagnosis, he is alive and well, and it looks as though he will live at least another five to ten years, maybe more. And we are still very, very happy together.

Looking back, it's all very strange how it happened. If David hadn't had cancer — which meant he gave up work and got his pension early — he wouldn't have been living on a boat close to my home so that we could meet... If I hadn't been snowed in that day, I wouldn't have seen David's profile when I thought I'd given up dating websites, and I wouldn't have accepted that half-price subscription... If we hadn't had a hard winter, David wouldn't have moved in with me relatively soon after we met... If he hadn't changed to a doctor in my area, he would never have gotten the second opinion that caused him to get treatment after all and prolong his life.

All the right things had to happen to make our love a reality. Truth is indeed stranger than fiction, and oh, so much better.

~Helen Krasner

52

No Glass Slippers

My knight may not wear a coat of shining armor,
but his code of glowing honor will never fail to protect
us both from evils far worse than any
fire-breathing dragon.
~Richelle E. Goodrich, Smile Anyway

Trembling, tired, and damp, I looked down at my husband's shoulders from my convenient seat on a bedroom bench. This was my daily spot after a shower so that he could dry my feet and put on my shoes and socks. Our destination was my physical therapist, whom I visited three times per week.

My car wreck and resulting broken back were a shock to both of us. After surgery and inpatient rehabilitation, I was sent home in an enveloping, three-month back brace with instructions for daily living. Of course, I was unable to perform many tasks alone. Jim did the best he could to adapt the one small bathroom in our house to my needs, but the shower bench on the hospital instruction sheet couldn't be done. My occupational-therapy lessons on showering alone were for naught.

So, every morning my husband of thirty-five years would set up my shower needs, help me get on the "okay enough" shower bench, supervise and help me off the bench—a nervous and exhausting process in the early days of my recovery. Once I was clean, we would move to the bedroom where I did as much of my own dressing as possible. Each morning, he would kneel near me, and dry my feet one last time before helping me into my socks and shoes.

That morning, I looked down at my husband — the man to whom I'd promised my love, devotion, and life. When we're young, we don't realize that while the commitment part of the wedding vows don't get stale, day-to-day living sure can. Average days filled with conversations about household chores (and who has done more), work schedules, stress over bills and each other's family can get mundane. We had been wandering into that territory of taking each other for granted just before the wreck. It was ironic that this day, as he performed this simple task of slipping on my shoes, I was overwhelmed with new love. My standard-issue, familiar husband became my hero in that moment. I fell in love all over again.

Tears filled my eyes and voice as I touched his shoulder lightly and said, "Thank you so much for doing all of this."

Without looking up, he modestly mumbled something like "no problem."

With urgency in my voice, I said, "No, honey. Thank you." He looked up, and our eyes met. In that moment, we stopped pretending that this was anything except a tremendously difficult experience for us both. I remembered the emergency room and the raw fear in his eyes; the comfort of him holding my hand as I faded in and out the day before surgery; and his relieved greeting as I awoke from surgery.

We looked at each other that morning, both of us struggling with our emotions. I surrendered to open weeping. My husband, who doesn't like to show his emotions, had shiny eyes and a husky voice as he told me, "I love you, and this is where I'm supposed to be."

What does love look like? Well, to others it could be expensive gifts and expansive gestures. To me, it is a partner who appreciates the good times and shines like a star in the terrible times. The dream of a prince with a glass slipper is fun, but I like the memory of my husband kneeling in love, morning after morning, helping me with plain cotton socks and tennis shoes.

~Billie J. Mitchell

53

Through Thick and Thin

Gratitude is the memory of the heart.
~Jean-Baptiste Massieu

The doctors faced us across the steel table in a small, gray office at the Veterans' Hospital. They looked at us for a long moment and then began to go over the results of the mental test they had administered to my husband, John.

"While some of the tests are normal, most of them show you have weakened abilities in the areas of memory and judgment, sir." The doctor paused and took a deep breath.

John felt for my hand and held on to me tightly.

"I'm sorry to tell you that the final diagnosis is 'advanced cognitive impairment with significant short-term memory loss.' This will probably progress into dementia."

I felt like they had kicked me in the stomach, and I couldn't breathe. It seemed like all the air had been sucked out of that small space. I felt John's hand tightening painfully on mine, and then it began to shake uncontrollably. I wanted to grab him and run out of that place, away from them and their calm, clinical words that would change our lives forever.

Instead, we stood, thanked them and walked slowly as John maneuvered his way down the hall with his right hand on his cane and his left arm looped through mine. We didn't talk as we clung to each other all the way to the car.

"What are we going to do?" John asked me on the drive home. "I don't want you to have to take care of me for the rest of our lives!"

I had loved this man for twenty-six years. We had met in the Angels Booster Club and grown close through our common love of baseball. We moved slowly in the relationship since both of us had been through painful divorces. I came to know him as an honorable, kind and thoughtful man. His parents and my mom and sister grew to love each other as well. I adored his daughter and John was excited to be a stepfather to my children and grandchildren. Our wedding was a true blending of our families as the minister placed everyone's hands on the Bible and declared, "I now pronounce you one family brought together by God."

We had taken care of my mother, and then John's parents and my sister at the end of their lives. We had always told ourselves that our time would come to enjoy our freedom and travel when we retired.

Then I had colon cancer surgery on our twenty-fifth anniversary and had to postpone our dream trip to New England. "Don't worry," John had told me then, "we will be able to travel later. You'll see."

So the following year, we planned a trip on a paddlewheel boat up the Mississippi from New Orleans to Memphis with ten friends from our church. A few weeks before we left, I developed a painful kidney stone. When the doctors went in to remove it, they found another tumor that had to be removed. Again John told me, "Don't worry, you will be up and around in time for our trip."

His positivity must have worked because we went on our trip and had a lovely time. I did notice, though, that he had more trouble walking and was confused on the boat about where our cabin was. On the trip home, John lost his balance and took a bad fall in the Dallas airport as we hurried to change planes on our way back to California.

When we got home, the doctor scheduled a three-hour mental evaluation for John. It seemed the results of that test would derail the future we had planned together.

All of this flashed through my head as we headed for home after the doctor's crushing diagnosis.

John put his hand on my knee as I drove, waiting for me to answer.

"Okay, that was the medical diagnosis, but they don't know us," I told him. "We have weathered every storm together, and this will be no different! We will eat healthy and exercise every day. Maybe the extra oxygen will help your brain stay clear longer."

"This is not the future we had planned, and I don't want you to be saddled with caring for me," John whispered.

"We are stronger together, and I wouldn't want to be anywhere else except with you in this fight," I assured him. "Besides, I wonder if anyone really ever ends up where they planned to be later in life."

We have developed ways of dealing with the memory loss by making lists and using calendars to remind him of plans. I administer his many medications, sit in on all his medical appointments, and encourage him to participate in activities with our church, relatives and friends.

This once proud, decorated soldier is slowly fading away. My heart hurts for him, but there is nowhere I want to be except by his side. I'm not always patient or the perfect caretaker, but our love and commitment are strong, and we are quick to forgive each other for our mistakes. We've learned to be grateful for the time we have together and we manage to live joyfully.

~Judee Stapp

Two Coffee Shops, Two Couples

When one is in love, a cliff becomes a meadow.
~Ethiopian Proverb

L ife is funny. If my parents hadn't met in a coffee shop on Halloween night forty-six years ago, then I'd have never met the love of my life either.

Forty-six years ago, my dad was a sound engineer, asked to help out with repairing a speaker system at the local coffee shop for his college. The music was good, the company was better, and the pay was decent, plus my dad loves to tinker with stereo equipment. And on a night when half the town was out partying, it was as good a way as any to get out and about.

Everything was going fine, right up until my dad went looking for his screwdriver, which had disappeared off his worktable. He found it... in the hands of a pretty little blonde with bright hazel eyes.

My mom was taking a break from serving snacks and drinks in the same coffee shop. She was tired and a little bored, so she picked up the first thing she found to occupy her hands and her attention. The only thing out of place in the shop was my dad's tools.

And the rest, as they say, was history. My normally possessive father, rather than being upset, quietly asked for his screwdriver back with a smile on his face. My shy mom, normally not much for speaking to strangers, gave it back and struck up a conversation. They discovered they both loved music and books. They exchanged information and agreed to meet again.

Two years of laughter, learning, and loving later, they married. I was there to help them celebrate their twenty-fifth wedding anniversary, and with any luck I'll be there to celebrate their fifty-year "golden" anniversary, too.

And they'll be helping me celebrate my tenth wedding anniversary — hopefully in the coffee shop where I met my husband — the coffee shop my parents bought four years ago.

At that time, my parents were visiting a friend and heard about a coffee shop and bookstore that were on the market. The current owners were looking to retire and either close the business or pass it on to someone else. My parents, closing in on retirement age, thought that a coffee shop like the one they'd met in was a fine retirement project. There were books to pursue for their varied interests (they're both voracious readers), and the nostalgic scent of coffee in the air, an aromatic reminder of the day they met. The only hitch: They weren't quite ready to retire.

At the time, I was recovering from some financial issues, a psychological breakdown, and the discovery that constant upper respiratory illnesses, including multiple bouts of pneumonia, had reduced my lung capacity by twenty-five percent. So, my parents offered me the chance to work at their new coffee shop as the owner/manager. With an endorsement from my doctor, who said that small-town air would definitely agree with me better than the city, I moved 140 miles and took over the new family business.

Six months later, a group of men walked in, looking for a hot drink on their way to work. One of them looked more interested in the books than the menu, ordered tea instead of coffee, and introduced himself as Ronnie.

A week later, he was back for another cup of tea, a book recommendation, and a lively discussion about the merits of our favorite science-fiction novels. A week later, he brought some books in to donate to the store, and another debate developed — this time over the merits of video games versus writing, and the rankings of our favorite comic and cartoon characters.

Two weeks later, we went on our first date.

Two months later, I suffered another breakdown. Over the next year I struggled with severe depression, resulting in violent mood swings, anxiety attacks, uncontrollable explosions of temper, and frequent attempts to isolate myself from everyone.

I was losing my mind, but somehow I never lost him. Or perhaps, Ronnie never lost me.

He turned out to be my anchor. In spite of the strains on our relatively new relationship, Ronnie never gave up on me. And as things evened out and I began to recover, I was never more grateful. With Ronnie's steady presence and unwavering support steadying me, I went from losing my mind to losing my heart.

One year later, we moved into our first house together, right down the road from the coffee shop where we first met.

Two years later, we married.

My husband and I celebrate our anniversary two weeks after my parents celebrate theirs. And I thank God every day for Ronnie and his patience, love and support.

We wouldn't be where we are today but for two coffee shops — one today and one forty-six years ago — where my parents and I met the love of our lives.

~Caitlin Finley

I Am Beautiful
to Him

Two souls, one heart.
~French saying

A letter to my beloved husband:

    On February 17, we celebrate our anniversary. Ah, the red rose Valentine's Day wedding. Seventeen years. To some, that's nothing. To others, that's something. To me? That's everything.

Everyone knows that marriage is hard work. You and I have witnessed many marriages crumble over time, and we've seen other marriages shatter into sharp shards of brokenness under the weight of circumstances and the dissolve of unity. Marriage is not for the faint of heart, but rather it demands a relentless reach toward one another in the thick throes of a merciless world. And sometimes, arms get tired. Other times, one gives up, while the other desperately stretches over and over again to grasp what little it can.

We've danced through many seasons, with this delicate balance that sways back and forth — at times, reaching relentlessly toward one another — raising our hands in the folds of hard decisions and, other times, grasping with what little we had to give. Marriage does that.

I'm just so grateful we're still reaching, still dancing.

As we celebrate seventeen years of doing this daring dance together, I want you to know that through each and every turn, lift, carry, and fall on the dance floor, there has always been one consistent and unfaltering way you have loved me. It has been the greatest, most enduring part of our history, but more importantly — it has nourished the woman in me and gifted me with a message I believe all women deserve to hear — but don't.

You always tell me I'm beautiful.

This may sound like a simple and easy thing to do, but you will never truly understand what it means to me...

You see, I believe you.

I believe you, not because when I get all dressed up and "feel" pretty, you say it.

But rather the opposite. When I've been at my ugliest, you've meant it.

Standing in the shower, trembling from pain, unable to move...

Broken and bruised.

Stitched up and swollen.

Empty of all that made me a woman.

The tears never stopped, and the humility drowned my voice.

The mirror's reflection revealed a hideous beast of a body that replaced what once was. I hurt. Oh, how I hurt. I couldn't raise my arms to wash myself, or bend over without enormous pressure bellowing toward my chest, so every day you would climb into the shower and take my hand to escort me there.

Groggy from the narcotics that dulled my balance and fueled my nausea, I could barely stand. You held me up until I felt centered enough not to fall. Taking the soap into your hands to make a lather, you gently stroked my skin and ran your fingers down my bloated broken body, tenderly touching all the bumps, the bruises, the stitches, and the dried-up blood.

And while you bathed me, I moaned and cried, soaking in the warmth of the wetness and the assurance of your whispers...

"You are so beautiful."

Over and over again.

In Sickness and In Happiness |

"You are so beautiful."

For weeks, this was our routine. For weeks, you couldn't wait to wash me. For weeks, you would say over and over again as you bathed me...

"You are so beautiful."

Thank you, my love, for always making me feel beautiful. You will never know the power of your words and how deep they go.

My sister was diagnosed with Stage 3 breast cancer. After finding out she had the BRCA1 mutation, she begged her three sisters to get tested. My test came back positive. After previously finding one abnormal growth in each breast, my maternal grandmother dying young of this monster, and the clear research data that demanded my attention, I sought a breast surgeon's counsel. She urged me to take immediate action and get rid of it all.

I did. I chose to let go of all the parts and pieces that defined my womanhood, for the sake of my precious family and for the hope of a future. I had three surgeries with three surgeons all at once — a double mastectomy, complete reconstruction, and a full hysterectomy at the age of forty-two.

It wasn't easy, but it was what needed to be done. My sister gave me and my other sisters the gift of knowledge. She says this was the one great accomplishment that came out of her plight — saving us sisters from the monster she continues to fight.

I knew, of course, I would always be a woman without my breasts and uterus.

But it was and always will be my husband who makes me feel like a woman.

I am beautiful to him.

He reminds me all the time.

~Christine Carter

Full-Blooded Love

Love is a disease no one wants to get rid of. Those who catch it never try to get better, and those who suffer do not wish to be cured.
~Paulo Coelho, The Zahir

The soft light of a January morning shone through my window. Dust motes danced in the air. I thought about the coming weekend, when I would walk down the aisle to marry the man who had made me fall in love with his kind, twinkling eyes. They were the colour of the ocean on a calm day.

Absentmindedly, I stroked the large bruise that had formed in the crook of my elbow. The nurse had been gentle during the blood-draw, yet my vein had rebelled. I had to find a way to hide the bruise. It wasn't going to look attractive in my wedding photographs.

Slowly, I pulled on my cardigan. Despite the warmth of summer, I was cold and tired. I had no idea how to muster up the energy for the urgent pathology appointment I had to attend. My doctor's voice on the telephone the previous afternoon had sounded strained. "I am sorry, Liezel, but it's important that you have this biopsy done. It's just a precaution — probably nothing."

Shaking off the apprehension, I drove to the laboratory. I was there alone because Craig was away on business. In the waiting room, I thought about our coming honeymoon. We had booked a quaint cottage in a tiny mountain hamlet called Hogsback.

In Sickness and In Happiness | 203

"Liezel," a booming male voice announced, "we're ready for you. Come through."

The room was chilly, or perhaps it was just me. The doctor gently explained the procedure that he was about to perform. After anaesthetizing a small area on the back of my hipbone, he extracted a thin core of bone marrow that would be sent for further investigation. I hoped I wouldn't end up with a bruise on my back as well. The procedure was over quickly, and I set off for home. There was still so much to do before Saturday, but first I needed a nap.

Just wedding nerves and a bit of stress, I told myself. *Nothing to worry about.*

I was roused from a deep sleep by the telephone's insistent ringing. I heard my mom answer softly. "Hello, doctor. You've got the results back already? She's sleeping. May I take a message?" I could hear concern in her voice. "We'll see you later then. Thank you."

"Mom?" I asked sleepily. "What did he say?"

My mom, her face pinched and drawn, shook her head. "I don't know, but he said that it's urgent. He's on his way over."

Fifteen minutes later, the doctor arrived. He joined my parents and me in the lounge, took a deep breath and said, "Liezel, I have bad news, my girl. Your biopsy shows that your bone marrow has stopped functioning. You have severe aplastic anemia, and it's a very serious condition."

I struggled to make sense of what he was saying. His next words hit me like ice water. "My girl, you have to cancel your wedding. I am sorry, but you are extremely ill. You need a bone-marrow transplant. It might be the only way to save your life. Without a transplant, your prognosis is about three months."

I didn't hear much more after that. My world came crashing in. I vaguely heard arrangements being discussed: flights that needed to be booked; a wedding reception to be cancelled. Questions flew around the room.

"Craig. I have to call Craig!" I whispered. I got up to go and make the call, but it was as if my brain wouldn't, or couldn't, get my body to move. My dad got up and just took me in his arms. I felt so broken.

A few minutes later, I managed to dial the number that connected me to Craig.

"Craig, love, you have to come home. I'm very sick. The wedding is off. I can't marry you." I was sobbing.

"Liezel? What's happening? It's okay, love, it's all okay. We'll sort this out."

I could barely speak.

"Liezel? I'm on my way. I'll leave in the next ten minutes. I'm on my way! I love you!"

I spent the next two hours in stunned silence. Phone calls were made to family and friends. Arrangements were cancelled. New ones — life-or-death ones — were urgently made.

I knew in my heart that I couldn't ask Craig to go through with our wedding. Marry a woman who had no guarantee of surviving the next twelve weeks? No, I couldn't do it to him. He needed his freedom, and I would give it to him.

When he walked through the door later that evening, exhaustion etched on his face, he took me in his arms, and I clung to him. He was an anchor in the roughest seas I had ever experienced.

"You can't marry me, Craig," I whispered. My throat was raw from crying. "The doctor said I might only have three months to live. Twelve weeks. I can't let you marry me. What if I die? It's not fair to you."

Pulling me closer, he gently kissed me on the forehead and whispered, "I would rather be married to you for three months than not at all. Our wedding is not cancelled. We'll get married tonight. I'll call the pastor. We'll do it right here. I don't need a fancy wedding. I just need you."

In that moment, I knew what love really is. It isn't flowers, a diamond ring, or a wedding reception in a fancy hotel. It was this man holding me up — clinging to me as much as I was clinging to him. The only thing left that I could give him was three months of my life, and it was enough for him.

We exchanged our vows that night — dressed in jeans and T-shirts and barefoot in my parents' lounge.

"For better, or worse, in sickness and in health." Suddenly, these words held new meaning.

The following day, we flew to Cape Town, and I started what turned out to be two years of treatment. We often joke about our honeymoon spent in an isolation unit.

In the end, it was everything I needed and nothing I wanted, but I learned what real love is. And nineteen years later, that love is still alive today.

~Liezel Graham

57

Shave and a Haircut

One love, one heart, one destiny.
~Bob Marley

My husband stood behind me as I perched on a kitchen stool. *Click.* A soft buzz filled the air as he switched on the hair clippers, then turned them off. He changed an attachment and set down the clippers.

"Are you ready?" he asked.

"Just a minute." I took the scissors and hopped off the stool, heading for the bathroom.

"You look beautiful!" he called after me. As usual, I didn't believe him. The numbers on my bathroom scale kept creeping upward, and my gray hairs and wrinkles were multiplying. After twenty-two years of marriage and three children, our lives ran on a parallel track as we navigated work, church responsibilities, and busy teenagers. We moved in different directions with hardly any time together. If my husband joined me to watch a child compete in an afternoon swim meet, it meant he would work late into the night to meet a deadline and I would fall asleep alone.

Our relationship was stretched thin, like a rubber band — until that night in Banff, in our vacation condo, when I lay in the dark and whispered, "I found a lump." In that moment, the stretched rubber band released its tension, and we pulled back together. When we returned home, our lives merged onto a single track of doctor appointments, surgery, and chemotherapy.

My husband tapped lightly on the bathroom door. "You okay in there?"

"Yes, I'll be out in a minute," I replied.

Cancer treatment had changed my body, and now chemotherapy was claiming my hair. My eyes were bright in the mirror. "Do *not* cry," I told myself. In a few minutes, I would be posing for photographs at our shave party, and I did not want tear stains running down my cheeks.

I took a deep breath and looked at my reflection. Maybe I could wait a few more days. Running my fingers through my hair, my hand came away with more strands than yesterday. More even than this morning. My hair was coming out, and my scalp was tender. It was time.

I took a section of hair and braided it with shaky fingers. Securing the end with a rubber band, I stretched it out from my head and picked up the scissors. Cancer could take my hair, but it could not have this braid. I thought about my last visit to the hair salon. My hairdresser had advised me not to wait until my hair was coming out in clumps on the pillow or in the shower to shave it. "Too depressing," he said. "Come in. I'll do it for you, and you'll look fine. No charge." I thanked him, but I knew I wouldn't be back any time soon. I had gone home and asked my husband to wield the clippers.

I hacked at the braid with the scissors, and it fell away from my head, limp in my hand. My throat burned, but I forced a smile and left the bathroom. I handed the scissors to my husband and resumed my perch on the kitchen stool. He secured the cape around my neck and began cutting away lengths of blond hair.

"Can we do a Mohawk?" I asked.

"Sure," he said. "I've never done one before, though." After cutting my hair to a three-inch length with the scissors, he switched on the clippers and began shaving the sides of my head. The mound of hair on the floor was growing. "Try that," he said. I returned to the bathroom to style what was left of my hair.

When I emerged, I gestured at my Mohawk. "It's a little floppy," I said. "I don't think we own hair gel strong enough to hold the shape. Hurry with the pictures before it falls over."

The camera clicked away, and together we viewed the images on the camera display. My smile was tentative in the shots. "Let's do a dramatic one," I suggested. I put on dangling earrings and touched up my make-up, adding smoky eye shadow. My husband grinned his approval.

After a few more photos, I returned to the stool for the final trim. My husband adjusted the clippers to the closest shave setting and ran them over my head. I closed my eyes as strands of hair hit the cape and slid down to my lap. He slowed as he buzzed around my ears, moving carefully. The buzzing stopped as he switched off the clippers. Taking up the scissors once more, he trimmed a few stray hairs. A layer of fuzz was all that remained.

"All done," he said, brushing hair off my neck. He picked up the broom, and I watched the hair pile up as he swept. It looked like a small animal curled in the dustpan. My hair was really gone. My head felt cold.

"Well?" I asked him, afraid to pick up the mirror.

"Good thing you don't have a weird, bumpy troll head," he responded, setting aside the broom. I recognized his attempt to make me smile. Standing up, I turned to look at him, needing to know the truth.

"Do I look okay?"

He ran his hand over my soft, fuzzy head. "You are a hot bald chick," he replied, the heat of his hand warming me.

This, I thought. *This is all I need.* In all the craziness of life, it was easy to forget how much he meant to me. Over the years, it had been easy to take each other for granted. But at the most fragile time in my life, he was there for me, solid and certain. Time felt precious, and I treasured every moment.

"Really?" I asked again.

"You're beautiful," he said, giving me a hug. And this time, I believed him.

~Amy Newbold

In Sickness and In Happiness |

The Miracle *of* Love

Meant to Be

58

Kismet

Love at first sight is easy to understand; it's when two
people have been looking at each other for a lifetime
that it becomes a miracle.
~Amy Bloom

I hadn't wanted to attend the wedding that night, and I discovered later that he hadn't been keen on it either. I would have rather gone to my friends' annual Ugly Sweater Christmas Party with my closest and rowdiest friends than get dolled up and make small talk with people I didn't know. I barely knew the groom; I had yet to meet the bride; and the last thing I wanted to do was pretend to recognize fellow guests as my mom presented them to me.

Don't get me wrong, I am in no way anti-social or a Scrooge. Quite the opposite, actually. It was two weeks before Christmas, and I was head-to-toe, inside-and-out, chockfull of holiday spirit, which meant Christmas music, Christmas movies, Christmas cookies, Christmas sweaters, and Christmas parties. I didn't want to miss a single candy cane, ornament exchange, or verse of "Rudolph the Red-Nosed Reindeer" the entire month of December.

But when your mother asks you to be her date at a wedding, you go. It's not a debate. There's no question about it. You just go. So, off I went to the wedding where I would know seven people — including my mom and myself. I eased into the car, careful not to slip on the ice or fall into the foot-and-a-half of snow that had blanketed Chicago earlier that week. There I was, in my black-and-silver dress, an elegant overcoat that in no way kept me warm, my curls pulled into a loose up-do, and my feet shoved into Jewel bags and then into my black, fuzzy winter boots. What can I say? I'm a classy chick.

I gazed out the frosted car window, listening to Brenda Lee singing about how she was rockin' around the Christmas tree and imagining my friends doing just that. I had hoped that my mom and I could bail after dinner so I could still make it for most of the party, but we were carpooling with my mom's friends, so I was on their time. No telling what that could mean. I was lost in thought, imagining the warmth of my friends' basement, decorated with multicolored Christmas lights and garland, the TV playing *A Christmas Story* in the background, and everyone standing around laughing and noshing on chili and artichoke dips, pizza, and homemade cookies and cakes, when I heard my mom say, "…so maybe you'll like him. We'll see."

Her words shook me from my reverie. "Like who?" I asked. "Are you talking to me?"

My mom was fiddling in her purse in search of gum as she repeated, "An old friend of mine… She and her husband are going to be at the wedding, and they want to introduce you to their son."

"Mom!" I gasped. If I hadn't wanted to go to the wedding before, this made me want to leap from the moving car.

"Oh, relax," she said, popping a piece of Trident in her mouth. "Just say hello. You don't have to do anything you don't want to do."

That wasn't the point. I hated being put in situations like that. My mom knew it. My friends knew it. Everyone who knew me knew it. Lately, however, it seemed like people were trying harder than ever to find me the "perfect guy."

About four years earlier, my decade-long relationship with my first and only boyfriend came to an overdue end, and I hadn't dated, in the conventional sense, since. Not a boyfriend. Not a real date. Not even a friend-with-benefits in nearly four years, and apparently everyone but me found this worrisome.

The funny thing was, I was actually happy being single. I know, I know… single people often say that to mask the fact that they haven't found the right person. And everyone around them rolls their eyes. But the truth of the matter is that I really *did* feel that way. I spent twelve years with the same person, and I needed time now to just be me.

There was a lot I needed to learn about myself and what it meant to be fully independent and self-reliant, so that's what I did for the four years following my break-up. I learned. I traveled. My social calendar was jam-packed, and not just on weekends. I had something going on every night of the week. And despite the fact that I was always exhausted, I loved every minute of it. I took advantage of every opportunity life afforded me. I said "no" to nothing — except dating. And this drove my friends crazy.

When we entered the reception hall a half-hour later, that couple and their son happened to be among the first guests we encountered. Luckily for me, he was extremely shy and didn't so much as look up when his mother introduced us. I nodded hello and, when he looked down, I took the opportunity to make a beeline for the coat check.

My mom knew so many people there; so I followed her around the room as she kissed and hugged everyone, and it turned out that I knew more people than I anticipated. But that didn't stop me from checking my phone every so often to see how quickly time might be passing. We all moved toward the back of the ballroom where the ceremony took place, and once it was over, we found our seats near the bar.

My mom and I had been seated with people we didn't know, and that isn't necessarily a bad thing if the people are friendly; however, this group seemed like they intended to talk amongst themselves. Suddenly, we heard someone calling my mom's name from the table beside ours.

"Maria! Maria!"

We turned to see a petite blonde in a tight, black dress waving us over.

"We have two empty seats," she said in Spanish. "The couple isn't coming. Why don't you and your daughter sit with us?"

Mom took the seat beside her friend, and I took the only remaining seat left, next to a handsome guy who appeared to be around my age. Even seated, it was clear that he was tall with a medium build and, in my opinion, resembled soccer great Leo Messi, but even better looking. I noticed a stunning, svelte blonde seated beside him, whom I assumed was his girlfriend, so I didn't bother making conversation. I surveyed the ballroom, admiring the Christmas lights and decorations, listening to bits and pieces of conversations, mainly in Spanish since most of the guests were from Argentina, and every so often, stealing a glance at "Leo."

As I was buttering my bread, my mom made eye contact with him and said in English, "Hi, I'm Maria. And you are?"

He smiled and said, "Pero yo soy Argentino." *But I am Argentine.*

They shook hands, smiled, and a look of recognition suddenly crossed my mother's face.

"Sos el hijo de Donato y Lourdes?" she asked. *Are you Donato and Lourdes' son?*

"Si," he replied. "Soy Marcos." *Yes, I'm Marcos.*

"No lo puedo creer! Como esta tu mami?" she asked. *I can't believe it. How is your mom?*

And with that, Marcos moved the centerpiece to reveal his mother sitting beside the svelte blonde. My mom and Lourdes exchanged hugs and hellos, and soon our table was bubbling with conversation, laughter, and reminiscing. I soon learned that Luz, the blonde seated next to Marcos, was simply a good friend of his, and so I felt more comfortable conversing with him. I was captivated by his charming Argentine accent as well as the way he spoke with confidence and honesty. We talked throughout dinner, and I realized that, for the first time in years, I had met a guy with whom I didn't want to stop talking. We could've sat there all night, and I would have been content.

At one point, Luz asked Marcos if he wanted to go outside and have a cigarette, and he replied, "No, I'm okay right now."

He turned back to me.

"You don't smoke?" I asked him.

"No, I do," he said, "but I want to stay here and talk to you. Is that okay?"

My heart leapt. I couldn't remember the last time I felt that way. Happy. Calm. Enchanted. And, most important, not afraid or hesitant.

It was the strangest feeling, but it felt as if I had come home. Something about him was so familiar, so comforting. I had known him for only a couple of hours, but I felt at ease, as though my heart had found its beat.

We spent much of the evening talking and flirting. At the end of the night, he came up to the bar where I was chatting with old friends to say goodbye. The music was blaring, so as he leaned in to speak in my ear, all I heard was "your number."

"You want my number?" I asked him, smiling.

"No," he said. "I have your number. Maybe we could have dinner sometime."

I wrinkled my brows, confused. I was fairly certain I hadn't given out my phone number that evening.

"I didn't give you my number," I said.

"I know," he said. "Your mom did."

Leave it to my mom. She knows me better than I know myself.

On the car ride home that evening, I said to her, "Mom, I have a feeling that Marcos is going to be a significant part of my life. I don't know why, but something tells me that I have not seen the last of him."

Two years later, during that same pre-Christmas week, Marcos and I married.

Throughout our courtship, we came to learn that our paths had crossed long before we were born. Our families are from a small town in southern Italy called Ripacandida, and our grandfathers knew each other well. Eventually, they immigrated to Buenos Aires, Argentina. Marcos' grandfather was a tailor, and he made the suit that my grandfather wore when he married my grandmother.

In the early 1980s, Marcos' parents decided to move to Chicago, and Marcos was born in the hospital where I was born. We were even delivered by the same obstetrician. His family lived here for approximately four years before returning to Argentina, and during that time, my grandparents and parents shared a friendship with Marcos' parents — so much so that Marcos and his brother called my grandmother "Nonna" (Grandma in Italian).

Our families were overjoyed when Marcos and I started dating. Just before we got engaged, his father visited us from Argentina, and he brought with him a photograph of us when we were little. We were on a carousel at a neighborhood carnival. I was three at the time, and Marcos' brother was four, and we sat side-by-side on horses with my dad standing between us. Only eighteen months old at the time, Marcos was sitting on a horse behind his brother as his mom propped him up. Currently, that photograph is tacked to our refrigerator, and I often look at it in amazement. Who would have thought that, thirty years earlier, I was sharing a carousel ride with the man who would be my husband?

Fate is a funny thing. A beautifully funny thing. Just a few short years ago, I was desperately trying to get out of going to a wedding where I would meet my future husband, the man my heart had been seeking. I believe that Marcos and I were truly made for each other, that our souls had been searching for each other throughout our lives. Our history is proof of that.

On our wedding day, as we recited our vows to each other in English and Spanish, I remember thinking to myself, *This is where I was always meant to be. All the ups and downs, the questions, the doubts, were leading me down the path to this moment and this man. My husband.* He was already a part of my history, my blood, and my story, woven into the fabric of my life.

Never did I imagine on that frigid winter night, while my friends were sipping eggnog and drunkenly singing Christmas carols, that my soul would find its mate — and my life would be forever changed.

~Vanessa Angone-Pompa

59

Bollywood Dreams

Our soul mate is the one who makes life come to life.
~Richard Bach

They meet, break out in choreographed dance with beautiful music, and fall in love. Then the movie ends, and we turn off the TV. That's love in the world of Bollywood.

Growing up in America in an immigrant family, I was in love with my Indian culture. I helped my mom cook, watched Bollywood movies like it was my job, and even danced and performed traditional Indian folk dances.

One day, I knew, I would marry my "Bollywood Princess." I had posters of Kareena Kapoor on my walls, and when I hit my early twenties, my family started introducing me to potential brides to meet from the arranged-marriage system of aunties, who were excited to play matchmaker. The plan was to marry the perfect bride: a great cook, beautiful, with a love for family. Of course, she would be Indian. And not only Indian, but from Gujarat, the state our family is from. And not only Gujarati, but also a Patel — and ideally a specific Patel from these five villages my family comes from. Simple, right?

But it didn't happen. By my late twenties, I had written two books and was traveling as a speaker and trainer. More books were written, and soon I was called to speak around the world. Instead of flying back and forth to home for a couple days, I decided to live on the road full-time as a nomad. Traveling made my heart soar. My family was happy about my success, and yet very concerned.

"Jaymin, when are you going to settle down and get married?"

"No one will want to marry you if you keep traveling everywhere! Get a job in one city where you can start your family."

For nearly a decade, I had happily met the women my family members set me up with. I "courted" here and there, but no relationship lasted. It was the same story each time. She wanted me to settle down, and my soul wanted to travel. It felt like I must live my passion *or* find love and start my own family. I just didn't see why I would have to give up what I loved doing to have a family. I was ready to give up hope. I was slowly coming to terms with the idea that perhaps my exciting, purpose-filled life would be spent alone.

Then, one weekend, I was invited to speak in Seattle. A friend had been trying for years to introduce me to a woman who lived there, but geography had never been on our side. I reached out, and we carved out a couple hours to connect with each other.

In that short time, we learned we had grown up with many similarities and interests. We had attended grad school to get our MBAs the very same years. We had even attended some of the same conferences without knowing it! We graduated with nice corporate jobs, which we then quit to travel around the world. Eventually, we became coaches and speakers because we wanted to help others with our life's work. It was like meeting the female version of me!

More importantly, I couldn't forget how she made me feel. She had this amazing presence and warmth that invited me to show up fully and authentically. She was gentle, curious, open and accepting. In those few short hours I spent with her, I felt so safe and seen. It was a magical feeling.

Soon after, we found ourselves speaking in San Francisco at the same time. We made plans to connect. What was supposed to be a lunch date on Sunday became lunch and dinner on Sunday, exploring the city on Monday, supporting each other's speaking events on Tuesday, enjoying a lovely picnic on Wednesday, and postponing my Thursday flight so we could also spend Friday together.

That evening, after one of her workshops, she took me in her arms and asked, "Do you want to be my partner?"

Partner? I was stunned. I wanted to say yes, but this wasn't happening like my Bollywood dream. She was so amazing, but she wasn't a Patel from the five villages, she wasn't Gujarati, and she wasn't even Indian! She was a mix of Polish and Swedish heritage, with bold blue eyes and curly blond hair. There was no way my family would accept me marrying her, so why date her? But the feelings from spending the entire week together could not be denied, and I followed the voice in my heart and said, "Yes!"

Six weeks later, we were back in Seattle brushing our teeth, and it hit me. I turned to her and said, "Just so you know, I'm going to marry you. How long do I have to wait before I ask?"

Her eyes flashed a smile, and being a relationship coach, she said, "Well, we are currently enjoying 'new relationship energy,' so I would say it's too soon right now. You'll have to wait at least six months."

I nodded, smiled, and kept brushing my teeth.

After what felt like the longest six months, we were engaged. What was supposed to be one lunch date had turned into a week, and had now turned into a lifetime. My friends couldn't believe it — I was finally going to get married! My family was less excited by my actions. They were hugely disappointed that I didn't choose a wife from those five small villages in Gujarat as they had expected me to do.

I had taken a bold step. It was not the Bollywood dream I had imagined, but I listened to my heart and knew it was the right decision.

My wife is the most amazing person I've ever met. She is medicine and magic. She has taught me that people do not *fall* in love; they *rise* in love. Anything feels possible with her.

Together, we are raising two children as we travel the world full-time as nomads. We have published a total of nine books, and continue to coach and speak everywhere we visit, sharing our story and our message to inspire others. It's a bold move, and not always an easy one. We face the same issues that all parents face — no sleep at night, sickness, bumps and bruises and crying, in addition to scheduling problems and travel upsets as we move to a new home every few weeks. But it's all worth it. I learned that I can, in fact, have it all. I just needed to follow my heart and say "yes" to the moment.

I was always told life was about making tough choices. I never felt like I could have it all. Finally, through meeting the woman of my dreams, I've proved the old adage wrong. You can have it all.

I did have my Bollywood love story. We met, we fell in love, and now we're dancing in sync to the beautiful music of life's ups and downs together.

~Jaymin J. Patel

The Face in the Window

A dream you dream alone is only a dream.
A dream you dream together is reality.
~John Lennon

I was divorced, thirty-four, with a beautiful son, when I first attempted to decipher the chaos of my many dreams. Surely, there must be messages there or something my subconscious was attempting to convey. At that time, I was not involved in a relationship, and I certainly had no wish for another failed marriage. I hadn't even dated for a couple of years and concentrated only on meeting the needs of my child and clearing my head of old, muddled thinking. Even so, I was open and interested in meeting a man of honesty and honor.

Then came the night of *the* dream—a dream so piercingly clear that it would alter the course of my life.

In this dream, I was engaged to marry a young sailor, complete with sailor cap, navy shirt, white pants and a neatly trimmed beard. The year was sometime in the 1940s. The place was Pearl Harbor, Oahu, Hawaii. The sailor's name was Johnny, and he was on a short leave for his birthday. I had made a birthday cake and decorated the dining area with brightly colored strips of crepe paper and balloons.

When he walked into the small bungalow and came directly over to me, I stretched out my arm, which came to rest on his. I could feel every single hair on his arm right down to the texture and the downy feeling of the hairs. The sailor spoke not a single word; he merely stared into my eyes with bold, fierce strength. I could feel the sense of his love wash over me and I knew that this man loved me truly and without question. The message was undeniable.

Just as quickly as it had begun, the dream was over. But the lasting effects of that dream stayed with me, day in and day out. I wrote down every detail that occurred in the dream, every movement, every emotion. It felt so very real, and I knew this dream held profound secrets for me. As to the secrets, I knew nothing. I only knew that the sailor, Johnny, loved me, and that felt as real as any moment in my life had ever been.

Days and weeks passed, and I found that I looked for Johnny's face and his sailor cap in crowds wherever I was — at the grocery store, the mall, social gatherings. I felt a strong need to find him. I also felt I might be losing my mind — looking for a person from my dream was ludicrous. One day, I became certain I was losing my grip on reality. I stood at my kitchen sink and looked over to a nearby sliding glass door — and saw Johnny's face in the reflection of the glass. It was plain as day — the face, the beard, the sailor cap — it was all there.

The following day, Johnny's image reappeared in the same location. That night, I saw his reflection in my bedroom window. He was seemingly following me as the days and nights flowed into weeks and then months of seeing Johnny's face nearly anyplace I traveled. I was absolutely certain I had lost my mind, but decided to put this to a test. On a business trip, I joined a co-worker in Oregon to help her coordinate a surgical convention. On our last day, we enjoyed a wonderful lunch along the coastline. Johnny's face appeared in the window as we gazed out over the beautiful beach scene. Finally, I asked my co-worker if she saw anything unusual in the window glass. She said no, she'd seen nothing out of the ordinary. I was devastated and certain I was indeed insane and had lost my mind. I cried and grieved for days.

Finally, I confessed everything to my best friend, whom I had positioned to stand at my kitchen sink and look over to the sliding glass door. However, she saw absolutely nothing. With this, I decided that I needed professional help, and I scheduled an appointment with a psychiatrist.

A group of friends was planning to gather at my apartment once a week for several weeks for numerology classes presented by a psychic whom I had come to know and appreciate. I was looking forward to having good friends around me to share some happy times and ease my worries. One of these friends brought along another friend, a girl named Sherry, whom I had never met. Sherry was a bright and cheery soul. When they first entered my apartment, she came right over to me as I prepared food items at my kitchen sink. She put an arm around my shoulder, introduced herself, and then grinned like crazy and asked, "Who's the sailor dude in the window?"

I nearly fainted. *Did I hear Sherry correctly?* I had. She went on to say that she clearly saw a dark-haired, bearded man with a sailor cap, and this image had been reflected in the glass of my sliding door. I nearly wept right on the spot, but kept my emotions under control throughout the remainder of the evening. The following morning, I canceled the appointment with the psychiatrist. Although I could not explain the image appearing in glass, the message was crystal clear. The man from my dreams was following me and making certain his image was kept fresh in my mind.

Life returned to normal, or what felt nearly like normal. One of my friends and co-workers attempted to set me up with a blind date, but I continued to say "no" for many weeks. Finally, I relented. Larry, I was told, was newly divorced and eager to meet me. My friend's husband knew him quite well and vouched for his character.

Soon, the night of the blind date arrived. When I opened my front door, I was not prepared for the sight before me. Without question, the man was identical to Johnny — right down to the hair, the beard, and the stature — but without the sailor cap! I was completely stunned.

The blind date continued at the seafood restaurant Larry had chosen. Once seated, we began to talk and shared many things from our childhoods. It turned out that Larry had wanted to be a sailor and always wore a sailor's cap until his mother finally took it away from him at age seven! I confessed that I had wanted to be a professional dancer, and although I had been given a full scholarship to a dance academy in San Francisco, I was unable to attend as my family moved soon after to another state.

Back at my apartment, Larry and I talked endlessly. He mentioned a childhood friend he always dreamed of — a little blond girl who always wore a two-piece, short red outfit and always had the smell of old shoes around her. That set me to thinking, and I brought out an old photo album filled with some pictures from my childhood. When Larry browsed through the pages, he stopped abruptly on one and said, "This looks just like the girl from my dreams — the girl with the red outfit."

The picture was black and white, but he was correct: My short, little outfit was indeed red! And as my father owned a shoe-repair store at that time, the smell of old shoes permeated those years of my life. Larry could not have known these things, but somehow he did.

We talked until we heard the birds chirping at dawn. We both felt like we had known each other before from another life, and perhaps we had. I now believed that anything was possible.

Eight days later, Larry got down on one knee and proposed. We were married soon after in a small wedding ceremony on Orcas Island in the San Juan Islands off Washington State. The witness, who was unknown to us, sat down at the piano and played a beautiful Hawaiian wedding song, which reminded me that my dream had been set on Oahu.

The man of my dreams had become real, and we shared a real love. It felt exactly like the love emanating from the sailor in my original dream. Larry and I were married for twenty-eight years before his death.

Dreams really do come true.

~Louetta Jensen

I Almost Gave Up on Romance

First romance, first love, is something so special to all
of us, both emotionally and physically, that it touches
our lives and enriches them forever.
~Rosemary Roger

It had been five years since my last real date. The post-divorce rebound taught me to be cautious, and looking online left me feeling empty, so I tried not to want a man in my life. Maybe I was better off single. Maybe the dogs, my most loyal companions, would be enough.

In January 2011, I promised myself I wouldn't look anymore, at least until my daughter graduated from high school in June.

Six months after I made that promise, on the Tuesday night after my daughter's graduation, I sat down at the computer in the hallway alcove. It had been another long day at work. My hands ached, and my eyes wanted to close as I scanned my in-box and then diverted to Facebook, hoping to relax.

A private message was waiting for me. I clicked the icon and stared at the name for several seconds as my weariness evaporated. My heart pounded as I read the message: *Greetings to you! After many years, I hope you are well. Take care and be safe!*

I looked at the name again, and then sat back from the computer. Could it really be him? My first love in high school? I took a deep

Meant to Be | 227

breath. Maybe I was seeing things.

Like a skeptical jeweler studying a diamond, I moved closer and read the name again. I'd typed that name into the computer a few times, but gave up after seeing how many people had the same name as my first love. And besides, I was the one who wrote to him last in 1972, so it was his turn. Now, in 2011, he was finally getting back to me with this simple message that made my heart feel like it was going to leap out of my chest.

David was a good guy when we dated in high school, but so much time had gone by. A person can change a lot in thirty-nine years. But the timing was too much to ignore.

Wow! It's so nice to get your message! I typed, and then added a little about sweet memories and high-school friends. I sent him a friend request, figuring he was still far away. If he turned out to be a jerk, I could simply unfriend him.

As we progressed from Facebook to phone calls, David didn't sound like a jerk at all. He sounded very interesting. He worked as a firefighter/EMT in Connecticut, and he had three dogs. He talked about his dogs like they were family. Beep, his ten-year-old Australian Shepherd mix, couldn't climb the stairs anymore.

"Yep, I carry the old girl upstairs to the bedroom every night," David told me.

My heart wanted to melt, and my toes tingled at the image of him carrying his old dog upstairs at bedtime. "Must love dogs" had been on the top of my list, the one I made in case I ever decided to take a chance on love again. As David and I talked on the phone, a tiny ember of hope — almost forgotten after so many years — glowed in my heart.

Still, I kept reminding myself to stay grounded, to keep my ears open and my brain fully engaged. I asked a lot of questions, and he didn't mind answering them. "Nothing's off the table," he told me.

One night, David had a question of his own. He asked me what I was doing on Friday, July 15th. He said he had some time off that weekend and wanted to take me out to dinner. I was hesitant. Talking on the phone was one thing, but…

"Are you still there?" he asked.

"You want to come all the way from Connecticut to North Carolina just to have dinner with me?"

"Yep, with one catch."

"What's the catch?" I tried to sound businesslike.

"I'd like to spend time with you on Saturday, to sit and talk, to find out what has brought you to this point in your life."

I had to take the chance. I agreed. It was a date.

And a wonderful date it was! We ate dinner at a cozy restaurant near the river. As David talked about his career and the lessons he had learned, I realized he had become a man of integrity. After dinner, we walked along the riverfront, and then sat on a bench to watch the golden sunset. I leaned back against him and let his strong arms hold me gently. The natural scent of his skin, which must have imprinted itself on my teenaged brain, was intoxicating. His kiss awakened feelings I had not felt in a long time.

David was a perfect gentleman on our first date, and on all the dates thereafter. He flew down from Connecticut about once a month, and I flew up to meet his friends and family, including the dogs. We talked on the phone every night between visits, asking questions, giving honest answers, and sharing our hopes and dreams.

On December 9th, three days before my birthday, David joined me on a church outing to Brookgreen Gardens in South Carolina. After dinner, we strolled under the live oaks lining the walkway. Twinkling lights and luminaries transformed the gardens into a land of magic as musicians played holiday melodies on flutes and violins.

We meandered to a path less traveled near the back corner of the gardens where white globes on poles stood like giant lollipops.

"What do you want your future to look like?" David asked.

"I want you to be in my future," I smiled, wondering what he might have in mind.

"I want you in my future, too," he said.

We stopped to gaze at the moon, and then David turned to face me. I looked up into his blue-grey eyes and noticed the moonlight gleaming silver on his hair.

"Will you marry me?"

"Yes," I answered without hesitation, and then added on impulse, "but you have to get down on one knee."

"Do you want me to ask you again?"

"Yes."

He looked around. No one was watching except the moon. David granted my request and asked again, "Will you marry me?"

"Yes!" I laughed. "Of course, I will!"

One year later, after I'd almost given up on romance, I married my first love, my last love, the love of my life.

~JoAnne Macco

62

Random Certainty

Do you think the universe fights for souls to be
together? Some things are too strange
and strong to be coincidences.
~Emery Allen

I met him the evening before the second semester of my junior year in college. I had seen him the night before at tryouts for the drama department's spring production. When the director introduced him as a sixty-hour major with professional experience, I remember whispering to a friend, "Sigmund Bonebrake... that's got to be his stage name. Nobody could have a name like that."

Even though his acting was excellent, he looked so young, like a fourteen-year-old. It did not seem plausible that he could have much experience. He was an enigma.

I met him the next evening in the Den at the Student Union. When the students he was sitting with left, a friend of mine brought him to my table. Don introduced us and promptly left as well. I began chatting with him tentatively, a bit shy at having to entertain someone I didn't know. I began by asking him how he liked the school so far and what he thought of tryouts. When I found myself more at ease, I asked him to tell me more about himself. He told me he had spent four years in the Army, attended three colleges for a brief time, worked in Kansas City as a cab driver and a printer, and lived in Australia for two years where he was part of a trapeze act in a carnival and was in a couple of movies. Looking across the table at him, I found his story difficult to believe. After all, he looked barely old enough to drive.

I was skeptical, but when I questioned the veracity of it all, telling him he couldn't have done all that since he was too young, he grinned and pulled out his driver's license. I was shocked into silence as I saw he was not fourteen, but almost thirty. In order to break the awkward silence, I suggested we go bowling at the lanes adjacent to the Den. Later, he walked me back to my dorm.

As classes began, I found that Sig was in four of mine, and he managed to find a seat next to me in each one. I actually began to believe he was as old as he claimed because he had impeccable manners. He carried my books, opened doors for me, and pulled out my chair at tables — all behaviors most boys my age had never learned or practiced.

We became almost inseparable. We had breakfast together in the college cafeteria, took our classes together, and met in the Den for suppers before rehearsals where we worked lights and sound together. During quiet times, we learned about each other, our likes and dislikes, past adventures and misadventures, and hopes and dreams for the future.

Then, one day, I discovered two bits of information about him that I felt were signs that our relationship was meant to happen. The first sign was that one of the productions Sig had been involved in during his fifteen years in theater had won a competition that had been broadcast on national television. Remarkably, I remembered seeing that broadcast and even specifically remembered his portrayal of the character in that production. I remembered explaining to my sister that they must have used a trampoline to accomplish the spectacular jumps his character had made.

The second sign we were meant to meet revealed itself when we were sharing our love for writing poetry. I told him I had been published in a book of Iowa poetry three years earlier, and I was eager to show him my poem. He told me that he had also been published in two subsequent issues of that same publication. While he returned to his dorm to get his copies of the books, I retrieved my copy to show him. I read his poems first and was amazed at their beauty and complexity. When he wanted to read mine, I found I was almost embarrassed to show him my simple poem. But I let him read it, and he was most complimentary.

Then he said, "I think I'm published in this issue as well."

"No," I replied. "I read this issue cover to cover when I got it, and I'm sure you aren't. There aren't any poems by a Sigmund Bonebrake in this book. I would certainly have remembered that name."

He flipped through the book slowly, looked at me, and then smiled. "Yes," he said. "Since I was in Kansas City at that time, my aunt in Iowa published one of my poems under her name."

And then he showed me his poem. As I read it, my heart stopped. Of all the poems in that entire edition, his poem had been my favorite.

Two weeks later, when he asked me to marry him, I thought again of those signs—and I said, "Yes." Thanks to random certainty, we'll be celebrating our fiftieth anniversary soon.

~Sue Bonebrake

63

Ooh La La

*Romance is the glamour which turns the dust of
everyday life into a golden haze.*
~Elinor Glyn

O oh la la —*how romantic these Italians are!* That was my
thought as I watched a carload of Italian construction
workers disembark at my hometown train station in
France.

World War II had just ended, and Europe was in the midst of
rebuilding itself. It was a monumental task that moved a lot of skilled
craftsmen throughout the various countries.

After a wartime period when most men were off fighting, it was
a joy and a relief to finally have them back. First, the good-looking
American soldiers came through, liberating France in the process.
Then the builders arrived, often romantic Italians with bedroom eyes.
It was almost too much for a gal to handle.

I was a young French woman at the time, working at a factory
job all day, while helping out at home in the evenings. All my earnings
went toward helping with the family's household expenses. In order to
purchase anything extra for myself, I worked extra hours on weekends,
harvesting crops in the fields or doing other odd jobs. It was a tough,
hardscrabble life, but we were young and could manage.

As a result of my heavy work schedule, contact with others came
in the brief moments between jobs, as I bicycled from one workplace
to another. When I zipped home in the evenings, I would see groups

of other workers who were also getting off work. Among them, the dark-haired Italians would stand out, chatting between themselves as they were taking in their unfamiliar surroundings.

From time to time, I'd see a particularly attractive Italian fellow who caught my eye. I was still pretty naïve, so I didn't really know how to get his attention. My flirting skills left much to be desired. I knew that the construction workers moved from town to town, repairing and rebuilding as needed. So I had a limited amount of time to figure out how to get noticed by this lad.

Daydreaming of this handsome Italian filled my workdays, as I imagined what my conversations with him would be like once I got to know him. I couldn't wait for the end of the day when I could whiz by on my bike to my next assignment and hopefully catch sight of him. Snatching the odd glimpse of him kept me going through long months of hard work.

Finally, there came the time when I didn't see him around anymore. As I had feared, his job probably ended in our area, and he was on to the next place, most likely never knowing I even existed. I was dejected and inconsolable. This faux romance had kept me going for so long.

Time passed, but I never forgot about my ideal Italian man. It seemed absurd, but I felt I truly loved him from afar. I swore I would never forget him, and I did not want to befriend anyone else to take his place. I constantly kicked myself for not being bolder while I had the chance.

My father tried to console me, saying there were plenty of fish in the sea. Like countless others, he also worked in construction, so he knew many single young men were out there looking for love. In fact, he said, a very nice Italian guy was working on his crew. He would bring him home for dinner one night.

I didn't want to know about any other Italians, nor did I want to cook a special dinner for an unwanted guest. I had enough work to do. I was looking for fun and love, and I had just lost my greatest opportunity.

Nevertheless, against my wishes, my father arranged a date to bring home his young work colleague. I made sure to make a plain, unappetizing meal, hoping to dissuade my father from ever doing it again. It was my form of passive-aggressive protest.

On the evening of the dinner, I stayed in my factory work clothes, refusing to dress up for company. It was bad enough that I was stuck making dinner for everyone in the family, plus an unwelcome guest. I didn't want to expend any more energy than I had to.

Finally, my father and his young worker arrived on their bicycles and came in the door. You can imagine my surprise when I found myself face-to-face with the very same Italian I had been swooning over for the better part of a year.

Dinner and the rest of the evening were a blur. The young man seemed truly appreciative of a home-cooked meal and being amongst a family, despite my earlier efforts to make things less than hospitable. We finally managed to break the ice that evening and get to know each other a little.

It was the beginning of a romantic love affair that lasted a lifetime.

~Denise Del Bianco

One in 300,000

*He stirred my soul in the most subtle way and the story
between us wrote itself.*
~Nikki Rowe

A quick slap from my best friend, Christine, caught me off-guard. "What was that for?"

"He's leaving." She bobbed her head a few times in his direction. I peered over her shoulder and saw the man she was referring to, phone to his ear, lingering near the garden exit.

I pursed my lips and gave her a shrug. "Maybe it's just not meant to be."

"You have to talk to him!"

I gave him another glance. He was handsome. I crossed my arms and slowly tapped my foot at her. "He didn't talk to me. And besides, if it's meant to be, I'll see him again."

She shot me her sweet look of disapproval. I gave her one back and turned to resume my stroll through the gardens. It wasn't long before I heard her little heels clicking behind me.

"Dar, this is the third time you've run into him. In a city of thousands and thousands of people. Three. Times." She waved her three little fingers in my face as if I couldn't hear her.

My cheeks flushed. She had a point. "Oh, yeah, I can see it now. He looks like he's with his parents. 'Mom. Dad. This is Darla... We met in a bar....'"

She squared her hands on her hips. "We are grown-ups, for God's

Meant to Be | 237

sake. And it wasn't a bar. The first time was a restaurant."

I nodded. I remembered it clearly. It was a restaurant — Primanti Bros. in Market Square. I ran inside that night to take cover from the rain. My co-workers and I had ventured to the square for happy hour as we did most Friday nights in the summer, but we were met with a sudden downpour. All of us, dripping wet, squished into the area in front of the registers. That was when my slightly intoxicated co-worker got a little too silly telling a story and hit a young man in the back of the head. He turned, and our eyes met. I promptly pointed to my friend, Lori, but being seven years her senior, I still felt slightly responsible and apologized for her behavior.

He smiled with his hazel eyes. "It happens." And then he handed me his phone. "It's John. Can you talk to him while I order?"

Before I knew it, the phone was in my hand, and the man turned back to the server where he continued to place his order. I chatted with John for a few minutes, at which point I found out the man whose cell phone I held was named Chris.

As quickly as it started, the rain stopped. Chris thanked me, took back his phone, and resumed his conversation. My friends and I went on our merry way.

"Dar?"

I shook off my thoughts and turned back to Christine. "Sorry. Yes. It was a restaurant, but the second time was definitely a bar."

"Yeah. And you never did get his number."

"That was your fault," I reminded her. We both laughed.

She and I continued to wander through the gardens. We were there to hear live jazz, not chase men. But I couldn't help thinking of that second time I saw him. Christine and I had accepted a ride from the guy she was dating. He took us to the Boardwalk on the north side of town, where nightclubs and bars were lined up along the river. Christine wandered off with her date as I lingered near the bar. I felt a tap on my shoulder and turned to see the man with hazel eyes. It had been three weeks since our Primanti's encounter, and I honestly could not place him. He could tell.

"You don't remember me, do you?"

I bit at my lower lip and shook my head. Nothing.

"Primanti Bros. A couple weeks ago. Your friend smacked me in the head."

"Oh… right."

We laughed and made small talk the best we could, but the people and the noise cut short our conversation.

There was something about him I liked, though. His eyes focused solely on me. He had an air of confidence, but wasn't pushy. His dark hair complemented his tan skin.

"Can I get your number?" he asked after a while.

"How about I take yours?" I countered.

He patted his pockets and chest. No pen. No paper. "I'll be back. Wait here?"

"Sure."

No sooner did Chris slip off into the crowd when Christine grabbed me. "We have to go. Our ride!" she yelled while pointing toward the exit.

"Hold on." I looked in every direction, trying to see over and through the crowd. The man with the dark hair and hazel eyes was nowhere to be found.

"Now!" she demanded again. "Our ride!"

I followed Christine and her date into the night, figuring if it was meant to be it would somehow happen.

Christine and I spent the rest of our day in the gardens unhurried and unworried about the man known as Chris. I never did talk to him that day. And he left without saying a word to me. That day marked seven weeks since I had run into him the first time, but we still had not exchanged last names or phone numbers. That encounter was number three in a city of 300,000 people, and now he was gone… probably forever.

I took that as a sign that we weren't meant to be.

That is, until about two weeks later…

I had returned yet again to Market Square with my co-workers. This particular Friday was special as one of the younger guys in our group was turning twenty-one. I congratulated my friend and offered to buy him a drink. He accepted, and so we headed into the 1902

Tavern. We wound our way through the many people in the entrance, trying to make our way to the bar. And then I saw that man with hazel eyes and dark hair, standing directly in front of me at the bar.

I stopped dead in my tracks. Speechless.

He smiled. "Are you stalking me?"

"Me? Are you sure it's not the other way around?"

To make a long story short, my friend got his birthday drink. As for Chris and me, we left the bar and spent the rest of the evening sitting in the window seat of a local coffee shop chatting the night away. It's been seventeen years now that we've been married, and we have four precious children. As we navigate the ups and downs of marriage, I always remind myself that we were meant to be together. What other explanation could there be for running into the same person four times in three months in a city of 300,000 people?

~Darla S. Grieco

65

Long Odds

Accept the things to which fate binds you, and love the
people with whom fate brings you together,
but do so with all your heart.
~Marcus Aurelius

In the spring of 1989, I was, like almost everyone else in the world, glued to my television set, watching the astonishing events unfolding in a large public square in the heart of Beijing called Tiananmen. I had a personal interest in China, for I was about to embark on a new career as a college teacher in Xinjiang Province. But after June fourth, when Chinese troops moved on Tiananmen Square to disperse the students, killing hundreds possibly thousands of people (we will never know the exact number), my Canadian sponsor phoned to tell me that, due to political uncertainty in China, the contract had been cancelled. Broke and disheartened, I moved into my mother's basement and found work as a costumed interpreter in a museum run by Parks Canada.

But as the saying goes: When one door closes, another opens. As it happened, my supervisor at the museum was on maternity leave, and the supervisor from Bethune Memorial House, another national historic site, had been asked to fill in temporarily. One day, this acting superintendent walked into the lunchroom with a fax in his hand and asked half-jokingly if anyone would like to go to China and teach English. "It seems that the Bethune International Peace Hospital is looking for an English language instructor. Anyone interested?" This fortunate coincidence came about because the Canadian surgeon Dr. Norman Bethune had served with the Communist Eighth Route Army during World War II and had established the first front line mobile army surgical hospital.

So it came to pass that in a few weeks, I found myself in Shijiazhuang, a grimy, industrial city of over a million people located some 280 kilometres south of Beijing, standing in front of a class of doctors and nurses, teaching conversational English.

The China I experienced was not like China today. This was old-style Communist China — perhaps more so because the events in Tiananmen Square had prompted a conservative backlash. Foreigners were only permitted to stay in government-approved accommodations. The hospital, because it had an international connection with Bethune, often had foreign guests, so it had a special hostel within the walled grounds for foreign visitors with its own segregated dining room where we had to eat all of our meals. My movements were very restricted. I was not allowed to visit Chinese homes without permission from the local police bureau. There were no private telephones or private cars. All news sources were vetted by government censors, and this was long before cell phones and the Internet could circumvent such control.

In the room next to mine in the government-approved hostel lived another Canadian named Nancy, who taught English at a nearby medical college. Because of the restrictions on our movements, we ate every meal together in the hostel's dining room and spent all of our free time in each other's company. This might have been a recipe for disaster if we proved incompatible, but we hit it off right away. We felt immediately at ease, as if we'd known each other all our lives.

Before we knew it, our Chinese minders — khaki-clad romantics all — were matchmaking. They set up chaperoned dates, dance parties with our students, and cultural visits to the few local historical sites that had survived the ravages of the Cultural Revolution. Our contracts only overlapped by a month, but I promised to get in touch with Nancy once I returned to Canada. Today, she is my wife of more than twenty years, and we have three lovely children.

Consider this: If the protest in Tiananmen Square had not happened, then my contract in Xinjiang would not have been cancelled. If I had not been working in the museum on that particular day, and if my supervisor had not been on maternity leave, I would never have heard about the job at the Bethune Hospital. And if I'd had the freedom to choose my own accommodation once I arrived in China, I might never have met my future wife. My children would never have been born.

Yet if our freedom is less perfect than we suppose, we are still faced with choices. The students in Tiananmen Square could have chosen complacency, but instead they chose to speak out against entrenched corruption. And given the opportunity, I still had to choose to go to China. It is a decision I will never regret.

~Hugh Kent

66

Hey, Ma, I Called that Girl from the TV!

*I knew the second I met you that there was something
about you I needed. Turns out it wasn't something
about you at all. It was just you.*
~Jamie McGuire, A Beautiful Wedding

O kay, so let me admit up front that the above is a somewhat misleading title. I never really said that to my
mother (and even if I did, I would *never* have used
the expression, "from the TV!"). But it *is* true that the
first time I laid eyes on the woman who would become my wife was
when she appeared on my television set... and it was on my *birthday*
no less!

It was October 18, 1985, and it was indeed my twenty-ninth
birthday. But I was in no mood to celebrate that Friday night after
what had been an exhausting and frustrating week at the brokerage
firm where I worked. I just felt like zoning out in front of the boob
tube and watching my "guilty pleasure" TV series, *Dallas*. Normally,
I'd be checking out *Wall Street Week* on PBS just prior to it, at 8:30,
but after the week I'd had, the last thing I wanted to hear about was
the stock market.

I grabbed the remote and started flipping from channel to channel... until I came upon a friendly, familiar face. It was legendary music
promoter, Sid Bernstein — the guy best known for bringing The Beatles

to America. I had actually met with Sid about eighteen months earlier when I was managing a talented young singer. Apparently, he was now the host of this TV variety show here in New York. I decided to watch.

I seem to recall the first act on the show being a one-armed Chinese accordion player (although my wife, to this day, swears it was mega-hit songwriter Alan Gordon). Then Sid introduced a "bright new musical talent" whom he said he had just met earlier that day — Miss Dana Britten. I remember watching her sing and thinking, *She's kinda cute, and the melody is really catchy. But the lyrics kinda suck. I could definitely help that chick in that area.* After the girl finished singing, Sid spent a few minutes chatting with her.

Sid: "So tell me, Dana, what's going on in your music career these days?"

Dana: "Honestly, not much, Sid. Some stuff is brewing, but who knows if it'll actually work out."

I certainly was not used to hearing that kind of refreshing candor from an aspiring music artist. I liked her. I wrote the young lady's name on a short list I kept of promising young singers/actors/actresses to "keep an eye on."

Well, two months later, Sid had this Dana Britten chick appear on his show again. And then, in early April 1986, she was a guest for the third time. She sang another original song and chatted delightfully with Sid afterward. I remember thinking to myself that night, *Hmm… maybe I'll try and catch her if she's playing around town.*

It was the very next evening that I was in a car riding home from a concert. My date was driving, and we had on WABC radio. The interviewer, Alan Colmes, was talking to singer/songwriter, Rupert Holmes. A young woman caller asked Rupert about some obscure songs he had written for The Partridge Family. In my head, I was thinking, *This girl is as weird as I am with the music trivia stuff!* And her voice, for some reason, sounded strangely familiar. Then, as she was about to hang up, I heard Alan Colmes say, "Hey, thanks for calling, Dana."

And that, my friends, was the moment I absolutely *knew* that I had to call Dana. The synchronicity of the events leading up to this moment was too obvious to ignore. So that Monday, I decided to phone

Sid Bernstein. And he actually took my call.

Me: "Hey, Sid. I don't know if you remember me from our meeting a while back…"

Sid: "Oh, yes, Gary. I do remember you. How can I help you?"

Me: "Sid, I've really enjoyed that Dana Britten you've had on the show a few times."

Sid: "Oh, yes, she's a sweetheart!"

Me: "I'd love to see if she'd be interested in some co-writing. But her phone number is unlisted. Do you happen to have it by any chance?"

Without hesitation, Sid gave me Dana's unlisted home phone number. And that night, I left the following message on her machine: "Hi, Dana. My name's Gary Stein. Sid Bernstein gave me your number. If you want to hear a really interesting story, give me a call at 212-517 — ." Later that evening, Dana did return my call.

"I cannot believe Sid gave out my personal phone number to a complete stranger!" were the first words out of her mouth.

I explained to her why I was calling, filled her in on all the quirky coincidences leading up to that point, and asked if she'd be open to my coming by some afternoon to share some music. Dana was reluctant… to say the least.

"Umm… As long as you don't mind that my husband, four kids and two dogs will be there while we work."

I didn't buy into that "husband and kids" routine one bit. And, frankly, I didn't feel like dealing with somebody so suspicious.

"That's okay, Dana," I said. "Listen, I understand. It's probably best to leave things be. I wish you great success with your career." I hung up with no intention of contacting her again.

But, for whatever reason, Dana called me back.

"I apologize, Gary," she said. "I'm a little nervous about inviting over someone I don't know. But since Sid has met you… How about Saturday afternoon?"

And that Saturday in the spring of 1986, I showed up at Dana's Manhattan apartment… wearing a Zorro mask and dragging a ball and chain on my leg! Sick, I know, but thankfully, Dana opened the door and took my lame attempt at humor in just the right spirit. We spent the rest of the day listening to each other's music and enjoying each other's company. I'll never forget how Dana walked me to the bus stop, and as I was about to leave, she said, "I don't know why, but I have a feeling we're going to do something special together." And when I got home to my apartment and my roomie, Mike Katzke, asked me how things went, I remember my exact reply: "This one could be special, Katzke."

And here we are today... Dana and I will soon celebrate our twenty-fifth wedding anniversary! We've written a ton of songs together in that time. Although several have been recorded by other artists, none have become radio hits. But when two soul mates find each other, as Dana and I did that April day in 1986? Well, somehow they know in their hearts that *their* hit song of all time is already in the process of being written.

Dana never erased that first phone message I left on her answering machine over a quarter-century ago. We still have a copy of that recording as well as the other videotapes of Dana's appearances on that Sid Bernstein show. Sid passed away a couple of years back at age ninety-five. To the rest of the world, he will be best remembered for introducing The Beatles to America. But, in my mind, he will always be the man who introduced my sweetheart to me. And for that, I will be eternally grateful.

~Gary Stein

Chapter 9

The Miracle of Love

---◦◦◦---

When I Knew

---◦◦◦---

67

Meeting Earl

All love stories are tales of beginnings. When we talk about falling in love, we go to the beginning, to pinpoint the moment of freefall.
~Meghan O'Rourke

I was in a lunch meeting with two of my colleagues. The owner of the restaurant, whom I knew well, walked over with a tall, handsome man.

"Excuse me, ladies," Arlene said. She looked at my two female colleagues. "I must ask you to leave." All three of us were taken a little aback. "Not you," Arlene added, glancing at me. She turned to the others. "I have someone here who Jeffree needs to meet."

My two colleagues began snickering as they gathered their purses and stood up.

"Hey, wait a minute," I protested. "Where are you two going? We're not done yet."

"Oh, yes, we are." My boss smiled like the all-knowing Cheshire cat. "You're on your own."

The two women departed, laughing all the way.

Moments later, Arlene launched into matchmaker mode.

"This is Earl. You need meet and get to know one another," she stated matter-of-factly. She pulled out a chair and pointed at it, indicating that Earl should sit. As soon as he did, Arlene left.

We sat there staring at each other. Neither of us knew what to say. Finally, I asked, "What just happened here?"

"Not really sure," Earl said. "I just moved back to town. I'm a commercial broker, and I sold this restaurant to Arlene and her husband. When I lived here before, I met a nice woman that Arlene knows. I called Arlene to let her know that I had moved back and asked for the woman's phone number, but she wouldn't give it to me."

"Why not?" I asked.

"She said there was someone in the restaurant right now that I needed to meet, and I had to get over here right away before she left. Obviously, that was you."

"Unbelievable!" I said, shaking my head. "I've had people want to set me up before, but never like this."

"Yeah, it's a first for me, too." Earl grinned.

After that, we sat in silence. Every few minutes, Arlene would walk behind Earl, wink, and make a thumbs-up motion. I thought it couldn't get any more embarrassing when Arlene walked up and sat down on one of the empty chairs.

"How's it going, you two?"

We glared silently at her.

"What?" She looked at each of us. "Have you exchanged business cards?"

We shook our heads.

"Phone number? Jeffree, have you given Earl your phone number?"

Again, I shook my head.

"Do I have to do everything?" she admonished both of us, as though we were unruly toddlers. "Jeffree, give me one of your cards."

I knew I wasn't going to get out of the restaurant until I cooperated; I handed over a business card. Immediately, she gave it to Earl.

"You call her, Earl," she instructed him as though he didn't know the protocol.

With that, I got up and excused myself, saying I had to get back to work. As soon as I came through the office door, the two women who had abandoned me began laughing. I got back to work and shortly forgot about the whole incident until a couple of days later when Earl called. I barely remembered him until he reminded me of where and how we met.

"Hey, that was pretty embarrassing," he said.

"No kidding," I agreed.

"I was thinking that we should have lunch."

"Um, thanks, but no," I said.

"Why not?" he pressed.

"You're calling because Arlene pressured you into it. I don't need anyone setting me up on dates."

"No, I'm inviting you to lunch because Arlene is a savvy woman," he said. "Obviously, she sees something you and I don't, and she went out of her way to introduce us. What would it hurt to have lunch and see if we can figure out what it is?"

I thought about that for a moment and then decided, *What could it hurt?*

"Just one thing," I said. "I'll have lunch with you, but not at Arlene's restaurant. In fact, pick a place on the opposite end of town."

We met the next day for lunch. At first, it was awkward, but then we began talking, really talking, about everything. Two hours passed before I realized it.

"Look, I'm actually enjoying this, but I do have to get back to work."

He smiled and asked, "Can I see you again?"

I didn't hesitate. "Of course."

A couple of days later, we planned to meet at a promotional event I was staffing in the evening. As soon as he walked in, I rushed up to him.

"Look, I'm really sorry, but I can't see you tonight," I tried to say, as tears welled up in my eyes. "My dog is really sick. She seems to be dying, and the vet isn't sure why. I waited until you got here so you wouldn't think I stood you up. I have to go over to the clinic now. I can't let her die alone."

"Let's go together," he said.

"What?"

"You shouldn't do this alone. I'll go with you." He placed his hand on my elbow and guided me outside.

We arrived at the clinic in minutes. As soon as we walked in, one of the techs led us into a large room and pointed to a metal crate where

I saw Lucy lying on her side. I could hardly breathe; my precious dog was comatose and barely alive.

"Do you want me to take her out of the crate so you can hold her?" the tech asked. I could only nod; I knew if I tried to speak, I would start crying.

I sat cross-legged on the floor, and Earl sat down opposite me. The tech gently lifted Lucy and laid her in my lap. Suddenly, Earl picked her up and lowered her into his lap. He began speaking to her in a low, gentle voice.

"You gotta live," he told her, as he stroked her long, silver coat. "Think of all the living you still have to do. Balls and butterflies to chase. Mailmen to bark at. Bones to eat and bury in the yard. You can't die. You'll break your mama's heart."

At that moment, I fell in love with Earl. He was trying to coax my dog, who he had never met, into living for me. Who does that for someone he barely knows?

We stayed with Lucy for a long time. It became clear that she wasn't going to die as long as we were there. Before we left the clinic, I gave them explicit instructions to call me when Lucy died, no matter what the hour. They promised they would. The next morning, I awoke and realized that the clinic had never called. I phoned them and asked why.

"Your dog is standing up in the crate, wagging her tail and barking for breakfast," the tech said.

I dropped the phone, grabbed my keys and drove like a mad woman to the clinic where I scooped up Lucy in my arms. She showered me with doggie kisses. Then I called Earl and thanked him for saving my dog and giving her a reason to live. We married five months later. That was twenty-six years ago.

~Jeffree Wyn Itrich

68

The Hot Guy

No love, no friendship can cross the path of our destiny
without leaving some mark on it forever.
~François Mauriac

I first saw Jared in my high-school philosophy class. He was the hot guy — aloof, six feet tall, with a surfer swoop of blond-ish hair and sleepy blue eyes. He looked like Tim Robbins circa *The Player* mixed with the dark and brooding air of Judd Nelson in *The Breakfast Club*.

Since this was my third high school in three years, I was used to being semi-invisible. I'd wander the halls in 1980s Molly Ringwald–inspired garb — an oversized men's blazer my mom called the "rabbi coat," paired with a vintage skirt and giant leather belt — trying to navigate the social stratification. Boys hadn't shown an interest in me at my last school, but I'd just hit restart in Boston and felt hopeful about my chances with Jared.

While our philosophy teacher rattled on about Aristotle, I stole glances at my future husband. Slumped in his chair, he stared into space, lost in a teenage reverie. But when the teacher called on him, he always knew the right answer. He was chill, smart, and fine.

I wrote to all my friends that I had found THE ONE. If he would just look in my direction, maybe he'd realize it, too. And yet, no matter how many times I cruised past his locker or searched for his lanky figure in the quad, he remained elusive.

I'd like to say that we had a total *Sixteen Candles*–esque moment at graduation and rode off together on his skateboard, but sadly he didn't even sign my yearbook.

Flash-forward fifteen years. Following a series of heartbreaking entanglements, I ended up on an overstuffed white couch in a therapist's office. I discovered that I was a co-dependent personality, searching for lost souls to save and drawn to broken men. My therapist suggested I try dating a friend, someone whom I could trust.

Then one day, a web designer walked into my L.A. office for a work meeting. He displayed the stereotypical physical attributes of a programmer — out of shape, hair buzzed short, and ashy skin that emanated a slight bouquet of coffee and cigarettes. Yet there was something oddly familiar about his handsome face. It wasn't the hair or tortoise-shell glasses that gave him away; it was that Tim Robbins-ish nose.

"I know you!" I shouted. My heart ticked in my chest.

Under the fluorescent lights, beads of sweat formed on his brow. He looked as if he'd been fingered in a police lineup.

"Jared, right?"

He nodded.

"It's me, Hilary. We went to high school together."

His downcast eyes showed no sign of recognition.

"You don't remember me."

"I do… kind of," he said, slowly backing away before hotfooting it out the door.

I stared, bewildered, at the spot where Jared had been standing and wondered if it was something I'd done — something so awful that this man was still terrified of me fifteen years after high school. That seemed unlikely since he barely knew I existed back then.

Mostly, I was intrigued. The cool, hot guy had morphed into a disheveled dude who couldn't wait to flee the building. How could he not be at least slightly captivated by our serendipitous reunion? I considered some possible explanations. Maybe he was in the Witness Protection Program or wanted for identity theft. But the fact remained that, of all the offices in all the towns of the world, he walked into mine. It had to be fate.

Two months rolled by before he sent an e-mail apologizing for our awkward exchange and invited me to dinner. I wasn't impressed that he had waited so long to get in touch, but he piqued my curiosity. I had to find out what had happened to Jared since graduation.

As we caught up over small plates, it was clear that life's challenges had humbled the hot guy. He'd struggled with depression and been in therapy to get his life on track. While he affectionately stared at me across the table, there was no denying it. He was finally into me. Now I wasn't so sure about him.

We went out again, as friends. And then again. But he always insisted on picking up the tab. His intentions were clear. Every time we got together, our friendship deepened, and my attraction grew. But therapy had made me cautious of jumping into relationships, especially with someone still "working" on himself.

An entire year passed.

On New Year's Eve, we ended up at the same party. Feeling the Sodium Pentothal effect of several Cosmopolitans, I blurted, "I had a crush on you in high school."

Without blinking, he said, "I have a crush on you now."

The din of party laughter and popping champagne corks faded away.

I remember thinking, *If the house caught fire, he'd rescue me.* No man had ever made me feel so safe.

We kissed for the first time. Three years later, we got hitched.

Shortly afterward, we decided to get a dog. A friend sent a photo of a cute Corgi-Beagle mutt named Noodle in need of a forever home. Jared had his heart set on a Benji-type dog. We went to meet Noodle. I adored him. Jared said, "He's not Benji."

I'd become accustomed to dealing with Jared's "warming-up period." Even after buying a new shirt, he'd wait two months to wear it. But Noodle was a serious catch, and he was going to get snapped up if we didn't make up our minds soon.

At the doggie adoption fair, Jared spent most of his time playing with a white Terrier while I watched a middle-aged woman fawn all over Noodle.

It was like being in high school all over again, waiting for Jared to get on board with the preordained plan.

The woman in charge told us that Noodle had other suitors, but we were a better fit. Noodle suffered from separation anxiety and would benefit from having two people around so that he wouldn't be left alone as much.

Eventually, Jared agreed to give Noodle a try.

Life with Noodle hasn't been easy. He has leash aggression. His separation anxiety is extreme, causing him to bark for hours if left on his own. Attempts to work with trainers failed due to our inability to put tough-love principles into practice.

Meanwhile, Jared and Noodle bonded immediately. Noodle seemed to sense a kindred spirit in Jared — a hot guy who traversed a tough road to find a loving home.

When Jared leaves the house, Noodle stares out the window until he comes back. During the day, while Jared works in his office, Noodle camps out on a bed next to his desk. The dog barely looks in my direction unless I'm waving a treat in his face.

I've tried plying him with peanut butter, toys, and belly rubs, but he's just not that into me. Occasionally, I joke that Noodle is an ingrate who doesn't appreciate that I'm the one who lobbied to bring him home. Then again, it did take Jared fifteen years to fall in love with me. Maybe Noodle just needs more time.

That's okay. I'll wait again. I'm a very patient woman.

~Hilary Hattenbach

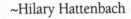

69

Flat-Out Amazing

I am my Beloved's and my Beloved is mine.
~Song of Songs 6:3

I met my husband 1,500 miles away from my hometown because of a flat tire. Twenty-three at the time, I was in an inaugural program to earn a four-year nursing degree in one year. The Accelerated Option was offered by just two schools in the nation—the other being 3,000 miles from home. I was a straight-laced, overly conscientious, somewhat socially awkward introvert. The year before, I had graduated summa cum laude from an Ivy League university with a Bachelor's degree in Psychology. A member of Phi Beta Kappa no less, I could not find a job in my field. I moved back home and spent the next twelve months cashiering at a gift shop and a chain-store pharmacy. My ego was bruised.

To make matters worse, my heart was bruised, too. As a sophomore, I'd met the guy who I thought was the love of my life. When the relationship ended, I was devastated. I stopped dating, eventually putting all my love into my car—an inanimate object that could not break my heart.

In the summer of 1983, I had two six-week sessions in which to complete full-semester equivalents of Anatomy, Physiology, Chemistry, and Microbiology—all with labs—and, oh yeah, an isolated Philosophy class that was also a prerequisite I was missing for the Accelerated Option degree that would officially begin in January. That summer, I allowed myself no life outside of classes and homework. This was no small feat considering that I was living in Miami with a big, beautiful ocean a scant few miles away.

I called my dad every night to say, "I can't do this!" To which he would unfailingly reply, "Yes, you can, honey. You just don't have to make all A's." Given my perfectionist personality, that really was not an option.

A scant few weeks into the start of the actual twelve-month program, I got a flat tire. I pulled into a nearby Goodyear for the repair. Keep in mind that I was still carrying a torch for my ex-boyfriend and still putting all that unrequited love into my car. With that mindset, I couldn't trust my vehicle to just anyone, so I crept into the bay area to make sure the person working on my car actually knew how to remove the offending nail from the tire and restore the radial to its former glory. Unbeknownst to me at the time, the person working on my auto was quite taken with my, uh, derriere, and was apparently quick to comment about it to a colleague as I slunk out of the bay and returned to the customer waiting area.

My car was pulled around, and I paid for the service rendered (just five dollars back then!). My copy of the invoice was lying on the passenger seat with a note penned on it: *The mechanic who fixed your car is Stan. We should get together for dinner sometime.* A phone number followed. Hmm. I hadn't dated in over three years, and I had never been anyone's "pick-up," but I was living alone in an unfamiliar city and supposed a meal out might be nice. I dialed the number. A man answered, and I overheard him ask, "Sweetheart, is Stanley home?" I thought with a smile, *He has parents who love one another.* And so it began.

I learned that Stan was living at home as he had just graduated from college, having delayed starting by serving in the U.S. Army. He was working at Goodyear while pursuing employment with a major airline. Over the course of that year, he was a good friend to me, and I do mean strictly a friend. I never led him to believe I was interested in him romantically, although it was evident to me and those around us that he felt otherwise. He never pressured me for more than the platonic relationship I was willing to share. He went on to be hired by Eastern Air Lines. I graduated (summa cum laude for the second time!) and began work as a registered nurse, choosing to remain in South Florida.

Almost another full year went by. Stan was deeply in love with me; I was still carrying a torch for the man I'd lost nearly five years earlier. Eastern had employee softball teams scattered throughout the country, and every year they met in a major city for a tournament. Stan played on one of these teams and, coincidentally, my ex-boyfriend was now working on his Ph.D. in that very city! I flew there with Stan, ostensibly to watch him play, but also to meet with my former love.

With Stan's full knowledge, I made arrangements to meet with my old flame. We spent the afternoon together on campus, and as time passed, I had a startling realization: I'd been carrying a torch for a man who no longer existed. Either I had changed or he had — or perhaps we both had — but I no longer had romantic feelings for him. I had so long ago placed him on such a lofty pedestal that I felt no one could ever compare to him, but the fantasy didn't match the reality. That was the turning point for me and Stan.

I went back to the hotel where the ball teams were staying, and I met Stan in the lobby. I realized that everything I wanted in a partner existed in the gentle man who had been patiently and faithfully beside me as a friend for almost two years. Less than two months later, we were engaged.

Stan loved me enough to risk my meeting with my former boyfriend. And it was that encounter that made me realize that the man I actually loved and wanted was Stan himself. That was more than thirty years ago, and that fateful invoice from Goodyear still sits on our mantel. I am married to the love of my life, my soul mate, my best friend. And because of a flat tire, my life has been, well, flat-out amazing.

~Sheryl Stone Clay

70

You Should Know Me

The beauty of love is that you can fall into it with the
most unexpected person at the most unexpected time.
~Ritu Ghatourey

Okay, I admit that I'm a notorious eavesdropper. The truth is, I've been one all my life; it's the way I learned about the world, other people and myself. So, there I was at twenty-seven years old, sitting in a café in Mill Valley, California, when I overheard a conversation. At a nearby table sat a tall, thin man talking about *Sesame Street.* By his conversation, I surmised he actually worked on the show. I was impressed. I had just begun my own children's TV show, *Buster and Me,* in Northern California. After listening to the man's private conversation, I marched right up to his table, looked him square in the eye and said simply, "Hi, you should know me." The look on his face was priceless, like I was a crazy person.

And that's how I met Brian Narelle, who would soon be hired to create animated buffers for my show, as well as write and act in several episodes. Brian and I became friends, and I never thought of him as anything else. While Brian was very talkative and expressive, sharing his feelings and stories, I found him overwhelming and annoying at times. Having had dyslexia all my life, I've struggled with various challenges, one of them being communication skills. With certain people and in certain situations, I can feel overwhelmed, stumbling through my words or clamming up and disappearing entirely. That's what I would do with Brian. He was a big presence, and I would shrink to the size of a pea.

Over the years working in the high-pressure world of television, I was forced to deal with my dyslexia head-on, learning to organize my thoughts and articulate my ideas and needs. I learned to deal with problems quickly, and my mental muscles and communication skills were sharpened as a result.

As Brian and I continued to work together on various TV and film projects, I was never very present with him. Instead, I felt impatient and irritated, and my pattern of clamming up and disappearing continued. But I knew Brian was very special. For example, he'd created a series of films using frog puppets called *What Tadoo* to help young children deal with child abuse. Brian played "What," and I played "Tadoo."

As you can imagine, the issue of child abuse is a very sensitive topic to convey to young children, but Brian handled it beautifully. One day, in real life, a four-year-old girl appeared in court before a judge and shared her story. She'd bravely turned in her predator. At one point, the judge leaned over and asked her, "How did you know what to do?" She said, "The frogs told me." Telling that story still makes me cry. That's the power of Brian's work.

In 1997, I was hired to help create a new children's TV show for the Discovery/Learning Channels to be produced in New Zealand. The show would be called *Bingo & Molly*. The show's producers informed me I could only hire one puppeteer from America; the rest of the cast I would hire overseas. Since I knew I would play the lead female character, Molly the rabbit, it was essential I find a great male lead to play her brother Bingo.

In a little log cabin in Mill Valley I auditioned seven of the best male puppeteers in Northern California. As it turned out, Brian was the best by far. Not only was he a brilliant actor and puppeteer, but he was also a uniquely clever and wonderful writer/cartoonist with a genius mind who would be invaluable to the project. Once I realized I had to hire him, it suddenly dawned on me, *Now I'm going to be stuck with Brian Narelle in New Zealand*. The thought freaked me out. I realized we'd be stuck together all the time in the same hotel, in a rented car every morning and evening, and in a TV studio all day long shooting the show for months on end. But the project came first, and I relented. I needed him!

When I arrived in New Zealand, a month before Brian flew over, I auditioned and hired all the puppeteers, helped design the sets, co-wrote some of the songs and worked with Richard Taylor of Weta (who designed the sets, masks and costumes for *The Lord of the Rings*) to create all the wonderful puppets, and then I continued working on all the scripts.

When Brian finally arrived, he irritated me right away. But with such a huge project to complete, there was no time for me to feel overwhelmed around Brian. I had to speak up for myself, and when I finally did, I found Brian to be completely receptive. When I stood up and challenged him, he'd say, "Oh, I never thought of it that way."

Suddenly, I realized a very cool guy was standing before me. I'd never noticed before because I'd never really given him a chance. Still, I only thought of him as a friend and nothing else. Toward the end of our production schedule, with only a month to go before we wrapped up the show, Brian and I found ourselves, on one rare evening off, in a small church in Wellington to hear Taizé chanting.

As I followed Brian down the long narrow aisle looking for an empty seat, I suddenly heard a strong, assertive voice announce in my head, *This is the man you're going to marry.* I was thunderstruck. *No way*, I responded to the voice. *That's ridiculous.* Now, hearing a voice was not new to me. Many times in my life, these strong directives have come through and proven to be miraculously accurate and intuitive, leading me to amazing synchronicities and blessings, and even saving my life a few times.

But this directive came so out of the blue that I was having none of it. "No way," I repeated. "No way." After the concert, I forgot about the voice and focused on getting *Bingo & Molly* in the can. But something had definitely shifted. I now found myself pulled to Brian, touching his back or his arm when I talked to him, wanting to be near him. Whereas before I wanted to get away from him, now I couldn't wait to be in his presence. The shift was profound.

One night in my hotel room, while we were working on a scene, Brian climbed under the counter to help me plug in the phone wire to my computer.

I was surprised that he didn't leave once he'd accomplished his mission. Finally, I asked, "Is there something going on here?"

When he answered, "Yes," I immediately admitted with great relief that the same thing was true for me. After all those years of friendship and working together, we found ourselves deeply in love. For the next few weeks, we tried to hide it from the cast and crew, but it was obvious.

Sometimes, I say to myself with eyes wide open, *I can't believe I'm married to Brian Narelle*, and then I smile and realize how lucky I am. It turned out I couldn't have found a more loving or supportive partner with whom to travel through this life — a sweet and gentle man with a beautiful heart. Believe me, we have our challenges, but we get through them with honest conversation and plenty of laughter. Since the day we were married, we trade "I dos" every morning before we speak another word. That's around 5,840 "I dos" as of this writing.

Now when I share our story, I always remind people that relationships can change and grow. Someone you might never have noticed before, or someone you actually found irritating one minute, could become the love of your life. Life is like that — a wondrous universe full of surprises.

Thank God, I'm a notorious eavesdropper. After all, you never know where you're going to find love!

~Robin Goodrow

71

This Is a Woman in Love

You know when you have found your prince because
you not only have a smile on your face,
but in your heart as well.
~Author Unknown

Getting cheated on sucked. But I recovered, and now I had a clear vision of what I didn't want in a man. I'd still get those waves of anger or sadness flowing through my mind, so I wasn't in the frame of mind to date anyone. But the universe sent him anyway.

We had been friends through a mutual contact. I'd see him in passing or on posts on Facebook. But, that August, everything changed.

I was getting ready to move away from home and start a new life. He was in the military fighting for our country. Our contact was usually limited to seeing how he was handling everything he was going through. I still wasn't ready to date anyone.

I was moving and it was my last night in my old bedroom. My entire life was packed up and ready to transport. I was so nervous I couldn't sleep, so I started looking at Facebook Messenger. I typed a message to him, but then I changed my mind and deleted it. Just as I was shutting down my computer a message came from him: "Hey you."

Four hours later, I felt better. We had chatted and he made me less nervous about my move. It felt like being on a first date. It was the first time in a long time I opened up to someone else.

I went to bed that night with butterflies in my stomach and a serious need for a good night's rest. My sleep was interrupted early in the morning by loud knocking on the front door. There was a giant brown box on the porch.

It was long with a flower logo on the side. He was the first thing to pop into my mind, but it couldn't be. He was in Afghanistan. I was here in New York.

I brought the box inside and set it down on the counter. I wondered what I had gotten myself into. I cut open the box to see it filled with red, long-stemmed roses and a teddy bear. The note read: "From a soldier far, far away."

My heart felt like it was going to burst out of my chest. My face was the same color as the roses, and my knees went weak trying to hold everything together.

My phone rang. I answered without saying a word. On the other line, I heard, "So, do you like them?" He was laughing. "It's the best I can do right now, but I told you I'd treat you like a princess."

That day felt like it was the first day of the rest of my life. It felt like I was living out the real-life version of a Nicholas Sparks book. Was this the true-life version of *Dear John*? And how ironic was it that they had the same name?

A few weeks later, his leave came. During that time, we had kept in close contact. Sparks flew every time we spoke. It was like my heart was permanently ready to explode. When the day of his flight home finally came, I went back to his family's house in New York to meet him.

This was the first time I'd lay eyes on him in months. I had imagined this scene over and over again. How was I going to react? What would be my first thought when I saw him open the front door? Would he pick me up? What if we fell over?

I answered the phone to hear his voice after hours of traveling. "Meet me at my house. I'll be there in an hour." There was no turning back now. I wasn't committed to him, but I was. He wasn't officially my boyfriend, but he was officially the love of my life.

I put on my tight blue dress with stockings and my knee-high boots. I wrapped a scarf around my neck and threw on my winter coat. I was ready. I stared at myself in the mirror with keys in hand. For a moment, I just admired myself. *This is what a woman looks like when she is in love. I hope this look never goes away.*

I raced over there. This was it. This was the first time he would kiss me. The first time we were going to be more than friends. The first time after months of online chatting we would be together in the same place at the same time. We no longer had to look up at the same moon in different countries.

As I approached the steps, my heart beat louder and louder. I thought I was going to keel over and pass out. He rushed out the front door and then he just stopped. He stood there staring at me with eyes of pure love. He wrapped me up in his arms and said, "I'm never letting go. Not now, not ever. You're the girl I'm going to marry."

~Sarahfina El

One Step at a Time

You know you found the right one when you stop
looking for "more."
~Laurel House

I remember the exact moment that I fell in love with my husband, Tom. We were having lunch at a Chili's in suburban Minneapolis. During a brief lull in our conversation, our eyes locked, and we smiled at one another.

Oh, no, I thought, *I'm in trouble.*

I had fallen hopelessly in love with this kind, hard-working, goofy man.

And it dawned on me that I never would have been in that delightful, life-changing moment, or have even met Tom, if I hadn't taken a job at Walmart seven years earlier near my hometown in rural Upper Michigan.

I was nineteen and excited to start my first real job, even though I had been assigned to work in the lawn and garden department — something I knew very little about. On my first day, I was told to work with Shawn, who would show me the ropes.

I liked Shawn right away. He was cute and confident, and he seemed to actually like me. So, when Shawn asked me to see a movie after just a few days, I was thrilled! It was a fine first date, and we made plans to go out again. This time, though, we invited some friends to join us for mini golf. He brought three of his friends, and I brought my best friend, Amie.

I was interested in learning what Amie thought of Shawn. But it turned out that Amie was more interested in getting to know Shawn's friend, Lee.

Over the next several weeks, there were a few other dates with Shawn, but I learned quickly that we didn't have much of a future. Amie and Lee, however, grew closer and began to date seriously.

During the next six years, Amie and I both graduated from college and began to establish our careers. In between working a part-time retail job and a part-time job at a local arts-and-culture magazine, I enjoyed living on my own in a 400-square-foot, ground-level apartment.

Amie put a lot of miles on her car visiting Lee, and I dated a few other people, though nothing lasted longer than a couple of months.

When I was twenty-three, my mom passed away after struggling with health issues for many years. Losing a parent is heartbreaking at any age, and I handled it the best I could. But that was an important time in my life. I was searching for my own identity and path in life. I desperately missed her support, advice and guidance, but I was forced to forge ahead without her.

Shortly after, I began dating a former co-worker who was a little more than twice my age. It was thrilling at the time, but I knew it wasn't the right decision for me. Again, we parted ways after only a few months.

When we were twenty-four, Amie and Lee announced that they were expecting a baby — and that Lee had been offered a good job in the Twin Cities. They were growing up and moving away, and I was feeling increasingly lost.

After Amie and Lee's son was born, I visited them in Minnesota. I picked up a copy of the *Star Tribune* and casually began reading the job listings. I had worked hard to earn a degree in English/Writing, and I was floored to see how many opportunities were available to me in the Minneapolis area.

Returning home from that visit, I couldn't stop thinking about Minnesota. I sought advice from friends, my boss and one of my mentors. They all told me to go. And when my former neighbors and close family friends, who now lived about forty-five minutes southwest of

Minneapolis, offered me a room in their home — for free! — I knew I had to make the move.

At the end of the summer, I packed my parents' old Dodge Intrepid as full as I could and hit the road. I cried for the first fifty miles, not knowing what was ahead. I didn't have a job, and I didn't have a plan. I just knew that I was meant to move to Minnesota.

Once I arrived, I was offered a great opportunity at a small community newspaper. Amie and Lee introduced me to some people, and they let me tag along on fun outings.

I dabbled in online dating and eventually joined a community-service organization, where I made some of the most wonderful friends. It had taken some time to adjust, but I loved the new life I was building for myself.

Amie called me one Saturday night, and I remember her exact words: "We're at a bar that Lee says is not too far from your apartment. And look hot because Tom wants to meet you!"

Amie had mentioned Tom to me briefly before. He was someone who worked with Lee, and Amie liked him a lot. She thought we would be a good match. I held my breath when Amie introduced us.

My first impression was that he had kind eyes and nice hands. He was well dressed, polite and genuinely interested in me. We chatted easily throughout the evening, and I knew that I wanted to see him again. But he was almost too polite when we said goodnight — he did not ask for my phone number.

I knew there was something about him, though, and I didn't want it to end before it had even begun. So when Amie called me the next day to see what I thought of Tom, I asked her to find his phone number for me. Nervously, I made the call, and Tom gladly accepted my offer of a first date.

Our first date led to a second, a third, and a fourth. About a month later, we had that life-changing lunch at Chili's.

Tom and I have built an incredible life together. We got married, adopted a dog, bought a house and, most importantly, welcomed two beautiful children, Noah and Natalee.

The road I traveled to find love was long, winding and a little bumpy, and many pieces had to fall into place to make it possible. But none of it would have happened if I hadn't taken that job at Walmart — where I met Shawn, who introduced me to Lee, who introduced me to Tom.

~Erin Elliott Bryan

73

Something Was Missing

Nothing is so strong as gentleness,
nothing so gentle as real strength.
~St. Francis de Sales

One evening, while dining with girlfriends, I complained to them that the men in our town did not know how to court because there were too many women from which to choose. One of my friends spoke up and said, "I teach school with a man that I would go after if I wasn't married. He says that he wants to settle down."

I replied, "Well, please give him my number." She did better than that. She arranged for us to have a blind date on my birthday. I was excited and happy that I would not spend another birthday alone.

Three days before the big event in October, Fred canceled. I would spend another birthday alone and I was sad. Several months later my phone rang and it was Fred. He explained that he had been dating another woman in October and his conscience wouldn't let him take me out. He scored ten points with me with that confession. My hurt had healed by then, so I decided to give him another chance.

We talked several times on the phone. I really liked his sense of humor and I sure needed some laughs. We decided to meet in the bar at the Red Lobster. I smiled at every man who entered that bar until one of them finally smiled back. It was Fred in his school coach jacket. He was a good-looking man, but the jacket threw me off a bit. I was expecting a sport coat. He suggested that we order a drink. I ordered a Kamikaze. I don't even drink. I guess I was trying to throw him off a bit.

That first date went well, so we decided to have a second, and eventually we became a couple. He continued to make me laugh, and I was happier than I had been in a very long time.

The problem was that I kept feeling as if something was missing in the relationship. I could tell that he was getting more serious than I was, and that bothered me. I told him that I had no intention of getting married again. That didn't seem to faze him. Fred attended the rehearsal dinner when my son got married. My two sisters-in-law kept jabbing each other and saying, "He's the one. We know he is the one."

I asked them how they knew, and they told me that it was the way we looked at each other. I told them they were crazy and we were just good friends.

I was in therapy at the time. I shared with my therapist that I was dating the nicest guy, but he was getting too serious for me. I just couldn't see a future with him because something was missing. I had to end the relationship because I didn't want him to get even more serious and be hurt any more than necessary. The therapist asked, "Did you see him last weekend?"

"Yes."

"Did you have fun?"

"Yes."

"How did you feel about yourself when you were with him?"

I had to think about this for a minute and responded, "Like a million dollars."

"Well," he said, "I suggest that you stop worrying about the future and just enjoy the present. If you have been upfront with him about not getting married, and he sticks around anyway and gets hurt, that is on him and not you."

The therapist and I went over this for several weeks. I even tried to set Fred up with another friend of mine while I wrestled with my decision. Then, Fred asked me to go to his hometown with him to explore the neighborhood in which he grew up. Being a psychotherapist, this was right up my alley.

As the trip progressed, I started to have very mixed feelings. I was enjoying myself immensely and felt completely at ease with this man. He expected nothing of me. All he wanted was the pleasure of my company. If he wanted to swim and I wanted to read, he went swimming alone. I could totally be me, and he was happy. I had never been more comfortable with a man before, and yet I knew I needed to break up with him.

On our way home, we stopped at McDonald's for lunch. As we were eating, Fred noticed that a fly was trying to get out the window. He stopped eating and spent ten minutes trying to get that fly into a cup so he could take it outside. During those ten minutes, I had an epiphany. I knew that if this man would spend ten minutes taking care of a fly, he would surely take care of me.

I also realized what was "missing" in the relationship — mistrust and pain. Throughout my life people had either abandoned me, emotionally abused me, or were very disrespectful while proclaiming love. Somehow, I had equated love with pain, and when there was no pain, I thought something was missing. I didn't know that true love didn't have to hurt.

In those ten minutes, I opened my heart to Fred just an inch. It took a while for me to trust and accept this new kind of love. We married the following year and have been together for twenty-six years. He still loves me unconditionally, lets me be me, and makes me laugh.

Thank you, God, for flies that need to be saved.

~Diane Henderson

74

The Best Offer

I was, and am, swept away. I believe there are some
things in life you can't deny or rationalize,
and this is one of them.
~Cate Blanchett

I watched my mother marry five times, each marriage more miserable than the one before. As a woman in her mid-thirties, I had resigned myself to my self-imposed spinsterhood. My daughter and a fantastic group of friends were all I needed.

But I still needed a date for my friend's wedding. I had responded with an optimistic "plus one" and had never done anything about it. I reluctantly turned to social media for help. "I need a date for a wedding next Saturday." It was an innocuous sentence that made my inner feminist ache. It was also the post that would change my life.

The first response was from my friend Johnny. We'd met through a mutual friend over a decade before and kept in touch online or at the occasional meet-up. "I have no plans for that day if you still need accompaniment," he stated kindly. "Unless you get a better offer…"

"I couldn't think of a better offer than you, mister," I replied. Many other friends agreed to go, but I happily told them it was handled. After all, I hadn't seen Johnny in months, but I vividly remembered how much fun I usually had in his company.

We spent the day together stuck on a boat full of strangers. The only person I even slightly recognized was the woman getting married. To fill the time, Johnny and I sent each other funny texts and played games like telling the other guests that we met on a safari or some other such adventure. We laughed away what would have been a boring day.

After that, we were in regular contact. My heart jumped every time I saw a text from him. When he came to visit me at work, the full-body hug I gave him was entirely real. We teased each other about past relationships and comforted each other when we had tough days.

He was just a friend, I thought. But then why was I listening to those sappy love songs on the radio? My confusion, plus waiting for more texts from him, kept me awake at night.

One night, my car broke down on the way to work. Then, after a frustrating ten-hour shift, I closed up the bar and got ready to face the long walk home at 3:00 in the morning. And there he was, my knight in shining... car. "I was in your area and heard that you needed a ride," he smirked, leaning confidently against the car. That was it. My heart was officially aflutter.

He drove the few miles home, and I asked timidly if he would like to come in. He agreed. We watched silly television shows, and the angst of my day melted away.

"It's a good thing we are just friends," he joked while sitting on my bedroom floor, "because I could *never* date someone whose room is this messy." To him, it was an off-handed jab, but to me it was a stab in the heart. Jovial conversation halted quickly, with him saying his goodbyes and me trying to mask the hurt from that comment. After he left, I spent the next few hours second-guessing myself and those strange feelings I had been having. I decided to close myself off and protect myself from getting hurt.

After a few days of being apart, my heart raced uncontrollably when I saw that my most recent text was from him. Tears welled as I read: "Look, we've been having so much fun not dating. Why don't we try going out on a real date?"

That was it. Within two years of that official date, I was surrounded by hundreds of our closest friends and family — reciting vows to a man who had been just a friend, but became my everything. It was the party of the century, with forty bridesmaids, twenty ushers, and family we hadn't seen in years.

We have since persevered through all the joys and trials that come with marriage. Financial turmoil, raising a teenager (mine) and which way to squeeze the toothpaste — all of it has been handled with the same humor and support that we'd always had for each other. Now we do it as a team.

A few months ago, I became ill. We had both been laid off from our jobs, so there was no health insurance. Assuming it was a common stomach flu, I lay in bed for days trying to let my body heal itself. Walking like a crone to occasionally use the restroom and/or vomit was the only time I left the bedroom.

After three days, I woke up on the bathroom floor to my husband in tears. "Baby, please let me take you to the hospital," he begged. The pleading in his eyes melted my normally stubborn demeanor. I agreed to go, if for no other reason than to prove that it was nothing and take away his worry. Within minutes, I was admitted, due to major problems with my pancreas. The doctor explained sternly that if I had waited another day, my body would have gone septic, which would involve major surgery or, worse, death. Luckily, I am here today to tell the tale.

Sometimes, the thing we aren't looking for is exactly what we need. Love can be found in unexpected places. A few simple words online changed both of us for the better. Now we truly know what it feels like to have a partner and, more importantly, someone to share this thing we call life. It may not be because of him that I am alive today, but it is definitely because of the life we share together that I can look forward to tomorrow.

~Jodi Renee Thomas

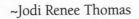

The Miracle of Love

Chapter 10

When I Least Expected It

75

My Second Chance

*Second chances do come your way. Like trains, they
arrive and depart regularly. Recognizing the ones
that matter is the trick.*
~Jill A. Davis

As we waited for our school's staff meeting to begin, I realized the English teacher was eavesdropping as I visited with the other automotive teachers. Then she interrupted us. "That's cool. I think you should do it."

The guys laughed. I was embarrassed, but tried to be polite. "Thanks. But it's impossible."

She smiled. "I'll pray about it."

The woman had no idea what she was talking about, but she was going to pray?

When I got home from work, I went down in the basement. My old 1956 Triumph sat in a corner covered with dust. I shook my head.

The next day, the English teacher stopped me in the hall. "I tell my students to go after their dreams. Maybe you should, too."

I grimaced.

The next night, I rolled my bike into my workshop, sat down, and stared. Restoring antique motorcycles was my passion, but I'd never restored one that was so old, rusty, and abused. But that wasn't the real problem. Since my wife Suzy had died, I just didn't care anymore. I preferred my recliner.

That night, I found myself staring at the old bike and talking to

Suzy in heaven. "Remember how badly I wanted this thing? I didn't fully appreciate what you sacrificed to give me my dream."

A few days later, I ran into the English teacher again.

"How's the motorcycle coming?"

I shook my head and walked away.

That night, I started cleaning the old bike while muttering under my breath. "English teachers understand books, not motorcycles!"

As I began taking apart the old bike, I thought about Suzy. That old Triumph was all we could afford. It needed tons of work. I spent extra hours at my job and used our spare money to buy new engine components to modify the chassis for racing. Suzy helped us economize by using our temperamental old washing machine and hanging up the wet clothes in our damp, smelly basement. Then, one night the motorcycle shop where I worked had a break-in, and my bike was gone. Suzy and I held each other and cried.

Years later, my friend Jim had called. "I bought an old Triumph, and it's been sitting in my garage for years. I'm never going to find time to rebuild it. Want to take a look?"

"Mmmm. Okay. But Suzy just commented that I'll have to live to be over a hundred to finish the projects I already have!"

Nevertheless, I went over to Jim's to look at the bike. Goose bumps popped out on my arms, and a chill ran up my spine. The bike was rusted and had missing parts, but I knew even before I checked the serial number that it was my old race bike. Someone had treated it badly, but I recognized my custom work. I gave Jim his money.

Then came Suzy's cancer diagnosis; I wheeled the bike into a corner and ignored it.

Now I was torn. I stubbornly stayed in my rut. Teaching automotive classes was my fourth career, and I liked it, but the rest of my life was spent in my recliner or with my grown children. When I saw the English teacher, I walked the other way. It would bring back too many memories. I was afraid to pour my heart into repairing that old bike.

Some evenings, I'd sit and stare at the old Triumph. This was the bike that made me a winner — that created my reputation as a mechanic and a racer. But the crazy teacher was wrong. Following one's dreams isn't always a good idea. I didn't need any more hurt.

One night, to my surprise, I found myself talking to God. "This is impossible. This bike needs too many rare parts." I went upstairs and studied eBay and Craigslist. Hours of searching didn't turn up anything.

But I kept searching, and a few weeks later I found an engine seal kit in England. At least the English teacher hadn't been sticking her nose in my business lately. I would have been embarrassed to admit that her big mouth pushed me into action.

A month later, after many computer searches, I found piston rings in California. The project was moving forward—at a snail's pace, but moving.

During Christmas break a year later, the teaching staff asked me to join them for lunch. I didn't realize the lunch was for a widow—an award-winning teacher—whose job was eliminated when her husband was dying of cancer. I found myself talking to her throughout the lunch and for an hour afterward. We had a lot in common. A few months later, the widow put a book on grief in my mailbox. When I read it, I started listening to the music Suzy and I shared—CDs I hadn't touched since her death. I wrote the widow a note thanking her for the book and closed it with the words: "You and I are kindred spirits." As soon as I mailed the note, I wished I could take it back. It was way too forward.

The beginning of May, the widow wrote me a letter telling me about the pain of having an auction to sell her husband's antique tractors—tractors he'd spent years restoring. "I just had a feeling you'd understand."

I did understand. My hands shook as I dialed her number and invited her to dinner. It had been fifty years since I went on a first date, and I was so nervous I only managed to eat a little of the breading off my fish.

My life was changing in ways I never could have imagined. First, I found myself talking to God, and then I made the commitment to rebuild my old bike. Next, I found myself falling in love, and now I was attending church every Sunday. What was going on?

Over the next year, the old Triumph came together slowly. Then, the finishing touch. Early in September, I found the tires I needed at a motorcycle swap meet in Iowa. The end of that month, I married the widow in a large church wedding with two of our children and fourteen of our grandchildren as attendants.

I'll never stop missing my precious Suzy, but I was blessed with a second chance at happiness.

And who is the widow? I'm sure you've guessed. I married the English teacher who prayed I'd rebuild my old bike.

And my 1956 Triumph? It's won trophies and blue ribbons at antique motorcycle shows all over the United States.

~Fred Prudhomme

76

Cloudy with a Chance of Love

Till I loved, I never lived.
~Emily Dickinson

I'm a planner. My weeks are planned down to the minute. I know who I'll be seeing when, and what I'll be eating where. I know when it's going to rain, and what the high will be on Thursday. I have a system, and it works for me. I don't do well with the unexpected.

But the universe doesn't share my need for order and procedure. If life had gone the way I planned, I would have finished my undergrad degree, gone on to get my master's, landed a well-paying, stable job doing something I loved, and spent a good portion of my discretionary income on food and travel. Eventually, when the time was right, a handsome man would have swept me off my feet, and we would have continued our life of adventure and exploration. Then a baby would come, and another. We would build a life together and be happy, well traveled, and well fed.

Luckily, my life took a very different turn and taught me to accept, if not embrace, the unexpected.

After high school, I left everything familiar in my life and moved across the country to pursue my education with no intentions or ambitions of settling down anytime soon. I enjoyed meeting new people and the occasional casual romance. I was never one for long-term relationships, and I tended to lose interest in a suitor quickly.

During a break from school, I flew home to visit family and attend a friend's wedding. Walking around the familiar landscape of home, hearing the sights and sounds of the Deep South, it was hard to believe I had ever left. The wedding took place on a perfect summer night and was illuminated by twinkling lights strung over the pool. I spent the evening catching up with old friends, laughing and reminiscing. Across the way, I recognized someone I knew as a teenager. He was the "cool guy"— the guy all the girls crushed on. A group of girls had even made "fan-club T-shirts" with his name on them.

The years had treated him well, and I was flattered and surprised when we started a conversation. He even remembered my name, although I had been painfully unimpressive in high school.

Determined not to be swept up in his charms and fawn all over him like the other girls, I responded with a lame "No, I need to drive my mom home" excuse when he asked me to go out with him later that evening. Not swayed by my rebuff (obviously used to getting his way), he persisted. "Tomorrow night then." Always the people pleaser, I agreed, but I promised myself I would cancel first thing in the morning when I could come up with a legitimate excuse. I was home to visit family after all, not to spend my time with this cocky, dark-eyed dream.

The next morning, my excuses fell flat. I decided to go through with the date, but was determined not to give the guy the impression I was smitten. Intending to play it cool, I invited my brothers who still lived at home to join me and this guy at an outdoor movie.

Wearing jeans and a T-shirt, with my brothers loaded up in our family Suburban, I drove away from our country home thinking how I'd never made less of an effort on a first date. My lack of effort came from truly believing this date was going to lead nowhere. He had asked me out from boredom. Or curiosity perhaps. This man was beautiful and athletic, and I believed him to be far out of my league. I wasn't a fool. I wasn't going to waste my time on someone unattainable.

My phone buzzed, and I saw it was him calling. Readying myself to answer with the intention of sounding disinterested and aloof, I prepared to tell him, "Oh, by the way, I'm bringing my three brothers along." But as his voice came through the phone, deep and marked with a hint of nerves and excitement, my stomach betrayed me as it began to flip. *Crap,* I thought. *He sounds nervous! Why does he sound nervous?* Horror struck me as I looked at my rowdy brothers in the back seat and checked my reflection with a critical eye. *This date could be for real. Perhaps I should actually make an effort.* My intentions to blow off this guy diminished. And, apparently with it, my voice of reason.

What happened next is the stuff of legends. The story has been told and retold, intensifying and morphing with each retelling. But I'm here to set the record straight.

No, I didn't ditch my brothers on the side of the road. No, I didn't dump them at the nearest gas station. No, I didn't tell them to hitchhike home. What I did do was what any clear-headed, responsible adult would do: I dropped them at a bookstore and called a friend to pick them up.

Then, slightly improved with a quick application of lipstick and a braid in my hair, I arrived to find my date waiting for me, tall and dreamlike. Side by side, we sat on the blanket, talking, laughing, and reminiscing. I was humbled to find this man, with his reputation for being a player, was nothing like what I had expected. What I found was a kind, inquiring, gentle person sitting next to me, interested in everything I had to say. As my giggles got more frequent and my hair flips more abundant, I moved my hand closer to his, tempting him to take it.

But he didn't.

He made me wait.

Maybe he wasn't a player after all.

We soon dated only each other. He finally held my hand and kissed me after what felt like an eternity. He was worth the wait. He was worth my life plan being thwarted. He was worth leaving my brothers on the side of the road… I mean, at the bookstore.

What was meant to be a quick trip home re-routed the course of my life. Everything I had planned and dreamed was re-evaluated. I wasn't finished with school. I hadn't landed that high-paying job.

I hadn't traveled the world and truly found myself yet. I was young, with so much life experience yet to attain.

Despite thirteen years of marriage and three beautiful children, life continues to be unpredictable. Through the ups and downs, health and sickness, joy and pain, we take each day as it comes and embrace the unexpected — because the unexpected is all part of the adventure. That's what I've learned, and although I checked and it's supposed to be partly sunny on Thursday, I accept that may not happen.

~Emily Rusch

Peel an Onion

Cowboys don't go around breaking hearts.
~Missy Lyons

H e leaned in and whispered, "You'll like me when you get to know me better. I wear well." I was speechless. *Get to know him better? Doesn't he know that I'm at the movie as payback for that favor he did for me? Get to know him better? Not in this lifetime, country boy. You are not my type.*

Not my type because he reminded me of my roots, which I had ditched thirty-plus years earlier. No more living in a small town. No more pastoral settings. No more boring weekends. My best girlfriend and I had headed to Columbus, Ohio — a metropolitan area booming with theaters, museums, and better job opportunities — the day after high-school graduation. We never looked back.

The first time I laid eyes on this man — John — he was wearing a white, short-sleeved T-shirt, paint-stained pants and Wolverine work boots. Bland. But it didn't matter; I was not there to see him. I was there to see his wife, Jan, who was housebound from undergoing a series of chemotherapy treatments for a recurrence of ovarian cancer. I was one of several volunteers from my church who made monthly visits to those no longer able to attend.

When I signed up for the program, I was already stretched as tight as a rubber band, yet I believed in it and wanted to serve. Never mind that I was a single parent of a twelve-year old boy and a daughter in college. I was taking classes two nights a week at a nearby college

When I Least Expected It | 291

while working full-time at a demanding job.

The only times John and I connected during the two years I visited Jan were when I arrived at their house and when I left. His greetings were the same: Thanks for coming, and thanks for the visit. A broken record.

My visits with Jan were helpful to her and heartwarming to me. We chatted about our personal lives and her condition. During one of our visits, she asked if I wanted to see her hair, which had fallen out and was now growing back. Before I could respond, she ripped off her scarf and ran her hand over a head full of gray one-inch curls! She beamed.

I was at night school when John called about Jan's death. He left a message with my son. "Tell your mom Jan passed away this afternoon. She was so good to her; I know she would want to know," he said. I attended the viewing. That was in May.

In mid-July, I gave John a call to see if he would assemble the still boxed stove hood that my dad had promised to install but never did. I knew through Jan that John was retired and a handyman. He agreed. I gave him my address, and we set up a time.

By the time the job was finished, I was feeling sorry for the poor guy. He gashed his head twice while maneuvering the hood — even drawing blood — and he had to go home once for tools he had left there.

He seemed distraught after finishing the job, so I offered him a beer. Before he even sat down, he began to reminisce about the good old days when he was in high school and worked for a gentleman farmer who raised and bred Black Angus cattle. He was animated as he talked.

I wanted not only to change the subject but to encourage him to leave, so I piped up, "John, you might want to grab a friend and see the new movie, *City Slickers*. It's about herding cattle on a ranch out west — right up your alley." I headed for the door, hoping he would follow.

He didn't. Instead, he blurted out, "I don't know anybody." Then he added softly, "Would you go with me?" Still feeling sorry for the guy, I agreed. We set a date and time for a month away. I was hoping he would forget by then. He didn't.

We went to see the movie *Mr. Roberts* in August. *Okay, one date,* I told myself. *I don't want to encourage this country boy who is clearly not my type.*

In September, however, I received an invitation to a wedding for November. It was addressed to me "and guest." It was going to be a first-class event, and I wanted to go. I hadn't met any single men at work, night school or the ball fields where my son played baseball. I doubted if "country boy" could even dance, but I asked.

"Yes, I can dance, and yes, I would like to go," he said eagerly, then added, "but I don't have anything appropriate for an occasion as 'dandy' as this. Would you go with me to pick something out?" *Would I? You bet!* I had visions of him dragging out a beige 1970s leisure suit for the occasion.

At the reception, as we hovered over the canapés next to a three-foot ice sculpture in the shape of Cupid, John turned to me and asked, "Wanna dance?" I placed my plate of shrimp tails on a nearby tray and followed him to the dance floor. The navy blazer, taupe slacks, striped shirt and patterned tie we had picked out earlier gave John a "natty" image. Gone was the country boy.

I could smell the Perry Ellis cologne we had picked out together especially for the occasion. The longer the music played, the closer he held me. His palms were sweaty, and I thought I could feel his heart beating. Or… was it mine? Nah!

Six months later, I was admitted to the hospital, a victim of exhaustion. The doctors told me I was overloaded with responsibility. Too much work, too little play. I also needed to learn to set boundaries. The superwoman lifestyle had to go!

On the first Sunday after my hospital stay, I spied John's smiling face and 6'4"-inch frame at the back of the church. He was wearing the same clothes he wore the night of the big wedding. "Will you go to breakfast with me?" he asked sheepishly.

At the restaurant, before I could even pick up the menu, he took my hand in his. "If I contributed in any way to your collapse, I'm sorry. I didn't mean to. I just wanted to be with you," he whispered, and then added, "I would like to help make your life easier. Will you marry me?"

I did not hesitate. Beneath the T-shirt, gabardine work pants, Wolverine boots and country twang stood a man of substance — a loyal, responsible, kind man. He was right when he whispered, "You'll like me when you get to know me better. I wear well." Lucky for me, he was just my type.

~Rosemary Barkes

78

Love Can Be Difficult

The consciousness of loving and being loved brings a
warmth and richness to life that nothing else can bring.
~Oscar Wilde

We both thought we were there to learn German. The Bosch company of Germany paid the way for about twenty German teachers from Virginia and Wisconsin to study at the University of Tübingen for four weeks in the summer of 1987. I hadn't been back to Germany since 1961, when I studied there as a university student. I'd taught German for a couple years, and then stopped to raise my two young daughters. I also taught Special Education for several years. In 1985, a position as a high-school German teacher opened in my district. I discovered that some of my students, who were the children of military parents, knew much more about German culture than I did. It was time to go back.

Sandy and I were two of three students in the program who lived in the old town center of Tübingen. The third one was an older fellow who spent most evenings in the German pubs. The other students lived a little way out of town, and because of limited bus transportation, usually headed right home after classes. So Sandy and I walked home together, usually ate dinner together, and then spent the evening together working on our homework or project. We had paired up to present information about "Freizeit in der kleinen deutschen Universitätsstadt, Tübingen" (Free time in the little German university city of Tübingen).

Because of our topic, there was much that we could do around the town during the evening. We went to movies, visited a different restaurant every evening, went to the pedestrian zone for shopping, and visited playgrounds, swimming pools and even a nearby campground.

After our first week at the seminar, other students started asking if we taught together or knew each other in the States. We explained that we had just met when the seminar started, but I'm sure some of them didn't believe us. We were so comfortable with each other from the very beginning.

During the four weeks, the seminar also provided us with tours of neighboring regions of Germany. We usually sat together on the tour bus and roomed together if we had overnight stays. One of the requirements of the seminar was that we speak German all the time. German teachers don't usually have colleagues in their schools to practice with, the way Spanish teachers often do, so this was an important part of our program. On one trip, when Sandy and I had been chatting well into the night, we finally broke the rule around 2:00 a.m. and spoke English because we were so tired.

I learned that Sandy had lived in Norfolk, Virginia, her whole life. I had grown up and lived in Michigan until I was forty and moved to Virginia for job opportunities. I was surprised that she didn't have much of a southern accent. I've since learned that what many northerners think of as a southern accent is either from the Far South or rural areas. Norfolk was neither.

While we walked around Tübingen and traveled to other towns, we picked up items that would be useful to decorate our classrooms. We packed several boxes of McDonald's tray covers, ads for concerts or products, and ticket stubs from train and bus rides — anything that could show our students what Germany was really like. We took the boxes to the post office one day and had them all sent to Sandy's house. Subconsciously, we were probably thinking that we would then have an excuse to get together again once we got back home. I was then living in Chesterfield County, outside of Richmond, Virginia, about ninety miles away from Norfolk.

During our stay, Sandy was keeping a calendar of our activities, and I had a mini-journal going. After a couple weeks, we both noticed, but didn't mention it to each other, that our events were more about "dinner with Marcia" and "visit to the library with Sandy" than about what we did. The "with whom" was becoming more and more important.

We all had home-stays, living with townsfolk. Both of our guest families soon realized that someone else was often tagging along with their visitor. There was a typewriter in my room, so we often went there to work on writing up parts of our project. Other times, we would spend the evening at Sandy's place, where we would work on getting the slides ready for our presentation.

Soon, our four-week seminar was over. Sandy flew home immediately, and I took a few days to travel to the little country of Liechtenstein by train. I enjoyed the little country, the majestic mountains, the flooding, the rushing Rhine river, and the colorful buildings. But I couldn't get my mind off Sandy and what was going on with my emotions.

I learned later that she was going through the same emotional upheaval. We were married, with children, and our lives were suddenly taking a 180-degree turn. We thought we were the only two women in the world who had ever gone through something like this. This was back in 1987, after all.

Back home, when our package of German-language posters arrived, I drove to Norfolk so we could share our treasures. That was the first of many trips across I-64 between Norfolk and Richmond. We would meet about every six weeks, sometimes in Colonial Williamsburg, which was halfway between us. We also wrote many letters each week — in German, of course — always fearful that we would be found out. Both of our families knew of our friendship, and we had all met each other. But the true fact of our growing love was not mentioned, seldom even by the two of us.

After about eight years, we still hadn't figured out what to do with our relationship. Sandy went into counseling to help her sort out her emotions. After a bit, she divorced her husband of twenty-four years. She just couldn't imagine the celebration of a twenty-five-year marriage. He was an alcoholic, and this made for a good excuse for her children and friends.

I still could not bring myself to ask for a divorce. Eventually, as I approached my fortieth anniversary, I knew that I, too, needed to take that step. I went into therapy for a while, trying to get permission to make that move.

Finally, seventeen years after meeting Sandy, I got up the nerve and admitted to my husband that I was in love with Sandy. It was the hardest decision of my life, but I knew I would never be truly happy until I could live the life and love that I truly felt.

Sandy and I have now lived together for fourteen years and were married in 2015. We went to the courthouse on June 26 of that year when the Supreme Court declared that same-sex marriages were legal.

Our families, friends and church are all supportive of our relationship. Even our ex-husbands have accepted our situation. Recently, at a dinner for my twenty-two-year-old grandson's engagement announcement, I asked him if he had told his fiancée about his grandmas' relationship. He announced proudly, "Sure, I've been bragging on you two all along."

"Bragging" about his lesbian grandmas. What a concept. Our long and difficult road to share our love openly had really turned out well!

~Marcia Slosser

79

What's in a Name?

What's in a name? That which we call a rose by any
other name would smell as sweet…
~William Shakespeare, Romeo and Juliet

Amy was excited. "Give me fifteen minutes. I'm coming over!" I put down the phone. Organising other people's lives was her forte, and having watched me fail miserably at dating for the last two years, she was itching to give me some pointers.

I poured a glass of wine and fired up my ancient laptop. I was ready for what Amy had already pitched to me as "the answer to all your prayers" — online dating.

I had considered this option before, but had never fully committed to it. The romantic in me refused to give up on the notion that "the one" was out there, and we would somehow be drawn together like magnets. Who needs a computer when we have fate? I had previously suggested this idea to Amy, who had laughed and choked on her coffee — always the realist.

I had tried. First, there was Luca — gorgeously tanned and all biceps and muscle. He was certainly a catch. The downside was, he knew it. Then came Gareth, who chipped away almost imperceptibly at my self-confidence, until I was convinced that I was the problem and not him. They were the most toxic in a long line of failed relationships.

When Amy arrived, she could see I was still doubting this whole plan. "You could at least pretend to be pleased to see me," Amy said with an eye roll whilst hanging up her coat.

"You know I am... I'm just... well, you know," I said with a shrug. I hadn't thought of a decent argument as to why I didn't want to try online dating, and I was reluctant to repeat the conversation that had made her spit out her coffee.

"Oh, come on, Carrie. How long are you going to pretend that Prince Charming is just around the corner, waiting to sweep you off your feet?" She wasn't being mean; she just wanted me to be happy.

"Umm..."

"Exactly." She didn't wait for me to finish. Instead, she went over to the table where the laptop was and made herself comfortable.

"Come on, you'll get into it once we've started."

She was right, of course. The wine started to do its job, and having let some of my earlier tension go, I started to get into the idea of "browsing for a man" instead of actually waiting for one. We giggled like schoolgirls as we filled in details and checked out some of those "looking for love." After all, they were like me — just normal people needing a helping hand.

Job done, we shut the laptop and collapsed onto the sofas. I actually felt positive for the first time in a while.

"So, just for laughs, what does your less-than-ideal man look like?" Amy asked casually.

"Someone with no hair, a bit overweight, plays golf and is probably called Alan, or worse, Colin," I said without hesitation. This description was the complete antithesis to every single guy I had dated up to that point.

"Okay, fair enough!" Amy laughed. Two minutes later, she was gone, swept back into the night like my Fairy Godmother.

Two months later... I was trying to leave a nightclub, dodging drunken New Year's revellers and attempting not to fall over. The music pounded, and my feet ached. It was the start of a brand-new year, and I was going home alone.

The dance floor smoke machine coated everyone and everything in a haze. People became odd, misshapen shadows in the mist, but as I stumbled my way along, I heard the unmistakable tones of Amy chatting to another woman. I hadn't seen her since she set me up online, and I really wasn't in the mood to explain to her that it had, so far, been a total disaster. My Fairy Godmother had other ideas, though...

"CARRIE!" she bellowed at me through the smoke.

I painted on a smile and greeted her, steeling myself for an interrogation. She got straight to the point. "Hooked up with Mr. Right yet? I bet you've had loads of admirers!"

"Yeah, loads!" I lied — badly. Good thing it was dark so she couldn't see my blush. The lie continued. "I was just on my way to the bathroom. I'll be back in a bit." I wanted to avoid a conversation with her at all costs.

"See you in a minute then!" she shouted.

In my desperation to get away, I burst through the doors of the nightclub into the cold air at such a pace that my heel got caught on a bit of stray carpet. I found myself grasping at nothing to stay upright before I was finally caught by the nightclub doorman.

"Steady on!" he chuckled.

"Oh, Jesus, I'm soooo sorry. I'm really not actually drunk, although I look it," I flustered. "I'm just in a hurry to go home."

"That bad in there, was it?" he said with another grin.

"Something like that." There was something warm and kind about his eyes.

"Look, are you okay? You seem a little upset," he asked with genuine concern.

"I think so. I'm just fed up and lonely." I sniffed.

"Well, you can hang out here with me if you like. Although I can't promise I won't call on you to help me break up a fight, you can be my wing man. Those high heels will probably come in useful as a weapon."

I laughed — a real laugh with no pretence. We chatted for the rest of the night. Something clicked. It was easy with him — no sleaze, no drama, no corny chat-up lines. He gave me his jacket when I started shivering and shared a burger with me at 1:00 in the morning. I knew it was the start of something special.

I married Colin ten years ago. He's a bit overweight, but I find that way he can envelop me in his arms protective and safe. He plays golf — it's his passion — and I love the way his eyes shine with excitement every time he goes out to play. He's bald, but I love stroking his smooth head. He opened up my heart to everything I thought I didn't want and showed me what deep and everlasting love really felt like.

A couple of months into our relationship, we were chatting over a lazy lunch in a local bar and recounting the moment we met.

"You know, I tried online dating before you decided to fall on me," he said with his customary wit.

"Really?" I said, wide-eyed.

He hesitated. "Actually, I never told you this, but I saw your online profile before I saw you in person. However, I thought I wouldn't like you as I could never see myself with a 'Carrie' who likes romantic fiction and hates golf."

What's in a name? Everything it seems.

~Carrie Roope

80

Taking a Chance on Love

*And think not that you can direct the course of love, for
love, if it finds you worthy, directs your course.*
~Khalil Gibran, The Prophet

L ike most little girls, I dreamt about falling in love with
Prince Charming and living happily ever after. As a teenager, my friends and I would squeal over teen magazines
or boys in our class. We would play games to discover our
true love's initials and draw hearts with our initials entwined. One
day, we vowed, we would find the man of our dreams.

In my twenties, I started to think that love was not in the cards for
me. I was incredibly shy and had no self-confidence or self-esteem. I
couldn't understand why a man could be interested in me. I watched
my friends find love, and it seemed like people were cars rushing past
me on a freeway, with me parked on the shoulder. I would tell the
world that I was waiting for Mr. Right, and I wasn't willing to settle.
I was also afraid of being hurt. I didn't want to take the chance that a
relationship wouldn't work out.

At that time, I worked as an office clerk in the plumbing industry,
which was a very male-dominated field. I took a chance on meeting
one of my customers for drinks, which turned our future telephone
conversations from light and friendly to stiff and awkward. When
my co-workers heard of my disastrous date, they looked at me with

sadness and pity. After that, I vowed that I would never try that again. I would stay on friendly terms with a customer — no mixing business with pleasure. I tried to convince myself that I was content to be single and that I didn't need anyone — until the day my phone rang and my life changed forever.

Fred was always in a hurry. He had a huge account for which he was the sole contact. I had spoken to him numerous times, quoting jobs and helping him obtain the product his customer required. Our conversations were always very professional but friendly.

On this particular day, just as I was about to end the call, he said out of the blue, "Would you go on a date with me?"

I was surprised and a little apprehensive. So I said what most people say when they're trying to avoid answering a question: "Let me think about it."

I was quite proud of myself when I hung up the phone. I had put him off just enough so I didn't hurt his feelings. I was safe.

Fortunately, Fred didn't take the hint. He called me back two minutes later.

"Did you think about it?" he asked. "I really want to go out with you."

I was surprised and intrigued. In all my life, I had never had a man pursue me like this. All my intentions to keep my dealings professional seemed to fly out of my head. The words "go, go, go" seemed to resonate in my brain. My heart was beating double-time, and I heard myself say, "Yes."

"Great!" Fred sounded so enthused. "Would you like to go for dinner and a movie?"

We proceeded to firm up plans, and after I hung up the phone, I was immediately flooded with remorse. I buried my head in my hands and groaned. What had I done? Didn't I remember the bad date with the other client? What was wrong with me?

For days, I fretted over my impulsiveness. I had the phone in my hand countless times, ready with a cancellation speech, but each time I put the phone back in its cradle. I had to get a grip on my fear and dive into the unknown.

Date night seemed to arrive quickly. Before I knew it, I was ringing the bell to Fred's apartment. The door opened, and a very tall, handsome man with dark brown hair and beautiful hazel eyes opened the door.

I was very surprised when a big grin spread across his face. His eyes looked at me admiringly. Could it be that he thought I was attractive?

Fred invited me into his apartment, and I stood at the entryway while he retrieved his jacket. When he walked toward me, he had three roses in his hand.

"I bought you these today, and each of them has a meaning," he explained. He handed them to me one by one. "One is for being so beautiful. One is for agreeing to go out on a date with me, and the third is for our perfect evening together."

We had a lovely dinner together and talked like we knew each other for years. At the end of the evening, he took me in his arms and kissed me goodnight.

"I really want to see you again," he said. "Are you free on Saturday night?"

Since that fateful phone call, Fred and I have been inseparable and very much in love. We just celebrated twenty-five years of wedded bliss. I often wonder what my life would be like today if I hadn't taken that leap of faith so long ago. I thank God every day that I overcame my doubts and fears and took a chance on love.

~Jill Berni

81

Programmed for Life

No one has ever measured, not even poets,
how much love the heart can hold.
~Zelda Fitzgerald

"I won't be able to come home for three weeks. See if you can figure out what this says while I'm gone." With that, my boyfriend handed me a dollar-bill-sized card covered with tiny holes.

A computer programming major in 1969, Talmadge had dropped out of school for a year to earn money for his education expenses. Despite the three-hour drive from an out-of-state job, he made it home most weekends.

A few days before handing me his puzzle, he showed me how the holes on a computer punch card corresponded to letters of the alphabet. Those were the days when computers filled an entire room rather than the palm of a person's hand and they were often operated by stacks of these punched cardboard cards.

Since I had plenty of time, I waited to work on his assignment until the Saturday night before his return. As on most weekends, I left my tiny college dorm room for my parents' home. Sitting on my bed with legs crossed under me and programming card in front of me, I began to decipher his message.

The first few minutes crept along while I reviewed his instructions. Brains may be computers, but mine took its time warming up. Finally, the pieces (or punched-out pieces) began falling into place.

As I figured out which letters were represented by those tiny holes, I jotted them down.

All the letters ran together at first. Then I started to see the words: WILLYOU.

"Oh, my goodness, is this what I think it is?" I kept going, and the message grew clearer.

WILLYOUMARRY.

"Eight letters… Why eight more letters?"

WILLYOUMARRYME.

"Okay, I have that much, but what's the rest?"

Hands shaking, I continued to compare hole punches with letters of the alphabet until I laughed in recognition. My often polite-to-a-fault boyfriend had done it again: WILLYOUMARRYMEPLEASE.

I sat there and smiled for the longest time while I hatched a plot of my own. I would not mention my discovery until he asked about it. Of course, those were also pre-cell-phone days when long-distance calls were expensive, so we did not talk much that week anyway. When we did, I held my tongue.

He picked me up the following Saturday night. Finally alone, he asked, "Did you figure out what the card said?"

"Yes."

"Yes, you figured it out, or yes to what it said?"

"Yes to both."

With that and a kiss to seal the deal, we programmed ourselves for a lifetime together. Computers have improved with time. So have our love for and commitment to one another.

~Diana C. Derringer

82

Just a Dance

Dancing with the feet is one thing, but dancing
with the heart is another.
~Author Unknown

"I'm not going home with you. I don't want to sleep with you. I don't want a relationship. I just want to dance." This was the very unromantic declaration I made the very first time I met the man I would end up marrying sixteen months later.

I was surprised at how blunt I was. Had I taken a moment to think about it, I probably would have come up with something better. At least what I said got right to the heart of the matter. I didn't want a relationship. And I really did just want to dance.

I gave myself points for initiating contact. Coming out of a divorce, the last thing on my mind was getting involved in a romance. I was reluctant to even go out that evening. My friend talked me into it. She and I ended up at a steakhouse that turned into a dance club after dining hours. As we stood together, feeling the beat of the music, my friend was also the one who suggested we should dance.

"Okay, how about those two guys over there?" I asked as I pointed toward two men who were standing alongside the dance floor. Before I had even lowered my finger, I added quickly, "But I want the cute one."

"Which one is the cute one?" my friend asked.

"The tall one. I want the tall one," I explained. Then I made my move. He appeared to agree to my terms, giving me a quick nod and walking me out on the dance floor. Although I thought we saw eye-to-eye on our arrangement, I found myself unable to look at him as we danced. I had to glance away several times, unable to stop the laughter when I saw he was staring back at me with a constant, dopey grin on his face. Months later, he told me he looked at me like that because he felt as if he had been struck by a bolt of lightning. He knew, in that very second, that I was the woman he was going to marry.

Still, it was just a dance. At the end of the night, I stuck to my word. I refused to give him my phone number, but I did agree to take his. And then I went home and lived my life for the next two months—until my girlfriend once again suggested we go out. Even worse, she said I should call the man I danced with last time and ask him to meet us.

"How can I call him? It's been two months! He probably doesn't even remember me! He might be dating someone else by now. I can't just call him up and expect him to be there!"

"Call him," she said.

For some reason, I did. Despite the fact I was nervous and didn't want to get romantically involved, and despite my embarrassment and fear of rejection, I picked up the phone and punched in the number. It went to voicemail, and I managed to stammer out a message. Five minutes later, he returned my call. He sounded excited to hear from me. He met us later that evening. Once again, we danced.

This time, at the end of the night, I agreed to meet him later in the week for dinner. I didn't see any harm. It was a public place. We both needed to eat. Anyway, I was sure it would quickly end once he found out I was divorced and had two young children. I told him at dinner. He didn't mind.

We started seeing each other, and I fell in love with him. My children did, too. He told me that he knew instantly he would marry me, and I laughed. I joked that it must have discouraged him when he didn't hear from me for two months, but he said he still knew. He said he looked for me after we met, even though he didn't have my phone number or know my last name. But he had escorted me to my car that first night and knew the make and model. He went for walks around neighborhoods in the area, hoping to at least find my car. I couldn't believe he would actually do that, especially since it was just a dance.

As we did a foxtrot in front of all the guests at our wedding, I looked at my new husband, amazed that I had found something I didn't know I wanted when I wasn't even searching for it. Our bodies moved to the music. He smiled. I decided maybe his grin wasn't so dopey after all. Then, looking straight into his eyes, I leaned closer and said, "I don't want to dance. I just want to have a relationship."

And I still do.

~Nancy Rose Ostinato

83

Testing Positive for Love

*The highest function of love is that it makes the loved
one a unique and irreplaceable being.*
~Tom Robbins

"I bet you want to go to Hawaii," said a handsome man sitting behind a table covered in travel brochures.

"Well, yeah," I smiled.

Wow, I surely hadn't expected this when I punched the time clock that morning to start my shift. I was just a nurse in need of the hospital's annually required tuberculosis skin test. A co-worker had informed me that I could complete this task in the conference room where an Employee Benefit Fair was being held.

Various vendors were set up at this fair, advertising their services to hospital employees. So I figured I would walk around and check things out... after having my forearm injected with a solution that, within three days, would indicate whether or not I'd been exposed to a deadly disease.

The "Hawaii man" was the first person I encountered, being that he was stationed beside the testing booth. This guy was a travel agent, representing a local travel agency. He was encouraging everyone to sign up for a chance to win a free trip — although it wasn't actually a trip to Hawaii.

Even so, I signed up to have my name entered in the drawing.

After the year I had endured, I would've been happy to win a trip to almost anywhere. I was in desperate need of a vacation! Only eight months prior, I had been "discarded" by my husband, a man I had been in love with since my junior year of high school.

While filling out my contact information for the drawing, "Mr. Hawaii" surprised me by commenting about the cross pendant I was wearing. He then asked me if I'd seen the popular Christian movie that was playing in theaters at the time. And there began a deep, amazing conversation that changed my life forever.

It was obvious that neither of us wanted to part ways, but I had to return to my patients. As I walked away reluctantly, I mentioned casually that my contact information was listed on the sign-up sheet for the free trip, hoping the guy would catch my hint. I knew his name and workplace by now, but being rather old-fashioned, I wasn't going to initiate anything.

I prayed all the way home from work that day, begging God for this man to call me. I called my lifelong best friend, telling her about the serendipitous encounter. "I just think he's the one," I kept saying. "There's just this 'knowing' feeling I have about it."

Two days crawled by at a snail's pace. Was he ever going to call? Should I start talking myself down off this cloud I'd been living on since meeting him? After all, the last thing I needed was to be disappointed and hurt again.

Even though that "knowing" feeling was there, it was time to get real with myself. What were the chances that my destiny involved a man who had shown up out of the clear blue sky? Through a random, fleeting meeting that would've never happened if not for me needing a tuberculosis skin test? For crying out loud! How could I believe in such fairy tales, especially after what had recently transpired in my love life?

No amount of rationalization could keep me from longing to talk with this man again… to feel the way I had felt in his presence for the ten minutes we had talked. Thankfully, I finally got my wish. He called me a couple of nights later.

My heart pounded for the four straight hours we talked. It was if I had known this guy forever. He could even relate to my misadventures in love, having been cheated on and divorced as well.

We were married eight months later in his childhood church in the mountains of North Carolina on a beautiful fall day. It was a simple ceremony with only a handful of close family and friends in attendance, most of whom were not too happy. Since we had dated for such a brief time, our marriage went against the wishes and advice of many of our loved ones. But, being the granddaughter of a couple who eloped in their teens, I believe it was in my blood to be a hopeless romantic… to believe in things such as love at first sight and happily-ever-afters.

Boy, am I grateful that I did! My husband and I celebrated our thirteenth wedding anniversary on November 13, 2017. We weren't even afraid of getting married on an unlucky date, knowing that superstition was no match for God and our love.

Though my life is far from perfect, my story is much like a fairy tale. My husband loves me with all of his heart and treats me like a princess. Even though I didn't win the free trip that particular day, I scored a prize that led to many wonderful adventures. Since then, "Mr. Hawaii" has taken me to Hawaii, and also to Italy, France, the Swiss Alps, Ireland, the Caribbean, Africa, and many other places around the world. Being that my husband is a travel agent, we are fortunate to be able to travel for free or at highly discounted rates.

Never would I have dreamed that a tuberculosis skin test would lead to the greatest blessing of my life, but it did. That's why I believe the test was positive, even though it wasn't positive for disease exposure, thank goodness!

~Mandy Lawrence

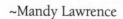

Chapter 11

The Miracle of Love

The Second
Time Around

84

His, Mine, and Ours

*Life is about timing, and timing is everything
in love and loss.*
~Barbara Kymlicka

My husband died in a helicopter accident in 1976 when our children were ages four, three, and one. After a while, I dated occasionally, but nothing serious. I felt I might open my heart to love again, and I knew the type of man I wanted: a family man who would love my children and me, exemplify strong values, and have a good work ethic.

Meanwhile, my brother and his wife had a new house they wouldn't be using for three years while he served in the Army to repay his dental school loan. They offered us the chance to live there while they were away. What a great opportunity to move closer to my family in California!

The children and I drove there from Utah in April. But as we drove past Salt Lake City, I felt an overwhelming sadness, a foreboding feeling that someone, somehow, might be in trouble. Would we have an accident? Was it a family member? I offered additional prayers of protection and comfort for whomever might be in need, and we arrived safely in California.

My parents drove us to see my brother's new house. I had been praying for a sure answer about our potential move, and when I saw the house for the first time, I was surprised by my reaction. We were not supposed to move there.

We drove back to Utah ten days later, and when we arrived home I got a phone call from a friend. "Did you hear about this man whose wife recently died in childbirth?" I had not. On Sunday at church, another friend mentioned, "This man's wife just died. You need to meet him!" Strange that two people had now mentioned the same thing.

I thought to myself, *How am I going to meet him?* Yet my heart whispered, *Perhaps this is why you are not to move to California.*

Late on Monday night, my friend Pauline called to tell me that her employer was this man's neighbor. They had arranged to have him come to her house the next day to interview her about becoming his housekeeper and providing childcare. She told me, "I am not interested in the job, but I am going to bring him over to meet you!" My heart literally skipped a beat, but I agreed to meet him.

Tuesday morning, I answered the doorbell to find an obviously grief-stricken young man. My heart went out to him immediately. In the midst of his extreme grief, he was trying to find a way to provide care during the day for his motherless children.

I invited him in. I listened with great empathy as he shared the tragedy that had befallen his family. His wife was well into labor when it was determined that the baby needed to be delivered by C-section. A healthy baby boy was soon born. His wife joyfully welcomed her newborn son. But due to complications following childbirth, she did not recover.

He explained his need for someone to tend to his five-year-old and the new baby; to be there when the nine-year-old and seven-year-old came home from school; and to do light housework and some meal preparation. He lived fifteen miles north of me. He asked if I was interested. I told him I would think about it and get back to him.

I began an intensive search into my heart and soul. I pondered and prayed. I determined that the timeframe for me to be at his home when his children got out of school would not mesh with my own children's school schedule. I called him to say I was sorry, but I could not take the job. I thanked him for even considering me.

Though he hired another woman for housekeeping and childcare, he soon began calling me in the evenings after his children were in bed. Gradually, a friendship developed based on our common loss of spouses, as well as having children of similar ages.

We dated during the summer. Our older girls bonded over their love of reading. Our sons became natural pals. Our younger daughters enjoyed playing together. Everyone adored the baby. I felt great love and compassion for these seven children, who had each suffered the loss of a parent in their young lives.

We decided to marry. To their credit, all four sets of grandparents supported us in this momentous endeavor. They treated each of our children as their own. With their blessings, we married five months after we met.

After a short honeymoon, we began the daunting task of merging his four children and my three children into a cohesive family. Blending our children — ages nine, eight, seven, six, five, four, and five months — was a labor of love. We embraced old customs from both sides of the family, even as we established new traditions together. I did indeed become their full-time childcare provider and housekeeper!

My heart rejoiced when his older son became the first to call me "Mom." I hoped that the children would feel equally cherished, for I loved them as my own. Years later, his deceased wife came to me in a dream. With tears in her eyes, she embraced me and thanked me for raising her children. I treasure that memory.

In the ninth year of our marriage, our oldest daughter graduated from high school a few weeks before our baby boy was born. Our seven children had an equal claim to their new brother. His, mine, and ours — eight children now spanning the ages from crib to college — are a testament to the divine timing and answered prayers that brought us together.

~Valaree Terribilini Brough

85

Pop

Vitality shows in not only the ability to persist
but the ability to start over.
~F. Scott Fitzgerald

orn to Swedish immigrant parents in 1908, my father-in-law grew up on the ever-changing streets of New York City. The best times we had together were when he'd reminisce about those good old days. Boy, did he have some stories to tell. He knew all about bathtub gin, street fights, sandlot baseball, Legs Diamond and how to make a cheap cigar last for two days. When he'd smoked it down to a tiny stub, he'd poke that stinky thing into his pipe. He never knew when he'd get another one, so he enjoyed every last puff of the one he had.

He was a young, married man during the Great Depression of the 1930s. He and my mother-in-law knew every which way to scrimp and save. These skills helped get them through the lean days. I think it's also the reason why Pop was a thief.

He hated to see good stuff go to waste, especially at work. He never let a can of paint, an extra wrench or a stray coil of copper wire feel neglected. He was more than willing to give them a home. The paint was for the outhouse door, the wrench came in handy for tricky plumbing jobs, and the copper wire? I always suspected he tried to hammer it into pennies.

When I first encountered this "rescue thief" mentality, I was aghast.

"That's stealing," I would righteously proclaim, and get a head shake and half-smile for my efforts. Clearly, he thought I didn't know how the real world worked. His stance was that his employer naturally expected employees to permanently borrow an item or two. How could I be so naïve? Eventually, I quit asking where things came from. Ignorance was bliss and might also keep me off the witness stand.

But Pop was another kind of thief, too — of hearts. This was evident when any upset baby or toddler within his grasp settled down as soon as Pop picked up him or her. He called them "little-ah-ones." He'd throw his head back laughing with them, and if his teeth stayed put, we'd all breathe a sigh of relief.

His charms were not lost on the opposite sex, either. One reason was due to his deeply held conviction that skinny women were always crabby. "They don't get enough to eat!" As a career dieter, this always annoyed me, but it sure endeared him to his plump wife and her friends.

Pop slid into retirement with ease and a few purloined hammers. He and my mother-in-law moved to their summer lakeside home near us. They bought a house trailer and spent winters in Florida. Then came his heart troubles and a triple coronary bypass. A few years later, my mother-in-law became ill and died.

And that's when Pop began to hunt in earnest for a new wife. He actually began bathing. He combed his hair and brushed his teeth. He'd done these things before, but sparingly. He harbored an old-world skepticism about baths and showers. He was certain they opened the pores, letting in disease and infection. But he must have known that most women preferred clean men.

He hit the bars and senior centers. He planted himself at the local Elks Lodge. He acquired a girlfriend. He broke up with her. He didn't have much time. He was well over seventy. Then one day, in late summer, he told me how it happened.

"Hey, get that thing out of my way," he said from his bar stool. Her gigantic handbag kept banging his knee. She was alarmed until she saw him grin. He was interested. She was plump the way he liked them, and she was enjoying her beer. They really hit it off, but there was a problem. She would be leaving in a few days to live with her daughter in Texas.

When Pop told me all this, I just smiled. Big deal. This poor old guy was infatuated with a woman he barely knew and had met at a bar, for crying out loud! What could come of it? Little did I know.

For some reason, he'd given his new crush our home address, hoping maybe she'd write. She did. At least twice a week, a letter arrived in our mailbox for him.

I'd call him right away. "Pop, you have another letter." Almost before I hung up, he was coming up our walkway. He'd grin sheepishly, take the letter, and hang around for coffee. But soon he'd be out the door, hugging that letter. This went on until late October when it started getting cold here in the Northeast. Then Pop announced he fully intended to drive to his home in Florida.

No amount of arguing could convince him otherwise. Pop loaded his car, locked up the lake house and came for lunch. It was time to say goodbye for the winter. We were anxious. What if he had a heart attack or an accident halfway there?

"Call us along the way, okay?" I smiled and worried.

"If I got a dollar bill, I can do anything," he said, shaking that imaginary bill at us. In his Great Depression mind, a dollar was still a big persuader.

The next thing we knew, he was in Texas — a state not on any previous route he'd taken south. When he called, my mouth dropped open.

"That's insane," I blurted.

"Heh, heh," he replied with a mischievous chuckle.

"Pop, what did you do?"

Turns out he'd showed up at the front door of his new love, Marie, and claimed her. Just like that. Wouldn't take "no" for an answer. With many giggles and her own disbelief, she packed up her bags, said goodbye to her daughter and drove off with Pop to Florida.

Two years later, Pop and Marie were married in our living room and were together for eight years, some of the best of his life. The last thing he said on this earth, as he lay dying in his hospital bed with her hand in his, was a whispered, "I love you."

And then the thief, baby charmer and wandering lover was gone. We sure miss that crazy, old man.

~Susan Sundwall

Waltz Partners Forever

To watch us dance is to hear our hearts speak.
~Indian Proverb

January 16, 2016

Before The Terrace roller skating rink, an old Toronto land-mark, was torn down in 1989, I'd been a regular skater for ten years. Like everyone who skated there, I grieved its passing like a dear friend. In fact, I was in a Facebook group that was dedicated to The Terrace.

I had joined a discussion recalling the old waltz songs we loved, and I had posted a link to my favourite: "Les Bicyclettes de Belsize," sung by Engelbert Humperdinck. And I allowed myself a moment to remember waltzing with Bruce. Then, suddenly, there was a post from Bruce! He posted simply, "Waltzing with Janet…"

I took a breath and posted back carefully, "Waltzing with Bruce… I can still feel it…" I heard my own words in my head like a whisper. Moments later, he posted: "Eyes closed, listening to the music… I can feel your warm breath on my neck…"

It felt like I'd been struck by lightning. Gasping, I shoved back my chair and shouted, "WHAT? What is this?" They say lightning never strikes twice in the same place, and yet… it just had. Time seemed to collapse, and the memories washed over me.

February 27, 1979

A girlfriend had convinced me to go roller skating with her, and when I walked through the doors of The Terrace and heard the music, I was glad I'd come. My five-year marriage had recently ended, and I was now on my own. I was twenty-eight.

We were standing in the snack bar when it happened. This guy simply flashed past the door, our eyes met for one split second — and lightning struck.

"What was that?" asked my astonished girlfriend.

"I don't know," I responded lamely.

"Do you know him?" she tried again.

"No, I've never seen him before."

Once on the skating floor, he skated for me the rest of the evening, and I knew it. As he flew around the rink, showing off, I thought he was the most beautiful boy I'd ever seen.

At 11:15, when the DJ announced the last moonlight skate for couples only, the guy finally approached me. "Hi, I'm Bruce. Would you like to skate?" Taking his hand, I replied simply, "It took you long enough."

We fell in love. Fast, hard, completely. He'd been skating since he was a boy — The Terrace was his domain. And he waltzed — beautifully. I began coming to the rink early for lessons at 6:30. Soon enough, he had me waltzing, and it was magical. The lights would go down, and then he and Elvis would sing in my ear… "Wise men say…Only fools rush in…" It was a high like nothing I'd ever known, and people watched us. We were good, and we were crazy in love.

In May, we spent a week in Vancouver. We skated the nine-kilometre path around the seawall in the spring sunshine, dancing along our way when the mood struck us. We drove up the Sunshine Coast to Halfmoon Bay and stayed at Lord Jim's Lodge. It was like a honeymoon, and we were oblivious to the deep issues we both carried that would eventually take us down. I'd never grieved the loss of my marriage, and by Christmas I was sliding back into the black depression that had dogged me for years. The six years between us seemed irrelevant, but at twenty-two Bruce was at a different stage of life and carrying a wagonload of invisible demons.

As the months passed, our passion for each other never wavered, but we both struggled. I finally sought help, which opened a space between us. When it all fell apart in the spring of 1981, my heart shattered so badly I thought I'd never be whole again.

In September, I left for Vancouver to heal. When I came home at Christmas, Bruce was engaged. He married the following year, moved outside Toronto and began his family. I filled my life with new relationships and challenges. And every so often, Bruce would call.

In the early 1990s, he began having brain seizures. The cause was unclear. When he told me he was scheduled for brain surgery, I was horrified. Afterward, both his long- and short-term memories were impaired, and he'd require drugs for the rest of his life. Worst of all, he now experienced seizures that were like psychotic episodes. Despite all this, he remembered who he loved. His family, his children — and he remembered me. From time to time, I'd hear from him. But as the years passed, the calls became fewer and eventually stopped. In 2007, we connected briefly again on Facebook. When my dad died in 2009, we exchanged e-mails, and I learned he'd been living on his own for some time with his two kids. But almost thirty years had passed, and I had moved on.

January 16, 2016

Awash with memories, I was reeling from being struck by lightning. "I often have difficulty remembering what I did before lunch," he wrote, "yet I can remember so clearly skating with you." I posted a link to Elvis singing, *"I can't help falling in love with you."* He posted back, "My favourite song to waltz to…" We carried on a bit longer, each post more intimate, until it felt like we were actually waltzing together — making love on our skates, not caring that we had an audience, just the way we used to. I went to bed in a daze.

In the morning, I still felt dazed and confused. Then my phone rang. As soon as I heard his voice, my heart somersaulted. Thirty-seven years had passed, but within five minutes we'd walked through a new door. That week, we spent hours on the phone trying to fill in the blanks from the lost years, including dealing with what had happened to us. He'd never truly understood it either, and eventually we chalked it up to his illness and some kind of karmic destiny. We forgave ourselves and each other, but with his seizure disorder and the associated disabilities and issues, could we really go forward? With a ninety-minute drive between us and me the only driver?

The following Sunday, I drove to Kitchener where he shares a basement apartment with his son. We spent the day together, going through the box of photos I'd kept that told our story. We held hands like teenagers, and discovered quickly that the love and passion were still very much alive. When I drove home that night under a canopy of winter stars, I felt a vast space open up in my heart and fill with grace, and a totally unfamiliar peace. The first time I brought him to my home, we played song after song that we used to waltz to, and simply held each other in awe — and danced — our hearts so full of love and gratitude we could barely speak.

While we definitely face challenges, true love simply prevails. Today, there's only one roller rink, and it's hard for us to get to. We've skated a few times, and even managed to waltz once! But the highlight was when we shared a family Christmas in my home with his adult daughter and son — an event that filled us both with joy.

The gratitude we share for this miracle of a second chance at love is hard to express. It's a love that somehow exists outside of time and space. We know it will always be with us.

~Janet Matthews

The Promise

Love makes your soul crawl out from its hiding place.
~Zora Neale Hurston

Before my husband Mark died, he shared explicit instructions about how I should go on living without him. His terminal brain tumor diagnosis gave us a short window, but we talked about things like money, work and family obligations. He suggested ways to handle our older son's determination and stubbornness and how to continually stoke the fire of our younger son's dreamy, creative side. We took a deep-dive into our consciousness, and no topics were off-limits.

"Promise me you'll date again," he said. "You need someone to take you out and spoil you. You need some fun in your life. This is the biggest thing I want for you. Please don't close yourself off from love. Promise?"

"I promise," I said half-heartedly. One should tell a dying man whatever he wants to hear.

Finding love again wasn't even a blip on my radar. Watching my husband take his last breath and enduring the horrific grief process that followed left no room for romantic thoughts. He knew this about me. He knew his death would leave a gaping hole in my heart and paralyze me. He knew I would make excuses.

"You're young and attractive," he had said. I was only forty-four. "You have too much to offer, and you shouldn't spend your life alone. Don't stop living while you're still alive."

Two years after his death, the heartache and pain continued to overwhelm me. My anxiety reached an all-time high, and I didn't know how to claw my way out of the grief abyss. The excruciating holidays passed once again, but February — the bleakest of the winter months — suffocated me with its ugly memories. Mark had been diagnosed on Valentine's Day and died one year later on Super Bowl Sunday.

Yet somehow through the brutal winters and never-ending tears, Mark's words echoed: *Promise me you'll date again. You need some fun in your life.*

I joked with my neighbor that she should introduce me to a doctor at the hospital where she worked — preferably an anesthesiologist who logged fewer hours but made good money. We laughed at the thought, but she didn't have a doctor in mind. She already knew someone else she wanted me to meet.

My heart stopped. "I'm just kidding," I said. "I'm not ready to date."

After several days, my neighbor gently brought it up again. She really wanted to introduce me to her husband's co-worker. "He's a good guy. Really sweet. A class act."

I thought about Mark's words. *You need someone to take you out and spoil you.*

Should I just get the first-date-after-the-death over with? I could bow out gracefully if things went south. I mean, I had a valid exit strategy in place, with the debilitating grief and all.

Tom called to introduce himself, and we talked for over an hour. He asked insightful questions about Mark's death and didn't change the subject during the darker moments. He seemed genuinely interested in learning everything about our family. We met for coffee. February didn't seem so bleak after all.

During our second date, I learned we were both born in Flint, Michigan. We are both fire signs. His ex-wife's name is Kim, too. We had so much in common that every other topic we talked about included a "Me, too!" or "I feel the same way!"

We even both love Dachshunds. Our Dachshund died the same year as Mark, but Tom's was just a puppy. That was another weird similarity. My husband was a single man with a Dachshund when I met him. What were the chances I'd meet another single man with a Dachshund?

The coincidences kept piling up. Mark liked vintage signs and old things like pinball machines and jukeboxes. He always talked about buying an antique gas pump, but we never got around to decorating our finished basement the way he wanted. When I spotted the jukebox and vintage signs in Tom's basement, my goose bumps got goose bumps. I almost fainted when I turned around and saw the old gas pump in the corner. What were the chances I'd meet another man who liked old gas pumps?

It occurred to me that meeting Tom was no fluke. It was almost as if Mark, working through my neighbor, put Tom directly in my path and conspired with the universe.

Don't stop living while you're still alive.

Tom is a fantastic human. He is kind, compassionate and thoughtful. He's adorable, funny and genuine. He's also a great kisser. His kisses remind me I am still very much alive, which is something I kind of forgot over the past few years.

Tom asked me one day if I ever felt guilty about dating after Mark's death. I said no, because Mark made it crystal clear that I shouldn't feel guilty about enjoying life. I shared a dream I had with Tom.

I stood in the middle of the road. Mark was on one side, and Tom was on the other. I couldn't understand why the pull to Tom's side of the road was so strong because Mark was still alive in my dream. But I kept inching closer and closer to Tom as if he was a magnet with a force too great to ignore. The more I resisted, the more the magnet pulled me closer. Mark understood my confusion, smiled and nodded to Tom's side. "It's okay. You can go," he said.

I woke up surrounded by a sense of calm I hadn't felt in years.

Please don't close yourself off from love. Promise?

I honestly didn't know if I'd ever find love again. Who was I to think I could have another shot at the kind of relationship that makes the soul sing? But I heeded my dear husband's advice and didn't shut the door on love. When I met Tom, I didn't know what to expect from a divorced father with adult children, and he didn't know what to expect from a widow with young kids. But two fractured souls took a leap of faith.

Tom and I still talk about Mark sometimes. He's never asked me to "get over" my husband's death or to stop talking about my past. He understands it is part of who I am. But our conversations don't dwell on the past as long as they used to. We like to talk more about what our future together looks like. It's so much brighter there.

When people ask Tom and me how we met, we tell them my neighbor introduced us. But I always like to add that we had some divine intervention assisting us, too. We both know we didn't really "find" love.

Love found us.

~Kimberlee Murray

88

A New Normal

*The mark of a real man is a man who can allow
himself to fall deeply in love with a woman.*
~Author Unknown

I never meant to meet someone and fall in love. Not yet, anyway. My husband had moved out just six weeks earlier, and
I was focusing all my love and affection on my two-year-old
son, Henry, and my new pregnancy. It was a bittersweet time,
yet I felt strangely relieved and content. One dream had crashed, but
deep down I knew it was for the best. My husband and I wanted different things in life, and we had grown apart.

For the first time, my husband was coming over to spend time
with our son, so I needed to go out. Feeling displaced and unsettled, I
decided to drive to a Caldor department store I never normally visited
and purchase some fabric to make myself an all-new maternity outfit.
I hadn't sewn in years, but I hoped the work would distract me and
the new outfit would lift my spirits.

The store was nearly empty. But as I found my way to the home-
and-fabric center, I was startled to see the familiar face of my sister-
in-law's brother. Having walked down the aisle on this man's arm at
my brother's and his sister's wedding ten years earlier, and having seen
him at numerous family gatherings since, I felt comfortable calling out
to him as I approached.

"Hey, Chuck," I quipped in a stage-whisper, "I hear we've both
recently had the same crummy experience!"

Surprised, Chuck looked up, caught my drift, and smiled. A month or two before my marriage ended, his long-term relationship had ended as well.

Conversation flowed easily between us. After his break-up, Chuck had moved to an apartment complex in a neighboring city. That particular night, in need of new drapes, he'd visited his local Caldor store, only to find that the drapes he wanted were out of stock. But after a helpful sales clerk called the store in my city and found them available there, Chuck hopped in his truck and drove to a store he never normally visited... and our crazy lives collided.

Before heading home — Chuck with his drapes, and I with my fabric — he invited me to a beach party at his camp the following weekend. My brother, his sister, and their two-year-old twin daughters were coming, he added, so Henry and I should definitely come.

The morning of the party, my son and I rode over to Chuck's camp with my brother's family. I expected Chuck to welcome us, make a few introductions, and then go about visiting his other guests. But to my surprise, he stayed by my side the entire day, even exploring the shoreline with Henry and taking me sailing on his catamaran.

It was a beautiful summer day, and relaxing at the lake was balm for my weary soul. Ever since my break-up, nothing seemed "normal" anymore. Even the most mundane tasks seemed drastically altered. For weeks, I'd been struggling to reclaim a sense of normalcy. But on that day at the lake, surrounded by dozens of people who knew nothing about my situation or me, I felt surprisingly normal and happy again. At day's end, as we piled back into the car, Chuck just stood there beaming at me with the biggest, brightest, sweetest smile ever. And as his warm brown eyes caught mine and held, I felt my heart stumble unexpectedly.

Chuck wasted no time in seeing me again. Some people are slow to think and act, while others just go with their gut. Chuck, I quickly learned, fell into the latter category. Not only was he interested in me, but he was delighted to get to know Henry and thrilled at the thought of another little person on the way. My mother once said that some men are not only ready for a family, but eager to jump in feet first. That

The Second Time Around | 333

was Chuck, one hundred percent. However, when he popped the big question just two weeks later, I went ballistic. *Are you crazy? It's too quick! Lousy timing! I'm married! I'm an emotional and hormonal mess!*

But Chuck, patient man that he is, was undeterred by my rant. And a few days later, when he beamed at me and said, "Wendy, I'm so happy I just want to write your husband a thank-you letter," my heart melted. At that moment, I knew Chuck was a keeper.

For all its joys, my life back then was incredibly stressful and awkward, and I'm sure many people doubted the long-term potential of our "rebound" relationship. But to us, strangely enough, it didn't feel like a rebound. It felt like we were meant to find one another... as if loving hands and a wisdom far greater than our own had directed each of us to an unlikely place where we would cross paths and begin a new life together.

When I told my mother that Chuck wanted to get married as soon as my divorce was finalized, and that he wanted (much to my dismay) a good-sized wedding, she replied sagely, "Well, *you* had the wedding that you wanted the first time around, but this is *Chuck's* first time. Why not let him have the wedding he wants?"

And so it was that I walked down the aisle eight months pregnant and balanced my food plate on my abdomen at the reception my parents hosted for us in their home. It was a lovely, fun and funny day, and Chuck and I are still going strong thirty-five years later. To this day, I remain awed and grateful that God guided us to cross paths that night. From the start, I felt an uncanny sense of certainty and peace in the midst of upheaval. Despite our whirlwind courtship, I trusted that Chuck and I could jump in with both feet and be just fine. As for that all-new maternity outfit I was going to sew to make myself feel better? It never got made. Somehow, after that night at Caldor, I just never found the time.

~Wendy Hobday Haugh

89

Falling in Love Again — Maybe

You didn't date someone to change him. You dated him
because you wanted him for the way he was.
Flaws and fears and all.
~Jean Oram, Whiskey & Gumdrops

I have a date tonight. It's the first date I've had in five years. A friend has arranged a blind date for me and her neighbor. Fred and I haven't met, but we've talked on the phone twice, and he sounds nice. We both lost our mates years ago.

I thought dating was hard when I was sixteen. I had no idea I'd be dating in my sixties, and it would be a hundred times worse. Every insecurity, doubt and anxiety is magnified.

The body I have now is nothing like the body I had when I was young. I have wrinkles, spots, lumps, bumps and stretch marks from bearing four children. I have scars from accidents and surgeries. I wear bifocals, and I'm thirty pounds overweight. If I laugh or sneeze, I have leakage problems.

Fortunately, the men haven't aged any better. They have potbellies; they are bald; they wear bifocals. Many have had surgery for various reasons. Some have pacemakers, and some have erectile dysfunction. Many can't drive after dark because they have poor night vision, so they can only have daytime dates.

We may look like the walking wounded, but we are survivors.

We might be old on the outside, but we are still sixteen on the inside, and still looking for true love. We still get butterflies over the first date, first touch, or first kiss.

I don't pretend to be anything other than the age I am, and I dress the way I feel is appropriate for my age. I don't want to go skydiving or skiing on a date; I might break my hip. I enjoy having a nice dinner and watching television. There's nothing wrong with being "comfortable."

If I invite a date to my house for dinner, I have to make sure I cook something safe: roast beef or chicken, nothing too spicy or with dairy that might cause him problems. I hide all my medication out of sight; my health is not something I want to discuss on a first date. I keep my calendar in my desk so it doesn't advertise my doctor and dentist appointments. I keep my photos of my kids and grandkids in my bedroom. Potential boyfriends don't see my children and grand-children as "cute"; they might see them as potential dependents if we ever get married.

If we fall in love, we have to think about our grown children and how they will react to their parents dating "at their age"! His children might think I'm a gold digger. My children might think he is looking for a nurse or a purse — someone to either take care of him or support him. Grown children worry if their parents remarry later in life because they might lose the inheritance they've been counting on. It could all go to this stranger, this intruder into their family circle. Most of us don't have much, but our children expect to inherit whatever there is.

We haven't lived this long without getting hurt, having our hearts broken, losing loved ones, and facing disasters, even death. Maybe these things make us softer, more patient, kind and gentle. We no longer expect people to be perfect.

So we keep trying. We keep looking for love in our sixties and seventies with the same hope and excitement we had when we had a date for the senior prom over fifty years ago.

I go outside and then come back inside as if I were a stranger. Does my house smell nice, or does it have the "old people" smell of BENGAY, bath powder and disinfectants? Everything is clean and uncluttered. It is welcoming and comfortable. The lights are low, but not so low he'll trip over the furniture. I wear a nice outfit, not too dressy, not too casual. I want him to feel I've dressed up for him and made an effort. I put out three different DVDs so we can watch a western, a mystery, or a comedy after dinner — his choice.

Yes, I've prepared my house, cooked dinner, and dressed up. I'm ready. This could be a pleasant evening with a new friend, or it could be the first date with the great love of my life.

I look at the clock, and it is 7:00 sharp. He should be here. I peek out my window and see a man pacing back and forth on the sidewalk. He opens a roll of breath mints and puts one in his mouth. He sucks in his stomach and holds his breath for just a few seconds, and then shrugs and lets out his breath. His stomach goes back to normal. He's carrying a bouquet of mixed flowers wrapped in the same purple tissue paper as the flowers sold at the convenience store on the corner. He's picking at the price tag on the paper and finally tears it off. He's nervous, and I find it endearing. He finally gathers his courage and starts up the sidewalk.

There's a knock on the door, and I open it. Fred is short and bald. He wears bifocals, has a potbelly, and is wearing khaki pants and a red plaid flannel shirt. He has a wonderful smile.

He's perfect.

~Kate White

Man on a Mission

*The heart is a thousand-stringed instrument that can
only be tuned with love.*
~Hafez

My husband and I were on a bus trip in Switzerland, high up in the Alps. About thirty people were on the bus, and we had gotten to know all of them over the past few days. One older couple, George and Mable, particularly caught my attention. She was short and petite, and he was tall and slightly bent over. They were always holding hands, and they seemed delighted to be together. It made me feel good to be around them.

I was a few decades younger than Mable, yet this cute, old, and in-love couple intrigued me. I wondered if they had been married for a long time. Mable confided that they were practically newlyweds, but had first met more than fifty-five years ago.

One hot summer afternoon, a few years earlier, Mable's phone rang, waking her from a nap. Her husband had passed away two years earlier, and she lived alone in the same house they had been in together for many years. Reaching for the phone that day, Mable had no idea that the call was going to change the rest of her life. The receptionist from her church was on the phone. They were good friends and talked frequently. Mable played the piano and organ, and provided music for their church.

The receptionist explained that a man named George had called from Pennsylvania, looking for someone named Mable who played the piano. He was calling all of the churches in the area, trying to find a girl he had met a long time ago. He didn't remember her maiden name and he didn't know her married name. George wasn't having any luck, and there were only a few churches left on his list.

Of course, Mable remembered George. He was her first love. They met during World War II, at a USO dance hall near the Air Force base where George was stationed. He was training to be a pilot and would soon be deployed to Europe to join the Allied forces.

George first spotted Mable sitting up on a small stage, playing the piano. She had recently graduated from high school, and music was her passion. Mable frequently volunteered to play the piano at the USO to entertain the troops, and she also played for her church on Sundays. She had been accepted to The Juilliard School in New York City and would be attending the school once the war ended.

George and Mable started dating, and her family quickly learned that George was a big practical joker. On several occasions, when Mable's family was at home together, the doors and windows would suddenly start rattling after dinner. George was out on a nighttime training mission and would intentionally buzz their house before flying back to base. Mable enjoyed the attention, but her father got upset every time George did it.

The war ended before George could be deployed, and he was scheduled to be discharged from the Air Force. Mable knew what was coming. George was going to "pop the question." She was afraid of the outcome because, either way, there was a lot to lose.

George, indeed, asked Mable to marry him. She wasn't sure what to do. She loved George and didn't want him to leave. Her father, though, didn't approve of George, and didn't think he had much potential. More importantly, there was Mable's love and passion for music. Her dream was to go to Julliard. After much deliberation, Mable decided to follow her dream. George went back home to his family, and Mable never expected to hear from him again.

Now Mable decided to call George back. Many conversations took place over the next several weeks as they tried to catch up on

The Second Time Around |

all of the things that had happened to them. Mable and George were getting along well on the phone. Unexpectedly, George asked if he could come for a visit.

The big day finally arrived. George was staying at a local hotel and was invited to Mable's house for dinner. Mable was both excited and nervous. She felt like a young schoolgirl all over again. Mable's children were at her house to meet George and had prepared a special dinner for the two of them. Her children served dinner in the dining room and quietly left the house so the two wartime friends might become better reacquainted.

George's visit went well that week. George suggested that he and Mable go on a cruise so they could spend some time together, without any friends or family, to see how they got along. The trip was wonderful, and they had a marvelous time.

Once again, George asked Mable to marry him. This time, she said, "Yes!" They decided to live part-time in each of their homes, to be near both families and sets of friends. Her one condition of marriage was that he buy her a piano for his home in Pennsylvania and designate a room as her music room.

~Barbara Dorman Bower

91

Desperately Seeking Soul Mate

When you realize you want to spend the rest of your
life with somebody, you want the rest of your life to
start as soon as possible.
~Nora Ephron

I had recently turned forty-eight and seriously contemplated placing a personal ad in *New York* magazine: "Fat, Forty, with Fibroids." I needed a little humor to keep me going. For the past sixteen years, I'd raised my son on my own, with summers off when my ex flew him cross-country. I'd had almost no dates the last six years. Men tended to drift away on the dance floor once I mentioned I was a single parent. I pretty much despaired of meeting a man, let alone a soul mate.

Occasionally, acquaintances would inquire, "Do you want to marry again?"

I'd respond, "I'd like to be in love...."

To make matters worse, my parents decamped permanently to Florida; my younger brother moved his family to the Boston area for a job; and my other brother lived in the Denver area. Recently, I teared up in a doctor's waiting room when asked to fill in an emergency contact person because I had no one to write down.

My son Alex called from college one Sunday night, hemming and hawing. "What is it you want to tell me?" I asked. A mother always senses trouble.

He took a deep breath. "Mom, this man is going to call you. His name is Shelly. He works for the city. He lives in Flushing."

My first thought: three strikes against him! It had taken me a lifetime to move away from Queens. But I listened as Alex explained he had asked a woman friend, a fellow artist, "Do you know anyone for my mother?"

She had screamed out, "Shelly!" She had this guy for me, the father of her best friend, going through a divorce, who also loved books, movies and music.

"So sweet of you both," I said, while thinking, *He'll never call.*

The next night, Shelly did call, and we talked on and on. He confessed later he was fist-pumping the whole time. I marveled at how normal and sane he sounded, a welcome change from the unsuitable men I usually met on my own — especially the ones who asked how I looked in a bathing suit or suggested we split the bill for coffee and a shared slice of pound cake.

Shelly and I arranged to meet the following Sunday at the Jewish Museum in Manhattan — an open, public place in case he turned out to be a maniac in spite of all evidence to the contrary. He called me several times during the week until I asked him to stop. I was getting too nervous. I told a friend, "He's going to have to look like Quasimodo for this not to work out."

On the corner of Fifth Avenue and 92nd Street, Shelly stood waiting for me. He was a good-looking fifty-three-year-old with a wild mop of charcoal grey hair, a trim body, and a welcoming smile. Immediately, he thrust a copy of *The Poetry & Short Stories of Dorothy Parker* into my hands. A gift! He pulled out pictures of his two daughters and went so far as to call his older daughter. He was psyched to let her know all was going well, and he put me on the line with her. Okay, a little awkward.

We ran up and down the stairs of the museum, visiting each display, and I was satisfied that he was viable and fit enough. We decamped to an expensive neighborhood Italian restaurant for a late lunch. Midway through the meal, Shelly shocked me with a proposal: "Why don't we go out again?" He was locking in a second date, and I hadn't had time to process this first one. Didn't he know he was supposed to wait, keep me guessing, and then call on Wednesday? But I agreed, deciding not to tell him how to play the dating game.

Eight months later, we were planning our guest list, only to panic when my parents announced they were getting divorced after fifty-two years of marriage. I felt confused, disoriented, and unsure. We put the wedding on hold. He moved in with me as I tried to figure out what I wanted. I teased him, "I know I like jewelry." I was set on getting an engagement ring, which I hadn't had the first time around. "And it would be nice to be married by a rabbi this time." Finally, when his younger daughter was bouncing around from college to college, trying to find her place, I suggested, "Let's get legally married before the start of a new semester. I'll be able to get children's scholarship money from my employer." So we corralled the kids to be our witnesses and got married by a judge in the White Plains courthouse.

Seven months later, we followed up with a small, wonderful wedding for our fifty-eight guests — the classiest wedding the caterer said he'd ever seen. I wore an antique lace gown and he looked simply dashing. We presented matchmaker awards to Alex and his friend, danced to 60s music, and videotaped our guests as they expressed their love and best wishes. We've watched that video many times over the years.

Twenty years have passed. So fast! As a couple, we've weathered health challenges, two moves, the deaths of three of our parents, and the "launching" of our kids. We've adopted several adorable kittens. Together, we've shared countless movies and books, delicious meals, and gatherings with friends and family. Every year, we travel to store up memories for the days when we'll be less mobile.

Shelly works two days a week in the local nursing home; I am fully retired and living the dream of writing full-time. We're adjusting to the changes that time brings and working hard at keeping active. We hike in the beautiful preserves of the Hudson Valley, work out at the gym a little less often than we should, and walk the Yorktown track.

Knowing the importance of a network, we cultivate friends at our writing, book club and acting groups. We get together with them to

The Second Time Around |

explore interesting upstate towns, and attend concerts, book readings, and craft fairs.

Is everything perfect? Pretty much. I feel blessed. Instead of an isolated and lonely middle age, I am one side of a loving partnership in which we share everything. People remark on how unusual it is that we both like the same things (with the exception of sports). My son adores Shelly; his daughters barely tolerate me. But his granddaughter and grandson, both Millennials, love me.

What more could I ask?

Finding my soul mate, that's enough for me.

~Janet Garber

The Miracle *of* Love

Keeping the Love Alive

92

No Compromise Date Nights

If you want to discover the true character of a person,
you have only to observe what they are
passionate about.
~Shannon L. Alder

"asketball? Really?" I asked my new boyfriend. "I told you the sound of squeaky sneakers on the court kills me," I added, emphasizing my disbelief that I was actually at a professional basketball game for the first time in my life.

"You can't complain; it's Wednesday," John reminded me. "There's no complaining on Wednesday date nights. In fact, you're supposed to pretend to have fun, even if you're not," he added, rubbing it in my face that I was the one who had created the rules in the first place. I had no choice but to close my mouth, sit back, and pretend to enjoy the game, squeaky sneakers and all.

When the final buzzer blew, John turned to me and asked, "Well? What did you think?"

"I actually had fun," I admitted. The rules had worked their magic. Not being able to complain, and having to pretend to have fun, had changed my mindset. I had actually enjoyed the basketball game, along with all the sounds and hoopla that went along with it!

I shouldn't have been surprised. John and I had been dating for three months. Each date thus far had been fantastic, especially the ones on Wednesday nights. When we were together on the other days of the week, we did the usual compromising thing that is essential to any healthy relationship. But Wednesday nights were different. They were "No Compromise Date Nights."

I had come up with the idea after our first date. I felt such a connection with John that I really wanted things to work out. But having spent years dating, with no long-term success, I knew I had to approach this relationship differently. I began to look closely at my past dating style. In doing so, I realized my biggest mistake was that I overcompensated.

Knowing that compromise was so important in a relationship, I would take it too far. I would defer to the other person's interests, sacrificing myself in the process. Each and every time, a day would come when I would wake up and not even recognize myself. I'd have completely lost myself in the relationship, becoming the person my then boyfriend wanted me to be. That was the day alarm bells would go off in my head, and I'd end it.

Having analyzed things backwards and forwards, I decided that in order to stay the person I really was at heart, I needed to be seen for who I really was. I needed my wants and interests to be known completely, without compromising them or watering them down. No Compromise Date Night was my solution.

My brainstorm went like this: Each Wednesday, the planner of the date would alternate. Rule #1 was: There was no consulting the other, and no compromising at all! In fact, we kept the plan a secret; the other didn't find out what the evening had in store until it unfolded.

Having a hunch that we were similar people at heart, yet having very different interests on the surface, I knew instinctively that each of us was going to plan events the other didn't like. Wanting John to appreciate what I planned meant I had to appreciate what he planned. So Rule #2 was: The other person couldn't complain. In fact, we had to pretend to be enjoying ourselves, even if we weren't. I knew the relationship had real potential when John agreed to my rules. So began our magical courtship.

Sometimes, we planned date nights all about ourselves, so the other person could see who we really were. If people had asked John if he would ever go salsa dancing, attend a performance by a mime, or walk a labyrinth on a moonlit night, he would have told them they were crazy. That is, until he did all those things and more on No Compromise Date Nights!

If someone had asked me if I would go to a Celtics game, mountain-bike through the woods, or hit golf balls at a driving range, I would have said no way. But lo and behold, we both participated fully in the other's interests, and our horizons expanded.

Other times, we planned date nights all about the other person, to show how much we cared. John put aside his own biases and took me to the Boston Pops and the Van Gogh exhibit at the Museum of Fine Arts. After I had mentioned I loved drive-in movies as a kid, he found one two hours away, and off we went.

For my part, I took John to an outdoor reggae concert and invested the dreaded physical energy it took to go cross-country skiing. Knowing he'd been obsessed with Bugs Bunny since childhood, I found a Bugs Bunny Film Festival in Boston and took him. I can't tell you how great it was watching the joy on his face as vintage Bugs Bunny cartoons played on the big screen.

The list went on and on, and the dates got more and more creative as time went on. It wasn't that we became competitive, trying to outdo the other; it's that we found we really enjoyed thinking outside the box.

Even when we did traditional date-night things, we'd get silly to make them more fun. When we went bowling, we had to wear nametags that said "Henry" and "Dolores." When we went out to an Irish Bar on St. Patrick's Day, we brought green food coloring to dye the beer green. When we went to the Planetarium, I had snuck into his apartment that day and placed glow-in-the-dark stars on his ceiling to continue the theme when we got home.

The time, effort, and love we invested in our dating life led to his proposal. I accepted, and here we are eighteen years later. We are happily married with three beautiful children. Although raising kids doesn't leave a lot of time for date nights, we're finding that, as parents, we're still following the No Compromise rules. The circumstances have just changed a bit.

For Rule #1, rather than spending time further discovering each other's interests, we're discovering our kids' interests instead. For Rule #2, when we attend the slew of events and activities for our kids, we can't complain, and we have to pretend to enjoy them.

It's such a gift to find that the rules still work their magic. It's in the pretending that our minds are opened, and we come to value and enjoy what matters to our kids. Consequently, the T-ball game doesn't seem so excruciatingly long; the whiny voices from the *Pokémon* movie don't grate like we know they should; and time spent building the millionth LEGO structure with them is still enjoyable.

Whether it's in friendship, dating, or raising children, when we're interested in someone, we should be intrigued by what interests them. When we love someone, we should try to experience what matters to them in hopes that it will matter to us as well.

~Claire McGarry

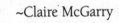

93

A Lifetime of Making the Bed

The greatest marriages are built on teamwork.
A mutual respect, a healthy dose of admiration,
and a never-ending portion of love and grace.
~Fawn Weaver

The bed, he insisted, must be made every day. Well, we were newly married and it was during the conformist 1950s, so I played along. I figured he took after his dutiful mother, rather than his slapdash father. Me, I took after my parents, who had the maid make the bed. But, of course, he and I had no maid. We were young and poor, and we made the bed in our third-floor walkup apartment early in the morning on weekdays before we went to work and later in the day on weekends.

Our habit of faithful bed making continued through the birth of three children and several moves in Connecticut. My mother reported that even when I was in the hospital having a baby (which I did three times in three years), Charlie made up our double sleigh bed without fail. Fortunately, he didn't check on the children's cots and cribs, which were often awash with blankets and toys.

Finally we made the "Big Move" and arrived in California. When we were asked to neighborhood dinner parties, I'd sneak down the hall for a quick peek at the hosts' bedroom. Most Californians, I discovered, just pulled a comforter or duvet over their messy bed and called it done.

Not us. We brought our more exacting Eastern habits with us when we moved west. We always had a proper bedspread, which we folded neatly over the pillows. It was easy with two of us working together.

Once, when we were having a cranky patch, I refused to be part of what I called "this ridiculous bed making fetish." Without snapping back or saying anything at all, my husband did the job alone until shame made me resume position on my side of the bed.

After we observed our fiftieth wedding anniversary, it occurred to me that the way we made our bed was like a metaphor of our marriage. Our style had always been the two of us working as a team. Charlie painted walls, created lush vegetable gardens, built bookcases and fixed everything that broke inside the house and out. I provided meals and most of the childcare, which wasn't easy with three children who loved to make things complicated. I also did the cleaning and shopping and made our social plans. This system worked well for us for many a year.

Of course, in due time the children grew up and moved out. Our gardening and shopping dwindled, and our meals became very simple. Still, we stood on both sides of our California King mattress every morning, neatly folding the top of the sheet over the blanket and pulling up the fitted bedspread to go over the pillows. Whenever I wanted to give up our daily routine out of sheer sloth and laziness, Charlie prodded me into stiffening my spine and helping him make the bed. It seemed important to his peace of mind.

But as he hit his mid-eighties, his legs began giving him trouble. The left one was losing feeling, and his balance suffered. He went from using a cane and a walker downstairs to needing a walker upstairs as well. Still, he'd gamely stand on his side of the bed every morning ready to do his part. I marveled at his determination.

Alas, the weakness in his legs finally conquered his urge to help. Now I make the bed alone. At night, I go upstairs before he does so I can turn down the bed and do a few other chores that help him get a good night's sleep. One evening, it dawned on me that by the time he arrives in the bedroom, the spread is already off, and the sheet and blankets are open to allow him to slide in without difficulty. It also occurred to me that since he rarely sees the bed in its made-up state, it would be easy for me to skip this chore. When I do it alone, I have to move from one side of the big bed to the other to pull up the sheets and blanket. Then I have to scoot around to the other side to pull up the spread. And back and forth, back and forth.

We've passed our sixtieth anniversary now, and everything has slowed down. Walking is really a challenge for Charlie these days, and I'm no Speedy Gonzales myself. We've signed up for a service that sends the ingredients for three meals a week and includes the preparation and cooking directions. Only one of us is driving. We've removed most of the small rugs from our house. We've bought a wheelchair. There are a number of changes in our lifestyle. But the bed, I've decided, will continue to be made every morning as long as I'm able to do it.

~Jean Adair Shriver

94

Like We Did

A successful marriage requires falling in love many
times, always with the same person.
~Mignon McLaughlin

W hen I first met Paul, he was as ambivalent about finding love as I was. Divorced for several years and just emerging from a difficult break-up, he was ready to give up on love. He just wanted to spend time with a puppy and be done with all things romantic.

On the other hand, I had been single for two lonely years after a series of failed, long-term relationships. I was spending my quality time with several pairs of comfortable stretch pants and obscene quantities of milk chocolate. I didn't think I would ever find my soul mate.

Luckily, we were both very wrong. On our first date, the hours we spent talking and laughing like dear old friends flew by as if they were mere minutes. After that first date, there were many walks on the beach, candlelit dinners, and heart-shaped everything—we had fallen in love. Two years ago, we decided to tie the matrimonial knot!

Recently, Paul and I got our annual blood work done based on our doctor's recommendations, since we're both around fifty years old. When we received our results, I was surprised to see that our cholesterol and A1C levels were the same! Initially, I thought this was just a cool coincidence. However, truth be told, there was a sentimental moment when I wondered if the phlebotomy gods, in all their infinite wisdom, were trying to tell us that we were meant for each other.

As I was thinking out loud about whether our highly synchronized blood work results were telling us that we were destined to be together, Paul said, "Yeah, we're physically deteriorating at the exact same rate." Then he went back to staring at the television, transfixed by his baseball game.

I looked over at him as he lay on the couch, with our half-eaten takeout food still scattered on the coffee table, strategically placed in front of the TV. This supper scene was our new norm. I realized that it had been a while since we shared a candlelit dinner.

Maybe I was expecting too much. Perhaps I wasn't assessing our relationship in a realistic way.

A few days later, Paul woke me with a tender kiss. I couldn't think of a more wonderful way to start my morning. And it ended as a fantastic day, filled with some small professional victories — but victories, nonetheless. Being my biggest supporter, Paul enthusiastically insisted that we celebrate those victories over the weekend. That was a sweet gesture on his part. I was touched.

When I suggested some restaurants and destinations that I knew he enjoyed, he said, "No. This is your celebration. I want to take you to places where *you* want to go." Again, I was touched — this time, by his selfless consideration.

That night, Paul asked me if I would like to have a foot massage as part of my "celebratory package." *Wait! Stop the presses! Did he say a foot massage? Who wouldn't like to have a foot massage?* My tired toes and I were positively giddy.

Casually, he also mentioned that we should make a special trip to the shopping mall so that we could pick up some of my favorite chocolates. This was part of my "celebratory package," too.

The meaning behind this "package" was not entirely lost on me. All these gestures were intended to show the extent to which Paul truly cared for me, cheered for me, and cherished me. His tenderness, adoration, and devotion made for an exquisite gift.

One morning, I left Paul a handwritten note to thank him for something nice that he had done. I left this note by his coffeemaker so it would be the first thing he saw as he began his day. He appreciated the note so much that he tucked it away in his special keepsake box. He could barely close the box because it had completely overflowed. Paul still keeps every note I have ever written to him. He says they touch his heart — which touches my heart.

Recently, I was so busy with work that I had to work on many weekends, leaving Paul to his own devices on Saturday and Sunday afternoons. One such Saturday afternoon, I received a text from him asking, "Have I told you today how much...?" I grinned. Paul and I often text each other when we are apart. It makes us feel like we are still together, even if we are many miles away. I receive this exact question from him almost every single day, which is heartwarming because the full meaning is: "Have I told you today how much I love you?"

It has become crystal clear to me that we are, in fact, two bodies, one heart. Just because we have some mundane moments here and there doesn't mean that our love isn't as romantic and tender as it always has been. Perhaps it just matured, like we did.

~Kristen Mai Pham

95

Anniversaries
by Halves

I'd rather have roses on my table than diamonds
on my neck.
~Emma Goldman

It was February 8, 1977. I was teaching seventh grade when I heard a knock at the classroom door. There stood my husband Michael with a long, rectangular gold box. The top had a clear, plastic window. Inside were a half-dozen long-stemmed, yellow roses, the same as the flowers I had carried in my wedding bouquet.

"Happy first half-anniversary," he said with a huge smile.

I was so surprised that I couldn't even answer. The flowers were gorgeous. The pale, yellow blooms glistened against the gold box. I stood there in front of thirty-five students with my mouth open and my heart beating very fast.

The first six months of our marriage had flown by. We taught at the same middle school, so we always had plenty to talk about. We enjoyed doing things together, including traveling, cooking, and going to the theater. I knew from the beginning that Michael was thoughtful, but these flowers were above and beyond. It was not only thoughtful, but so romantic.

Michael and I had met a year and a half earlier when we applied for the same teaching job. We hadn't known there were two teaching positions available when we interviewed. His interview was first, and mine followed. When we were finished, we found ourselves seated next to each other in the vice principal's office.

Smiling shyly at each other, we started chatting.

"How did it go?" Michael asked.

"Oh, fine," I replied. "It turns out there is a typing teacher position open. I told them I would take it if they needed me."

"Do you know how to teach typing?"

Luckily, before I had to tell Michael a lie, the vice principal appeared.

"I'm so glad you've met. I get to share the good news with you both. We've decided to have you fill both positions. You each will be joining us for the new semester. Michael, you'll teach all English. Ina, you will teach the typing classes and one English class. Classes start on Tuesday, with Monday an in-service teacher day. Welcome to our school."

This time, we looked at each other with big smiles, not so shyly this time, and shook hands. We were about to embark on what we had thought would be individual teaching adventures but turned out to be so much more. Who would have suspected that we would get married a year later?

As I went to take the flowers, my darling husband whispered in my ear, "You told me once that because we were married in the summer, you would never get flowers for our anniversary delivered to your classroom."

It was true. I had said that a bit off-handedly, so I was amazed that Michael had remembered. I just always loved the idea of flowers being delivered to my room so I could share them with my students.

"Oh, these are wonderful. It's the best surprise gift I have ever received."

Michael beamed as my students looked on. Then he kissed me. There was a round of applause from the kids.

It also was the start of a lovely tradition. The flowers that I received for our first half year together were just the beginning of many more bouquets to come.

Never once in all this time has he forgotten to have flowers sent to me! Through the years, the flowers have taken different forms. Some years, I have received a formal flower arrangement, with many gorgeous flowers, including roses, iris, orchids, and daisies. On occasion, a plant has arrived on my desk. Once, there were balloons and flowers mixed together.

Even when I left teaching and worked in an office, a vase of flowers would be waiting for me every February eighth. After a few years, the receptionist would call and say, "I think it's your half-anniversary today. There are some beautiful flowers waiting for you in the lobby."

One year, flowers arrived a week early. We were expecting our first baby right around February eighth. Michael said he didn't want me to miss getting flowers.

Every year for the last forty-one years, Michael has had flowers, always with a yellow rose tucked in somewhere, delivered to me wherever I am on our half-anniversary. And every single year, I am filled with joy and surprise all over again.

~Ina Massler Levin

The Unity Candle

*A successful marriage isn't the union of two perfect
people. It's that of two imperfect people who have
learned the value of forgiveness and grace.*

~Darlene Schacht

"Just let me know if there's going to be a wedding tomorrow," my dad said solemnly, as he turned off the kitchen
light and headed off to bed. My fiancé and I were trying
to argue quietly, but I guess my dad heard.

We were to be married in my home church in Concord, California,
at Fair Oaks Baptist the following evening—plenty enough time to
sort out our differences (or so we thought).

The tradition—at the time—was not to see the bride the day
of the wedding, so we had until midnight to get our "little" problem
straightened out, and it was already 10:30 p.m.

The argument was over a silly thing about the unity candle and
its placement. A "unity candle" is a three-candle set-up, with two tall
tapers on either side of a short pillar. The idea is that the bride and
groom each take one of the lit tall candles, and together, use those
candles to light the center pillar candle. Being Catholic, my husband
insisted that the candle be placed on the altar at the foot of the steps.
My church—being Baptist—insisted that we light one of the candles
behind the altar—preferably the three-tiered candelabra.

I'm not sure that our "discussion" on the matter led to any sort
of unity; in fact, I seriously doubted there would be a wedding the

following day.

Mark was holding his ground, and I was holding mine because it was my church that we were getting married in. Quite frankly, I didn't see that it mattered either way, but the bigger issue was: Why were we fighting about it in the first place?

If we couldn't resolve our differences over a unity candle, how were we ever going to come to an agreement on the things that really mattered — like having children! I think it was the latter that really concerned me — the big things, not the little things. But I had heard that unity over the little things was sometimes more important than the huge things in a marriage. Does he squeeze the toothpaste from the top, the middle or the bottom? Does he leave dirty dishes in the sink at night? Does he scatter his clothes all over the bedroom floor, or does he put them in the clothes hamper? Frankly, I didn't know the answers to those questions.

Mark stomped out of the house, and I was left crying and wondering if there would be a wedding the next day.

One of my bridesmaids was spending the night, and I didn't want to wake her, so I slept on the sofa in the living room. I tossed and turned all night, wondering how to call off the wedding over a unity candle.

In the morning, my dad was busy making scrambled eggs and bacon for everyone, and I heard the paperboy throw the newspaper against the screen door — a signal that it was time to get up. Dad didn't say a word when I wandered into the kitchen — still wearing my clothes from the night before. I grabbed a plate, poured some orange juice, and contemplated my fate.

"Oh, I forgot," Dad said, "this was on the front porch this morning." Dad handed me a white envelope with a single piece of paper tucked inside. On it were the words: "Connie, I'm so sorry for last night. I love you so much, and I want to marry you — if you'll still have me!"

Tears trickled down my cheeks. My dad smiled as he walked past me and whispered close to my ear, "I guess the wedding is still on, right?"

Smiling through my tears, I replied, "Of course. What else would we be doing?"

It's been forty-two years since I walked down the aisle — holding tightly to my dad's arm — with the pipe organ playing the classical "Trumpet Voluntary" by Henry Purcell. We had a candlelight wedding with the unity candle placed on the altar with two white taper candles on either side (not the three-tiered candelabra as Baptist tradition dictated).

I guess you could say we had a Baptist wedding with a Catholic twist, but it set the tone for our married life. Whenever we have an argument, we always get out the unity candle and light it. We may not have settled our differences, but somehow when the candle is lit, it really doesn't matter anymore. Our love for each other is renewed.

After all, it takes two to light a unity candle.

~Connie K. Pombo

This Is Us

*Marriage: Love is the reason. Lifelong friendship is the
gift. Kindness is the cause. 'Til death do us
part is the length.*
~Fawn Weaver

My make-up had been meticulously applied. My hair had
been styled by a French hairdresser — more of an artist,
actually. Not a gray hair was visible. The reflection in the
mirror pleased me. I didn't look a day over thirty-five.

Standing behind me, my husband Larry placed a stunning diamond
necklace around my neck. It must have cost a mint. The earrings matched
perfectly and dangled long and sexy.

We were cruising somewhere in the Mediterranean, on our way to
dinner at the Captain's table.

The ringing of the phone awakens me. I open my eyes. Instead
of cruising on the Mediterranean, we've been snoozing at our home
in Dallas, Texas.

I had fallen asleep on the love seat. Larry is across from me,
sound asleep and snoring on the sofa. Even Ollie the cat is asleep in
the sunshine on the windowsill.

The TV is on, blaring the sounds of a football game.

I reach for the phone on the coffee table, but it has stopped ringing.
A text from Sharon reads: "We're going out for lunch. Want to come?"

No, I do not want to go. Everything I need is right in front of me.
There is nowhere else I'd rather be on a Sunday afternoon than in my

own home with my husband and my cat.

The dream of the Mediterranean cruise was appealing, but this scene is better. I wouldn't trade it for anything in the world.

We are ordinary people, extraordinarily blessed. Of the thirty-two years that we've been married, thirty-two have been happy. How many can say that? Lucky me!

This morning we attended the Lutheran church down the block where we got married. After the service, we returned home and got comfortable. Larry put on jeans and an old T-shirt and I put on my yoga clothes.

I gave him an ice pack for his knee. Someday, he'll have it fixed. I don't force it. It's his choice.

I made coffee; he mixed our "special juice." He said it was beets. I called it his beetle juice. He had heard about it on the radio. "It will keep us young and healthy," he said.

What has kept me young and healthy is having a husband I can depend on, laugh with and trust.

He brought down our vitamins. Four for me. I had already forgotten which ones I took. "Just want you to know I've told everyone that you give me my pills. So if I'm ever poisoned, they will know where to look," I joked. "Who knows what you really give me?"

But, of course, I trust him like no other.

Half-heartedly, I made a fruit salad — fresh blueberries, orange slices, raspberries, cantaloupe and whatever else is in season. Every single day, I make a fresh fruit salad because he doesn't like it already sliced from the grocery store. Every single blessed day! A bit of a pain in the neck, but if my husband likes it, it's worth it.

Larry made the eggs. How many times do I have to tell the man to heat the pan first, or it will burn? He doesn't listen. But who cares? I can throw out the pan after a while, but I want to keep the man. So I gave up complaining about the pan. Considering this is the only meal he ever makes, I'd say he is doing well. The eggs always turn out delicious. Larry has always been the Egg Master. I love that he cooks Sunday breakfast for us — for me.

While he cooked the eggs I made the toast. The butter has to be just right for him. Lots of it! His toast was smothered. It doesn't do any good to nag that too much butter is bad.

We managed to get everything ready at the same time. When we finally sat down at the table, we talked. We don't talk about earth-shattering things; we make small talk. After thirty-two years, we have already said everything. It's just comfortable.

Then he brought his dishes and mine to the sink. Someday, I'll tell him we have a dishwasher. He doesn't know. He's never opened it. I like it that way. He'd only mess things up.

He doesn't know we have a washer and a dryer, either. He thinks the utility room is a place to throw dirty clothes. Miraculously, they come out clean and pressed — sooner or later.

Sometimes, he says something profound like: "We are in the last third of our lives."

He says it not with remorse, just nostalgia.

"Speak for yourself," I'll banter. "I'm younger than you!"

Perhaps he is right. Perhaps we *are* in the last third of our lives. But I like to think of it this way: We are in the *best* third of our lives.

This is love. This is all I need.

~Eva Carter

Love on the Parkway

I will love you until the stars go out and the tides
no longer turn.
~Author Unknown

It was a picture-perfect July day, and I'd spent it down on the Jersey shore with my mother, sister, and a friend from college. But it was a Sunday afternoon, so it wasn't long before we hit traffic on the Garden State Parkway.

My friend moaned, "Great, now what are we going to do?"

My mother replied jokingly, "Let's look for cute guys."

My friend then exclaimed, "There's one!"

We all looked to the left and, sure enough, a very cute guy in sunglasses and a backwards cap was driving a forest-green Explorer. I smiled and waved from the driver's seat of the purple Kia sedan; he smiled and waved back. We all giggled as this exchange took place several times over the next mile or so.

Traffic began to slow again, and my mother told me to speed up; my guy was slowing down for me to catch up. We stopped alongside each other and began to talk. We exchanged initial greetings, and then I asked, "Where are you going?"

He answered, "Lyndhurst." I'd never heard of it. He asked, "Where are you going?"

"Hackettstown," I replied.

He said, "Oh! I know someone in Hackettstown!"

To which I said, "Oh, really? Want to know me?"

Smooth, right? That's right about where smooth and I parted ways, because after he replied, "Yes!" I blurted out, "Follow me!"

He pulled in behind me, but as traffic slowed again, he pulled beside me once again and said my town was a little far for him to go. Instead, he asked me to take his phone number. My mom took an envelope from her purse and wrote it down. We went our separate ways, and I called him later that night.

We had our first date a week later. We both agreed it was the best first date ever: dinner and mini-golf. We ended the night with a hug. Something just felt right from the start. My soul rejoiced the first time he kissed me, and I remember thinking, *Ahh, yes, here you are.*

We've been together twenty years now. We've been through the usual ups and downs of life and marriage — children, celebrations, milestones, and losses. Through it all, we have been each other's best friend.

Our family is only as strong as our foundation, and we have always made our relationship a top priority. We nurture each other and our dreams; we lift each other up; we complement each other. Most of all, we make each other laugh. No one can make me laugh the way my husband does, and it brings me absolute joy when I make him laugh. It is a magical feeling when we laugh together and an essential element for keeping us young, vibrant and close as the years roll on. I'm grateful every day for the traffic on the Garden State Parkway that brought us together.

~Heather Kerner

Six Yards of Love

Preservation of one's own culture does not require
contempt or disrespect for other cultures.
~Cesar Chavez

I stepped into the white cotton slip and fastened it at my waist. Pale green georgette slipped through my fingers as I unfolded the six yards of cloth and started wrapping the sari counter-clockwise around me. My elbows bumped into the walls and door as I maneuvered the fabric into place. The tiny room and everything in it vibrated to the hum of jet engines.

Even an experienced Indian woman would have found it difficult to put on a sari in an airplane restroom. Yet, here I was, doing it for love.

In a few hours, Naresh, my husband of one year, and I would be landing in New Delhi where I would meet his family for the first time. He had taught me how to tie a sari, but I'd only worn one half a dozen times. Together, we purchased this one, with its dark green border and modern flower print, at a shop in Chicago. My mother and I sewed a matching sari blouse from a piece of dark green cotton. I intended to greet his family wearing it, but had postponed putting it on until now for fear of getting it wrinkled or dirty on the long flight.

Naresh and I had met three years earlier at a party in my apartment in Maine, on the day of his arrival in the United States. We immediately became friends and spent much of our free time together during graduate school. A Midwesterner by birth, I was curious to explore Maine and its environs. I packed my car with international students who were keen to see new places, too. Naresh was often an enthusiastic participant in these adventures. He learned how to cross-country ski, and we traversed the campus trails together. When summer came, we tried tent camping.

We also explored world cultures through our international friends and helped start the host family program at the university — matching local families with international students to foster friendships and cultural understanding. Together, we cooked our family recipes and sampled other cuisines. He was a lifelong vegetarian, and I wanted to explore this diet, too, as an ethical response to environmental concerns.

When I returned to Illinois after completing my degree, Naresh still had six months of school. I felt torn, as if I was leaving part of my soul behind. I don't recall the specific day we decided to get married, but by the time he was preparing to graduate we were planning our wedding.

His parents were not able to come, but they sent a beautiful wedding sari through friends. We held two ceremonies in my parents' living room: one Hindu and one Christian, with a feast of foods from our two cultures in between. This was back in the days when phone calls on the old overseas trunk lines required considerable planning, but that morning we finally connected with his family. We promised a trip to India to see them and celebrate the following summer.

Now our year-long wait was almost over.

I pleated the sari's front and tucked it into the waist of my petticoat. Gingerly, I held the loose end high, not sure of the floor's cleanliness after such a long flight, and wrapped it around one more time. I draped the loose end, the *palla*, over my left shoulder and, studying my reflection in the mirror, adjusted it in place. Pale skin, short dark hair: I didn't look Indian at all. I hoped it wouldn't matter.

Not trusting my ability to keep the loose end draped naturally over my shoulder, I fastened a safety pin through the blouse and the folds of the *palla* to hold the slippery fabric in place.

I checked the hemline as best I could without a floor-length mirror and took a deep breath. Would my new family be able to see how much they already meant to me?

The sari swished about my legs as I slowly walked back to our seats, saying a silent prayer that I wouldn't trip over it sometime that evening.

"How does it look?" I asked.

Naresh perused my work with both an engineer's and a new husband's eyes. "Beautiful. You know you don't have to do this if you don't want to."

"I know. I want to."

I squeezed his hand as we landed, the city lights shimmering in the dark. He squeezed mine back, and we were off the plane and into the chaotic crowds going through immigration and retrieving luggage. As we approached the exit from customs, he scanned the windows of the balcony above.

"There they are." He waved.

I smiled shyly at my new family, recognizing them from his photos.

Hot dry air and warm smiles greeted us as we stepped outside. We touched his parents' feet and greeted everyone with the traditional *namaste*, palms touching at our hearts, heads bowed slightly. My new family welcomed us with pungent garlands of bright yellow marigolds and the kindest compliments about my *namaste* and sari.

Amid the cacophony of honking horns and the crowds of people, we wove our way to the parking lot. We crammed our luggage and ourselves into two cars and headed to his sister's home. The ride was a blur of sensory experiences for me: the dry, summer heat; the dust; the acrid smoke of cooking fires mixed with an occasional whiff of sandalwood and curry; the buzz of scooters careening around us; and an occasional bicycle, even this late at night. Unfamiliar trees lined the dimly lit avenue, and more vegetation grew luxuriously from the pale earth. All the while, family chatted with my husband, and he regaled them with tales of his adventures since leaving for the United States.

To this day, however, the scene that stands out most in my mind is when we arrived at his sister's home. She stood in her sari in the darkened doorway holding a *thali* — a round, stainless-steel tray strewn with flower petals and lit with tiny clay lamps. She dipped her finger in a little *katori* bowl and smudged vermillion powder with a few grains of rice on the center of our foreheads in welcome and blessing.

A whole new world opened to me that evening. I had gained not only the love of my life, but a new family. Our love would continue to deepen as we grew together, and at the same time it would swell and expand to include those who loved us. And the ripples continue over the years, enriching our lives still.

~Susan Rothrock Deo

A Daisy a Day

*And what's romance? Usually, a nice little tale where
you have everything as you like it, where rain never
wets your jacket and gnats never bite your nose,
and it's always daisy-time.*

~D.H. Lawrence

"**I** wanted someone who knew agriculture, who was athletic, and who was musical," my husband confided several years after we were married. An image of a farmer choosing a heifer at a sale flicked through my mind, but I let it go. Being raised on a farm and a product of practicality, it seemed reasonable to know what one wanted. And through the years, we discovered that we both wanted the same thing.

1979: We first noticed each other on Ag Hill at Penn State. I would learn that he had been raised on a large dairy farm. He would learn that I had been raised on a farm, played field hockey, took the stairs instead of the elevator, and had piano books stacked in my dorm room. Forget that my family's farm was a hobby farm, that I had already had knee surgery, and that the piano books were dusty — he'd found his woman.

We discovered a piano just inside the dorm's back entrance. I proceeded to hammer out some good, old sing-along songs. We sang "A Daisy a Day" together, and I smiled when he reached around my shoulders to turn each page instead of simply leaning forward. My piano playing was adequate but, oh, his voice. I fell in love with his voice.

1981: While driving across the New Mexico desert, we heard the news on the radio. Pope John Paul II had been shot. I looked at my husband of one month to share the shock, but he remained stoic, his eyes on the road. I wondered briefly about this part of him, but then I noticed his hands gripping the steering wheel as the wind buffeted our truck, and I realized he wasn't being cold—he was just focused on our safety. I never again questioned his character or devotion.

1990: Our family of four settled on a twenty-six-acre farm, which soon became the best playground kids could ever want. Through our sons' middle- and high-school years, sledding turned into saucering off the barn's side roof, which led to big air ski competitions. It was my husband who waited at the bottom of the ski slope and ushered one of our sons into the lodge after he broke his nose. Even when he worked long hours in the spring, my husband supported our sons' pursuits, and the three of us could count on his calm demeanor—except on rare occasions.

2000: "Do you know what Matthew 5:30 says?" my husband said in exasperation. After a dusty sixteen-hour day, he was sitting at the kitchen table with an open Bible in front of him.

I had walked into this scene after a hectic evening of running our sons here and there. I glanced at the note on the table that noted the time a friend would pick up one of our sons for choral practice—Matthew 5:30. Valiantly fighting back hilarity but losing, I tried to explain the purpose of the note and make clear that the note hadn't been for him.

But exhaustion had apparently shut down part of his hearing because he continued, "Matthew 5:30 says that if your right hand offends you, you should cut it off. I just spent the last hour trying to figure out what I did wrong!"

He must have forgiven me for laughing so hard because he accepted my peace offering of a hearty bowl of homemade chicken corn soup—with rivels—a real sign of true love.

2015: Cancer. My husband's diagnosis of kidney cancer focused us on what mattered. One evening, I came into the kitchen to find a CD on our table with a note that said, "Let's dance." We did. For three minutes each evening, in reprieve, we breathed deeply, held each other close, and moved to the sound of a love song. He smelled of fresh outside air, hay, and home. Every evening, we slow danced to a different song — for about a week, then once a week, then when we'd remember and make the effort. As his health improved, we began again to count new blessings, make new memories, and dance — occasionally — to new songs.

I am thankful that our love has never required perfect gifts, words, or actions. For thirty-six years, we have simply nourished our shared desire to connect, and to give each other a daisy a day.

~Gail E. Strock

Live Without Regret

The best time to love with your whole heart is always
now, in this moment, because no breath beyond the
current is promised.
~Fawn Weaver

People were saying that I "glowed," and I sure felt that way. I was over forty and as giddy as a schoolgirl, because I had unexpectedly fallen in love — that over-the-top, can't-eat-breathe-or-sleep kind of love.

Since I'd been deeply hurt in my marriage, I had never planned to remarry. I was happy in my career and had just built a house. The man I fell for hadn't planned to remarry either, but then we found each other.

We were cautious, though. We read marriage and relationship books. We got counseling. We attended an eight-week premarital class. I even had thirty-four people interrogate my poor man, just in case they saw something I couldn't see. I was not going to live with regret again.

Finally, I felt sure it was right. One wonderful April evening, Dale got down on his knee and proposed. I said "Yes!" and we began to plan our wedding, excited to begin a long and happy life together.

But then, just a month after we got engaged, Dale was diagnosed with prostate cancer. Dale gave me the chance to back out of our plans, but I was committed to a man who gave me more love, joy, and peace than I'd ever known. His love healed so many broken places in my heart that, even if we only had months left together, it seemed worth the risk of losing him in order to know such love.

We moved forward with our plans, and married in July. Two months later, Dale started radiation and then had surgery in November. On our first Thanksgiving, we thanked God for Dale being alive. As he healed, we gathered our family together to celebrate Christmas.

Unfortunately, the New Year brought more physical challenges. In March, Dale needed to have rotator-cuff surgery. For several months, he struggled through the agonizing physical therapy that was required.

By springtime, we noticed that Dale's right hand had begun to shake, and his handwriting kept getting smaller and smaller. We were about to face our biggest challenge of all, for the love of my life was diagnosed with Parkinson's disease! The doctor told him he had three to five years to live. And although we now know that doctor was wrong, and that people with Parkinson's usually enjoy a full lifespan, his words were more than scary. We knew this would be a challenge we'd have to face — together.

Then it was my turn. In May, the doctor found skin cancer and cut out a pencil-eraser-sized hole in the tip of my nose. Dale loved me through the emotional trauma I faced. Thankfully, my nose healed, and on our first anniversary we celebrated life, love, and our commitment like few couples do.

This year, we are celebrating our fifteenth anniversary, and we'll continue to love and support each other through all the ups and downs of life. In the last decade and a half, Dale has had four melanoma surgeries plus eight other major surgeries, and he now has thirty-two Parkinson's symptoms, including some cognitive challenges. But our commitment to love each other is unwavering, solid, and sure, so we choose to allow each new challenge we face to bring us closer together instead of tearing us apart.

Our motto has always been "live without regret," but that takes intentional living. Because of this, we've traveled the world and built many friendships. We have completed our bucket list, and we have twenty-eight photo books filled with wonderful memories. Together, we have enjoyed many ups and down and had a lot of fun. We even wrote two premarital books together, hoping to help others experience this kind of love.

~Susan G. Mathis

Meet Our Contributors

Idella M. Anderson is a wife, mother of four, and advocate for women and children. She enjoys books, movies, reality TV, and spending quality time with her family. When she is not busy entertaining and being a personal Uber for her children, you can find her at her local café writing and enjoying a tea latte.

Vanessa Angone-Pompa received her MFA in Creative Writing from Columbia College Chicago in 2005. She is currently submitting the manuscript for her first novel for representation in hopes of publication. She enjoys writing, reading, traveling, and watching films. She and her husband are expecting their first child.

Dr. Colleen M. Arnold is a writer and family physician in Lexington, VA. She is also a widow and mother of three young adult daughters. She enjoys hanging out with family, taking care of her patients, writing, walking, and working on her blog, *Living and Loss: Learning Lessons, Finding Joy*, at colleenarnold.org.

Sandra Bakun is a retired newspaper reporter and medical secretary. She held the dual positions while bringing up her four children in Stow, MA. She retired to Cape Cod in 1995 and now splits her residency between the Cape and Myrtle Beach, SC. She loves to read, golf, and walk the beaches with Art.

Rosemary Barkes won the Erma Bombeck Writing Competition in 2000, which began a writing career. She subsequently published *The*

Dementia Dance: Maneuvering Through Dementia While Maintaining Your Sanity. She holds B.A. and B.S. degrees from The Ohio State University and an M.S. degree from University of Dayton.

Sarah Barnum is a freelance writer and editor with TrailBlaze Writing & Editing (www.trail-blazes.com). A lifelong horsewoman, she enjoys ranch life in Northern California with her husband, Michael, and Appaloosa horse, Ransom.

Jill Berni is an avid animal lover and history buff. She has spent many happy hours volunteering at her local humane society, historical museums and seniors' residences. Jill enjoys reading, writing, and music. She lives in Mississauga, Ontario with her husband Fred and their two dogs. She plans to write short stories.

Sharon Kay Beyer is a freelance court reporter in Appleton, WI and has a passion for journaling, gardening, writing and all things Colorado! Sharon enjoys summer hiking in the Rockies with her darling husband Tim, and is working on her first book, hoping to inspire others to uncover and manifest their dreams.

Sue Bonebrake received her BSE and MA from Northwest Missouri State University in 1969 and taught secondary and college English/Speech/Drama for almost thirty years. She and her husband have three children and three grandchildren. They have now retired and raise alpacas on a small acreage in northeast Iowa.

Michele M. Boom has taught elementary school both in the traditional setting as well as online. She also works as a freelance writer and is a frequent contributor to the *Chicken Soup for the Soul* series. She lives in Bend, OR with her family, two cats and two aquatic frogs.

LaRonda Bourn enjoys her life in a small Minnesota town that prides itself on its German heritage. She lives there with her husband, two daughters, three cats and three fish.

Barbara Dorman Bower is a CPA, and retired from the Financial Services industry. This is her second published story in the *Chicken Soup for the Soul* series. She enjoys having the time to explore her creative side, and likes to travel with her husband as often as possible.

Michele Brouder is originally from the Buffalo, NY area. She has lived in the southwest of Ireland since 2006, except for a two-year stint in Florida. She makes her home with her husband, two boys and a dog named Rover. Her go-to place is, was and will always be the beach. Any beach. Any weather.

Valaree Terribilini Brough graduated from Utah State University with a Bachelor of Arts in Elementary Education, and a dual minor in English and French. She enjoys reading, writing, sewing, playing the piano, researching family history, and serving others. She loves spending time with her family.

Erin Elliott Bryan earned her bachelor's degree in English/Writing from Northern Michigan University. She spent ten years as an editor of a community newspaper in Minneapolis and has worked in communications for a nonprofit. She lives in the Twin Cities area with her husband Tom, children Noah and Natalee, and dog Memphis.

Jill Burns lives in the mountains of West Virginia with her wonderful family. She's a retired piano teacher and performer. She enjoys writing, music, gardening, nature, and spending time with her grandchildren.

Christine Carter writes at TheMomCafe.com, where she hopes to encourage mothers everywhere through her humor, inspiration, and faith. She is the author of *Help and Hope While You're Healing: A Woman's Guide Toward Wellness While Recovering from Injury, Surgery, or Illness.*

Eva Carter is a freelance photographer and writer. She has a background in finance, having worked in the telecommunications industry for over twenty years. She is originally from Czechoslovakia, grew up in New

York and now lives with her husband in Dallas, TX.

Elynne Chaplik-Aleskow, a Pushcart Prize-nominated writer, is founding general manager of WYCC-TV/PBS and distinguished professor emeritus of Wright College. Her stories have been performed throughout the U.S. and Canada and are published in anthologies and her book, *My Gift of Now*. Her husband Richard is her muse.

Cindy Charlton is a person with disabilities and writes personal essay/ memoirs about her continued journey as a triple amputee. She works as the program director for Rehabilitation Services and Stroke Day Program through Easterseals Colorado. Cindy finds her work rewarding and is inspired daily by those she serves.

Dr. Jeanetta Chrystie has more than 800 published magazine and newsletter articles, plus devotions, poems, and anthology chapters. She is Assistant Professor of Management at SMSU and online adjunct faculty at Judson University. Jeanetta and her husband enjoy beachcombing, gardening, and watching plays and movies together.

Sheryl Stone Clay hopes to be blessed with a marriage to Stan that's at least as long ('cause it's definitely as loving!) as that of her late in-laws Foster and Louise Clay (fifty-five years) and her parents Lois and Gerry Stone (sixty-one years and counting).

This is **M. Scott Coffman's** third story in the *Chicken Soup for the Soul* series. He writes two blogs, *Truth Mission* (http://truthmission.net) and *Low-Rent Foodie* (http://lowrentfoodie.net). He is the ghost-author of *Called to CARE* by James P. Rousey, available from Chilidog Press. He lives in Central Illinois with his wife, daughter and two cats.

Darin Cook received his Bachelor of Arts in 1993 and has been writing and editing ever since. He draws material for his travel writing and works of nonfiction from all of life's experiences, whether travelling the globe, journeying into his past, or exploring the challenges of being a parent.

Sandra Croft is an English language arts teacher, actor, and a professional acting coach. Previously, she has written for Applause Theatre and Cinema Books, Contemporary Drama Service, and *The New York Times*.

Linda C. Defew and her husband enjoy a peaceful yet full life in the country. An unsolved murder committed on their farm in 1927 motivated Linda to dig deep into the past. She had her first book, *Murder in Little Heaven*, published in 2017, which opened the door for an exciting writing career.

Denise Del Bianco is a retired widow living in her hometown — Bischwiller, France — after traveling the world with the love of her life, Pietro. After meeting in France, he and Denise raised two children in Italy and Canada. She enjoys cooking, reading and cuddling her furry grandkids. Her twitter handle is @DeniseBecht1.

Susan Rothrock Deo loves exploring the world through friendships, travel and reading. Her publishing credits include three *Chicken Soup for the Soul* books, a short story in *Highlights for Children* magazine and a recurring children's nature column in a local newsletter. She and her husband live in California.

Diana C. Derringer is an award-winning writer and author of *Beyond Bethlehem and Calvary: 12 Dramas for Christmas, Easter and More!* Hundreds of her devotions, articles, drama, and poetry appear in forty-plus publications. She enjoys traveling with her husband and serving as a friendship family to international university students.

Lindsay Detwiler is a high school English teacher and a contemporary romance author with Hot Tree Publishing. Lindsay has published eleven novels, including her latest, *Still Us*. She is married to her junior high sweetheart, Chad. They live in Pennsylvania with their five cats and their Mastiff, Henry.

Janice R. Edwards received her BAT degree with honors in 1974. She taught English and Journalism before working for Texaco. She now writes for *Image Magazine* and has published eight other personal stories in previous *Chicken Soup for the Soul* books. E-mail her at jredwards@brazoriainet.com.

Sarahfina El received her Bachelor's in Communications with an emphasis on Journalism and Media Studies in 2015. She is a certified personal trainer and developing life coach whose goal is to write inspiring books to help others become healthy from the inside out.

Vancouver Island artist **Micki Findlay** dabbles in all kinds of creativity including song writing, jewelry design, and photography. She writes true stories based on her own life, her battle with depression, and her personal experience with miracles. Her aim in writing from an authentic place is to give hope to others.

Caitlin Finley currently resides in Buffalo, TX, managing the local coffee shop and bookstore. Recently married, she enjoys hosting local Open Mic and Game Nights, as well as other events. In addition to writing, her hobbies include glass painting, crochet, weaving, dance, and martial arts.

Lorraine Furtner is a playwright and former newspaper columnist who enjoys writing fiction and poetry, reading, and being outdoors with family. She hopes to complete her BSIS in Journalism and English at East Tennessee State University, where she's been enrolled in the "get a degree in thirty-five years or less" program since 1991.

Janet Garber received her M.A. in English literature from the University of Rochester. Her comic debut novel, *Dream Job*, has won two awards.

Janet enjoys hiking, live music, and her two rescue cats. Learn more at www.janetgarber.com.

Robin Goodrow is a four-time Emmy Award-winning writer, puppeteer and songwriter, whose children's show *Buster & Me*, was named "Best Local Children's Show in America" (the Iris Awards). Her music CD, *Amazing*, has been called "a superior album for children. Learn more at busterandme.com and hear her music at goodrowproductions.com.

Liezel Graham is married to Craig and is a homeschooling mom to their little boy. She loves words, whether writing or as a proofreader, and helping others weave delightful stories. She writes at "GraceGirl" on Facebook and enjoys long walks in the Scottish woods, reading, and gardening. She's also fond of a good cup of coffee.

Darla S. Grieco, M.S.Ed, is married with four children and resides near Pittsburgh, PA. In recent years she began writing, and is proud to be publishing her third story in the *Chicken Soup for the Soul* series. She has also been published in Guideposts' *Angels on Earth* magazine and shares lessons God has taught her at dsgrieco.com.

Hilary Hattenbach is the winner of the 2016 Mona Schreiber Prize for Humorous Fiction and the coauthor of *The Kitchen Decoded* cookbook (Skyhorse 2014). Her work has been published in *Chicken Soup for the Soul: Best Mom Ever!*, *Entropy*, and *The Eastsider*. She was recently a featured storyteller in KPCC's *Unheard LA* series.

Wendy Hobday Haugh writes short stories, poetry, articles, and books for children and adults. A naturalist at heart, she loves watching the wildlife in the woods around her home and observing their unique habits. Wendy resides in upstate New York with her husband and two crazy cats.

Joyce Ermeling Heiser is living her dream retirement as a published author. She is sharing her retirement with her husband Dennis and two tabby rescue cats in his hometown in South Dakota. She enjoys music, photography, needlework and reading. She is working on her first book. Connect with her at joyceheiser.com.

Diane Henderson, MSW, LCSW is a Speaker, Psychotherapist and Life Coach. She leads workshops on "Taking Care of You, So You Can Better Take Care of Others." She also manages a closed Facebook Group entitled, Women Exploring Empowerment. Diane is married, lives in Rocky Mount, NC, and has two sons and four grandchildren.

Miryam Howard is an active member of her community in Jerusalem, Israel. She enjoys traveling and meeting new people. She loves to write about her experiences and seeks the hidden treasures found in daily life.

Jeffree Wyn Itrich has been a professional writer for thirty years. Though writing nonfiction since the mid-80s, she's also written two novels and a children's book. When not writing she's a quilting maniac, a theme that carries through her blog, *The Goodness Principle*.

Jeanie Jacobson is on the Wordsowers Christian Writers leadership team. She's published in venues such as *Focus on the Family* and *Live* magazines, the *Chicken Soup for the Soul* series, and other anthologies. Jeanie loves visiting family and friends, reading, hiking, praise dancing, and gardening. Grab her fun book, *Fast Fixes for the Christian Pack-Rat*, online. Learn more at JeanieJacobson.com.

Maurene Janiece holds an MFA in Writing from Vermont College. She uses story to discover and communicate strength and connections through shared experiences. She lives in Montana with her husband and daughters, enjoying all that the Rocky Mountains offer.

Robin Jankiewicz lives a happily married life in Los Angeles, CA with her husband and two children. She looks forward to visiting Florida again someday.

Louetta Jensen has written four mystery novels, three screenplays and numerous short stories, most of which have garnered national and international awards.

Kathy Joyce is an organization development consultant, facilitator, and educator by day, writer by night. She has published essays and prize-winning short fiction, and is working on two novels. She lives in Michigan with two teenagers, one Poodle, and a very patient husband. E-mail her at kathyjoyce.writer@gmail.com or on Twitter @ kathyjoycewrite.

Megan Pincus Kajitani is a writer, editor, and educator. Her writing has appeared in several anthologies, including four other *Chicken Soup for the Soul* books, and publications such as *The Chronicle of Higher Education*, *Mothering* magazine, and *Huffington Post*. As Meeg Pincus, she also writes nonfiction for children.

Hugh Kent is a librarian who lives in Southern Ontario, Canada. He will be returning to China this summer to show his children the place where he met their mother.

Heather Kerner is a writer and school and group tour coordinator for a local farm who does her best to juggle marriage, motherhood, and everything in between with as much humor as possible. She lives in New Jersey with her husband, three kids, four dogs, cat, horse, and fish.

Alice Klies is president of Northern Arizona Word Weavers, a chapter of an international writers' group. She is a seven-time contributor to the *Chicken Soup for the Soul* series. She has nonfiction and fiction stories published in twenty anthologies, *Angels on Earth*, and *The Wordsmith Journal Magazine*. E-mail her at alice.klies@gmail.com.

April Knight is a freelance author who is currently working on a western novel. Her favorite pastimes are riding horses and enjoying nature.

Helen Krasner has a degree in psychology, and has worked at various times throughout her life as an occupational psychologist, market researcher, and helicopter pilot. She is now a freelance writer, writing mainly about aviation, travel, and cats. She lives in Derbyshire, UK with her partner David and their five cats.

Mary Ellen Flaherty Langbein recently received her Certification from Purchase College in New York and is a Certified Professional Stager. When she is not staging homes or decorating, she writes. She has been published in *Woman's World* and two *Chicken Soup for the Soul* books. Her greatest joys are spending time with family and traveling.

Tree Langdon is a Canadian writer and artist. Her short stories, poetry and sketches are inspired by dreams for the world and by her passion for shining a light on things that concern everyone. She studied Creative Writing and Forensic Anthropology in college. Curious about everything, she is always learning something new.

Mandy Lawrence is a registered nurse who considers writing to be her true calling. She is a Christian speaker and the author of *Wisdom from Wilbur: How My Dog Has Brought Me Closer to God* and the novel *Replay*. Mandy loves animals, chocolate, and traveling. She and her husband, Shane, live in Lexington, NC.

Ina Massler Levin was a middle school teacher and, later, the editor-in-chief at an educational publishing house. In retirement, she has been indulging her love of travel and ballroom dancing with husband, Michael. Travel is mandatory since her two daughters live on opposite coasts.

Anna M. Lowther graduated *summa cum laude* from the University of Central Florida before returning to Ohio. She is a wife, mother of four, and human to three cats and a dog. Besides having several stories published in the *Chicken Soup for the Soul* series, she has also been published in many anthologies of dark fantasy and horror. She is working on a collection of short stories.

L.M. Lush is an inspirational writer and teacher. After retiring from her career in IT, she started a spiritual business in New York and hopes to have her first book published soon. She enjoys playing the piano and cello, photography, and hiking with her dogs, Sadie and Oreo. Learn more at LMLush.com.

JoAnne Macco worked for thirty years as a mental health therapist in a nonprofit agency. Since retiring, she paints angels, volunteers with first graders, and has published her first book, *Trust the Timing: A Memoir of Finding Love Again*. JoAnne lives in North Carolina with her husband, David, and their two dogs.

Carol Marks is a Program Coordinator and freelance writer who lives in British Columbia. She has three grown children and three grandchildren. She enjoys hiking, biking, writing inspirational poetry and short stories and plans to have her work published in the near future.

Lisa Marlin's essays have appeared in *Writer's Digest* magazine, *The Dallas Morning News* and *The Denver Post*. She is a contributor for *Laugh Out Loud*, a humor anthology from the Erma Bombeck Writers' Workshop. She credits her family as her greatest source of joy, worry and writing prompts. She posts at www.lisamarlin.com.

Susan G. Mathis is a multi-published author of *The Fabric of Hope: An Irish Family Legacy*, *Countdown for Couples*, *The Remarriage Adventure* and more. Learn more at www.SusanGMathis.com.

Janet Matthews is the author of four Canadian *Chicken Soup for the Soul* books, an inspirational speaker and freelance editor. She is a certified canoeing instructor, plays her violin in two amateur string ensembles and, as a passionate roller skater, is overjoyed to be once again waltzing with Bruce. Learn more at www.janetmatthews.ca.

A former lay missionary, **Claire McGarry** now freelances for magazines, contributes to CatholicMom.com, and posts at ShiftingMyPerspective. com. She's also the founder of MOSAIC of Faith, a ministry with several different programs for mothers and children. She lives with her husband and three children in New Hampshire.

Linda A. Mikus's passion is discovering new people and places. She earned a degree in English language and literature and then was lured by the opportunity to meet others and travel the world. After a rewarding career as a flight attendant, Linda has retired her wings and picked up her pen. She enjoys travel with her husband.

Billie J. Mitchell is a retired community college administrator who earned her B.S. and M.S. as an adult student, and worked to help other adults do the same. She currently writes for pleasure, sings in several choirs, and travels with her husband.

Rae Mitchell graduated from the University of California, Davis with bachelor degrees in Comparative Literature and Linguistics. She is currently married to the wonderful Mr. Mitchell who has always been a source of inspiration and support for her writing. They currently live in Washington with their son.

Holly L. Moseley roams a ranch and its environs in the northern plains of South Dakota. Her poems have appeared in the anthologies *Granite Island, Amber Sea*; *Black Hills Literary Journal*; *Roots Grow Deep and Strong* as well as *South Dakota Magazine*, *Vermillion Literary Project*, and *Pasque Petals*.

Rachel Dunstan Muller is an author, storyteller, and personal historian. She and her husband of twenty-eight years continue to have adventures from their home on Vancouver Island, Canada. They have five children and three grandchildren. Learn more at www.racheldunstanmuller.com.

Kimberlee Murray is a proud mother of two fascinating teenage boys who are destined for great things. Kim's freelance writing has been published in *Chicken Soup for the Soul: Thanks Dad*, the *Detroit Free Press*, and *LongWeekends* magazine. Kimberlee is a widow who helps other widows navigate their new normal at www.widow411.com.

Amy Newbold is a cancer survivor, writer, wife, and mom. She is the author of two picture books: *If Picasso Painted a Snowman* (2017) and *If da Vinci Painted a Dinosaur* (2018). Amy lives in Utah with her family and enjoys reading, hiking, taking road trips, and sampling dark chocolate.

Nancy Rose Ostinato is a playwright and romance writer. In 2018, her play, *My Dream Husband*, was published and *Reflection of Me* was produced in Orlando. Her other writing credits include *Chicken Soup for the Soul: Divorce and Recovery* and *Belle of the Ballpoint*, a blog about fairy-tale romance in marriage.

Whitney Owens lives with her husband James in California and now has three kids, the oldest of whom was recently married. James is too busy with work and family life to make pottery these days, but that famed pot is still in their home. Writing assistance for this story was provided by Barbara Owens, Whitney and James' sister-in-law.

Jaymin J. Patel is the founder of www.JayminSpeaks.com. He travels around the world with his wife and two children helping people find wild success in their careers through his books, coaching, workshops, keynotes, and TEDx talk. He is grateful to his wife Eri for helping create this epic love story!

Suzanne Garner Payne, a North Carolina native and a teacher for thirty years, has always loved helping middle school students find their voices through writing. She has now found her voice by writing about her family, which includes two fine sons, Alan and David, and her true Southern Californian husband, John.

Kristen Mai Pham is a screenwriter and an author of inspirational stories. She is delighted to have several stories published in the *Chicken Soup for the Soul* series. Kristen enjoys laughing at her husband's jokes while devouring obscene amounts of milk chocolate. Follow her on Instagram @kristenmaipham or e-mail her at kristenmaipham3@gmail.com.

Connie K. Pombo is an inspirational speaker, freelance writer, and frequent contributor to the *Chicken Soup for the Soul* series. When not speaking or writing, Connie enjoys international travel with her "love-at-first-sight" husband of forty-two years and visiting her kids and grandkids in Lancaster, PA.

Mary Elizabeth Pope is a Professor of English and Creative Writing at Emmanuel College in Boston, where she teaches with her husband, Matthew Elliott. She is the author of *Divining Venus: Stories* (Waywiser Press, 2013) and her work has appeared in *The Florida Review, Bellingham Review, Ascent*, and many others.

Fred Prudhomme, a retired U.S. Air Force Sergeant, holds a Bachelor of Arts in Technical Education from the University of Minnesota. He raced motorcycles professionally earlier in life and continues to pursue that passion by restoring classic motorcycles. He has three grown children and lots of wonderful grandkids.

Carrie Roope is a magazine editor based in the UK and lives with her husband Colin and two boys, Alfie and Ollie. She enjoys writing, reading, and soaking up all the history and heritage the UK has to offer. One day she hopes to turn these historical adventures into a fiction book for children.

Emily Rusch is a mother to three boys, a cancer survivor, a group fitness professional and a health coach. She graduated with a B.S. in Health Science, and is passionate about health and wellness, travel, spending time with her family, and Disney World.

Jean Adair Shriver has published two middle grade books: *Mayflower Man* and *The Einstein Solution*. As her children are now grown she has time to write short essays about anything that strikes her fancy in and around her Southern California home.

Marcia Slosser is a retired school teacher, having taught mostly German, but also Math, Social Studies, Special Education and girls' P.E. (because she was the youngest female teaching at a small school). Since retirement, she enjoys knitting hats for the homeless, driving cancer patients to appointments, traveling, and journaling.

Jessica Snell is a writer who lives in sunny Southern California. She's the editor of *Let Us Keep the Feast: Living the Church Year at Home* and *Not Alone: A Literary and Spiritual Companion for Those Confronted with Infertility and Miscarriage*. She blogs about faith, fiction, and family at jessicasnell.com.

Glenda Standeven is an author and inspirational speaker who lives with her husband, Rick, in Chilliwack, BC. She is an amputee and bone cancer survivor who enjoys sharing her "choosing to smile" message wherever she goes. Her books are available online and on her website at www.glendastandeven.com.

Judee Stapp is a wife, mother of three, and grandmother of four. She speaks at women's events and retreats and is a previous contributor to the *Chicken Soup for the Soul* series and other publications. Through her speaking and writing, Judee's dream is to inspire people to recognize miracles in their own lives. Learn more at www.judeestapp.com.

Gary Stein co-founded an NYSE-member investment banking firm. He was a strategy advisor to Lionsgate, Miramax and Seventh Generation and built a thirty-time Emmy-winning kids TV business. Gary is a proud mentor to several outstanding young women, and has been a frequent contributor to the *Chicken Soup for the Soul* series. E-mail him at gm.stein@verizon.net.

Gail E. Strock lives in Belleville, PA, and enjoys finding humor in everyday experiences with her family and friends. A published freelance writer for twelve years and an editor for another fifteen (retired), she ensures successful writing and editing results for her freelance clients. E-mail her at strockgail@gmail.com.

Susan Sundwall is a freelance writer, blogger, speaker and the author of the *Minnie Markwood Comic Cozy Mystery* series. She writes from her home in upstate New York where she is working on the third story in the series. To read about her adventuresome outlook on life, visit, www.sundwallsays.blogspot.com.

Jodi Renee Thomas is proud to be part of the *Chicken Soup for the Soul* series. An award-winning novelist and playwright, she lives happily in Florida with her husband, teenager and two dogs that like to bother her while she is trying to write.

Many of **Susan Traugh's** stories have appeared in the *Chicken Soup for the Soul* series. She writes curricula for special needs teens, blogs for a mental health site, and wrote the award-winning novel, *The Edge of Brilliance*. Susan lives in San Diego, CA with her husband of thirty years and grown children. Learn more at www.susantraugh.com.

C.C. Warrens lives in a small town in Ohio, where she works as a waitress and a Christian author. She graduated from college with a B.A. in psychology, and loves spending her time writing, painting, walking, and volunteering.

Kate White was an only child who made up imaginary friends to play with. At a young age she began writing stories about her imaginary friends and when she was thirteen she sold her first story. Her lonely childhood made her a writer, and through writing she has made many real friends and has had some great adventures.

Kristi Woods, a writer, speaker, and Jesus girl, scribbles encouragement at KristiWoods.net, Crosswalk.com, and iBelieve.com. She is published in two previous *Chicken Soup for the Soul* books as well. Kristi, her husband, and their three children survived a nomadic, military lifestyle and have set roots in Oklahoma.

Joey Wootan works as an executive at the local utilities company. He enjoys hunting, fishing, and spending time with his wife and son. Joey loves his wife so much that when she talked about writing a love story for the book, he surprised her with his own.

Following a career in nuclear medicine, **Melissa Wootan** is joyfully exploring her creative side. She enjoys writing and is a regular guest on San Antonio television, where she shares all of her best DIY and decorating tips. Learn more at www.facebook.com/chicvintique.

Meet Amy Newmark

Amy Newmark is the bestselling author, editor-in-chief, and publisher of the *Chicken Soup for the Soul* book series. Since 2008, she has published more than 150 new books, most of them national bestsellers in the U.S. and Canada, more than doubling the number of Chicken Soup for the Soul titles in print today. She is also the author of *Simply Happy*, a crash course in Chicken Soup for the Soul advice and wisdom that is filled with easy-to-implement, practical tips for enjoying a better life.

Amy is credited with revitalizing the Chicken Soup for the Soul brand, which has been a publishing industry phenomenon since the first book came out in 1993. By compiling inspirational and aspirational true stories curated from ordinary people who have had extraordinary experiences, Amy has kept the twenty-five-year-old Chicken Soup for the Soul brand fresh and relevant.

Amy graduated *magna cum laude* from Harvard University where she majored in Portuguese and minored in French. She then embarked on a three-decade career as a Wall Street analyst, a hedge fund manager, and a corporate executive in the technology field. She is a Chartered Financial Analyst.

Her return to literary pursuits was inevitable, as her honors thesis in college involved traveling throughout Brazil's impoverished northeast region, collecting stories from regular people. She is delighted to have come full circle in her writing career — from collecting stories "from the people" in Brazil as a twenty-year-old to, three decades later, collecting stories "from the people" for Chicken Soup for the Soul.

When Amy and her husband Bill, the CEO of Chicken Soup for the Soul, are not working, they are visiting their four grown children and their first grandchild.

Follow Amy on Twitter @amynewmark. Listen to her free podcast, "Chicken Soup for the Soul with Amy Newmark," on Apple Podcasts, Google Play, the Podcasts app on iPhone, or by using your favorite podcast app on other devices.

Thank You

We owe huge thanks to all of our contributors and fans. We loved the thousands of love stories that you submitted and it was difficult to narrow down our choice to only 101. We were amazed by the variety of ways you met your soul mates and the interesting journeys you have taken through romance. Ronelle Frankel, Susan Heim, and Barbara LoMonaco read all the submissions, because we are always looking for new writing talent, so every single submission gets read!

Susan Heim did the first round of editing, D'ette Corona chose the perfect quotations to put at the beginning of each story, and Amy Newmark edited the stories and shaped the final manuscript.

As we finished our work, Associate Publisher D'ette Corona continued to be Amy's right-hand woman in creating the final manuscript and working with all our wonderful writers. Barbara LoMonaco and Kristiana Pastir, along with Elaine Kimbler, jumped in at the end to proof, proof, proof. And yes, there will always be typos anyway, so feel free to let us know about them at webmaster@chickensoupforthesoul.com and we will correct them in future printings.

The whole publishing team deserves a hand, including our Senior Director of Marketing Maureen Peltier, our Senior Director of Production Victor Cataldo, Executive Assistant Mary Fisher, and our graphic designer Daniel Zaccari, who turned our manuscript into this beautiful book.

Sharing Happiness, Inspiration, and Hope

Real people sharing real stories, every day, all over the world. In 2007, *USA Today* named *Chicken Soup for the Soul* one of the five most memorable books in the last quarter-century. With over 100 million books sold to date in the U.S. and Canada alone, more than 250 titles in print, and translations into nearly fifty languages, "chicken soup for the soul®" is one of the world's best-known phrases.

Today, twenty-five years after we first began sharing happiness, inspiration and hope through our books, we continue to delight our readers with new titles, but have also evolved beyond the bookstore with super premium pet food, television shows, podcasts, positive journalism from aplus.com, movies and TV shows on the Popcornflix app, and licensed products, all revolving around true stories, as we continue "changing the world one story at a time®." Thanks for reading!

Share with Us

We all have had Chicken Soup for the Soul moments in our lives. If you would like to share your story or poem with millions of people around the world, go to chickensoup.com and click on "Submit Your Story." You may be able to help another reader and become a published author at the same time. Some of our past contributors have launched writing and speaking careers from the publication of their stories in our books!

We only accept story submissions via our website. They are no longer accepted via mail or fax. Visit our website, www.chickensoup.com, and click on Submit Your Story for our writing guidelines and a list of topics we are working on.

To contact us regarding other matters, please send us an e-mail through webmaster@chickensoupforthesoul.com, or fax or write us at:

Chicken Soup for the Soul
P.O. Box 700
Cos Cob, CT 06807-0700
Fax: 203-861-7194

One more note from your friends at Chicken Soup for the Soul: Occasionally, we receive an unsolicited book manuscript from one of our readers, and we would like to respectfully inform you that we do not accept unsolicited manuscripts and we must discard the ones that appear.

Changing lives one story at a time®
www.chickensoup.com